KT-545-503

TOMORROW'S GOD

How We Create Our Worlds

Centre for
Faith and Spirituality
Loughborough University

LLOYD GEERING

Loughborough University & Colleges
ANGLICAN CHAPLAINCY

BRIDGET WILLIAMS BOOKS

To
Bruce and Jane,
Jessica, Zoe and Alice,
Emma, Gregory and David,
and in memory of Neil.

First published in New Zealand in 1994 by
Bridget Williams Books Ltd, PO Box 11-294, Wellington

©Lloyd Geering, 1994

This book is copyright under the Berne Convention.
All rights reserved. No reproduction without permission.
Inquiries should be made to the publishers.

ISBN 0 908912 66 8

Cover design by Mission Hall Design Group, Wellington
Internal design by Afineline, Wellington
Typeset by Archetype, Wellington
Printed by GP Print, Wellington

Contents

Preface

The material in this book was gathered and composed in the years 1992–93. During that time some portions were delivered in earlier draft form as lectures to the Sea of Faith Conference at Leicester, 1992, the summer conference of the Guild of Pastoral Psychology at Oxford, 1992, and the inaugural conference of the New Zealand Sea of Faith Network in Hamilton, 1993. The Oxford lecture was published by the Guild of Pastoral Psychology in 1993 as *The Spiritual Source of Our Symbol Systems*.

The author and publishers acknowledge with gratitude the following permissions to quote: Gordon Kaufman for quoting from his books *The Theological Imagination* and *Theology for a Nuclear Age*; Hodder & Stoughton for quoting from *Green Christianity* by Tim Cooper; John Wiley & Sons, Inc. for quoting from *Inventing Reality* by Bruce Gregory; Little Brown, London, for quoting from *Origins* by Richard Leakey; Macmillan London for quoting from *The Ape that Spoke* by John McCrone; the Oxford University Press, Oxford, for quoting from *And the Life Everlasting* by John Baillie, and *Mankind and Mother Earth* by Arnold Toynbee; Reed Book Service for quoting from *The History of God* by Karen Armstrong; SCM Press Ltd, London, for quoting from *In Search of Deity* by John Macquarrie, *Taking Leave of God* by Don Cupitt, *Radicals and the Future of the Church* by Don Cupitt, *Creation out of Nothing* by Don Cupitt, *What Is a Story?* by Don Cupitt, and *Gaia and God* by Rosemary Radford Ruether.

Introduction

What sort of existence is this which we humans experience? Is there any ultimate meaning lying behind it all? The answers to these questions form the content of what has commonly been called religion. If religion is defined as the human concern to find meaning in existence, then this book is about religion in general and Christianity in particular. Yet this book is in no way an exposition or defence of conventional Christianity; consequently it is not intended for those who are committed to the belief that the ultimate meaning of life has already been revealed by the God who created the universe.

The traditional religious answers to the basic questions of human existence no longer satisfy to the degree they once did, and an increasing number of thoughtful people tend now to say they are not religious. This book is chiefly for them. It nevertheless draws upon the Christian heritage simply because it is that which has mainly shaped Western culture and it is out of Western culture that, for better or for worse, a new kind of global culture is now emerging. The reason why the traditional religious answers no longer satisfy is that they were constructed to suit a world which looked very different from that we find ourselves now living in. The way we understand ourselves, the earth we live on, and our relationship to that earth, have been changing enormously in the last three hundred years. This change has come about largely through three revolutions of thought. First there was the cosmological revolution (pioneered by Copernicus and Galileo), by which the supposedly flat earth on which we lived was displaced from its privileged position as the centre of the universe, to be replaced by the vast space-time universe. Then came the biological revolution (most effectively promoted by Darwin), by which our understanding of the origins of planetary life, including our own, was changed from one of sudden creation not so long ago to one of slow evolution of species over billions of years. Third was the anthropological revolution (pioneered by anthropologists, psychologists and medical scientists) by which we have come to recognise ourselves as psychosomatic organisms whose individual life-span is bounded by conception and death.

The net result of these revolutions of thought, along with the many changes to which they led, has been a radical shift in human consciousness. In Western culture in particular, and to some extent in all cultures, people of the late twentieth century see and interpret reality differently from their ancestors. What had appeared to be unchangeable truths have been questioned and are being replaced by new ways of thinking. In no area is this more pronounced than in religious thought. It is almost as if religious thought has been turned upside down.

For example, it was traditionally thought by Jew, Christian and Muslim that the world and everything in it, including us, was made by God. It seemed to be so self-evident that it was rarely questioned. For Jew and Christian, the Bible was clear and convincing. It told just how and when God created everything. First God created light, then sea and land, and finally the many kinds of vegetation and living creatures. This description was found eminently satisfying and believable right down to the middle of the nineteenth century. The fact that this biblical account of origins could be so convincing, even to the most highly educated people, for more than two millennia is striking testimony to its power.

When, in the nineteenth century, the Darwinian theory of biological evolution began to displace the literal understanding of the biblical stories, which came to be regarded as myths (symbolic stories created by human imagination) rather than divinely revealed knowledge (to which even scientific knowledge should conform), there was heated controversy in the Christian community. In conservative Christian circles the evolutionary view of origins is still fiercely condemned.

More liberally minded Christians, however, came to accept relatively quickly the idea of a long evolutionary process and believed they could reconcile it with the theological doctrine of divine creation. Liberal Christians believed that Darwinism had changed simply the understanding of the process by which God had created the world and of the time-span in which he had achieved it; the fact of God's creatorship, in their view, remained unchanged.

The attempt to reconcile new world views with the traditional theological doctrines, however, cannot be achieved quite as simply as that. The reason why the new cosmology causes no theological controversy today may be that, in daily life, we continue to act as if the earth is still the centre of 'our' world. If we really think through the implications of the Copernican revolution, we may come to appreciate why Copernicus and Galileo caused as much consternation in Christian circles in their day as Darwin did in his. There is a deep-seated conflict between the biblical view of heaven and earth and the view of the universe opened up by Copernicus.

Similarly, the theory of biological evolution is not just an alternative view of how God might have created the universe. The theory contains an explanation of not only how, but also why, the species came to be as various as they are. The variety is due to chance variations and mutations rather than the activity of a cosmic planner. The creative and designing role of God has been rendered more and more redundant.

These revolutions in thought have led to a form of human consciousness in which awareness of a personal God, who is both creator and benefactor, has been fading. The role vacated by God has, to some extent, been taken over by the human species itself. Traditionally it was assumed that the human species was created by God. It now appears, by contrast, that the very concept of God was itself created by the human species. Traditionally it seemed self-evident that the world was made by God. Now it appears that the world in which we humans actually 'live, and move and have our being', far from having been created by a supreme divine being, is largely of our own making.

At first this statement may not only sound blasphemous to the ears of the traditionally religious, but appear a travesty of common sense and a manifestation of human megalomania. Certainly, it would be ridiculous to assert that we humans created the distant nebulae, the sun or even the planet earth. That is not what is meant by suggesting that we humans live in a world largely made by the species *Homo sapiens*.

Initially, and at a superficial level, there is a simple way to illustrate the truth of the assertion that we humans largely make the world we live in. It is this. We live in houses that we build. We dress in clothes that we make. Much of the food we eat does not come directly from tree or field but has passed through several stages of human processing. And the world which chiefly occupies our attention day by day – business, work, sport, entertainment, the arts, books, television, radio and so on – is all part of a culture created by our species.

We have no trouble in acknowledging the human origin of these aspects of the world we live in, but they constitute only the surface of a much deeper world which we humans have created. Much hangs, as we shall see, on what is meant by the ambiguous and many-faceted word 'world'. We commonly speak of 'the world' as if it were perfectly clear to everybody just what we are referring to. If we consult a dictionary, however, we find that 'world' is a very complex concept, whose meaning depends partly on the context in which it is used. Sometimes we mean the planet earth on which we live, sometimes we mean the whole physical universe, sometimes we mean a quite limited area of human concern, such as 'the world of politics', 'the world of sport' or 'the Muslim world'.

The reason for this ambiguity is that the very concept 'world' has a hidden subjective component. This is made clear by the etymology of the word, which is derived from the two Germanic roots, *wer* ('man') and *ald* ('age'); it refers to the age or context in which humankind lives. In similar fashion Hebrew (*'olam*), Greek (*aion*) and Latin (*saeculum*), while originally meaning an age or era, came to connote 'this present age' and hence 'this present world'. Whatever world one is thinking about, it is also tied to the dimension of time. Further, as we shall see in Part I, every world is, in part, a human construct, depending on how we have been conditioned both by our culture and by our own personal experience.

This deeper world is so important that without it we could not even become human. Yet it is a world which the human species as a whole, and over a long period of time, has slowly created. The world we live in is not an absolute, external reality which is independent of how we think and act; it is a relative world partially dependent upon us. This constitutes a strange paradox. We live in a world whose shape and meaning have been slowly constructed by the human species, yet it is only by means of this world that our species has in fact become human.

Traditionally, our forebears believed that it was God who created both us and the world, and that he did so for a meaningful purpose which he designed. A basic theme of this book is that we humans are slowly coming to realise that what each of us inhabits is a world of meaning which we ourselves have put together. There are many and various worlds of meaning; we humans, both collectively and individually, have actually constructed them all.

The reason why we are better placed than our forebears even to contemplate such thoughts is that, with the advent of modernity, we have entered into a vastly different world of thought. It is a cultural change just as radical as that which occurred in the Axial Period. This term, coined by Karl Jaspers, is now commonly used to refer to the few hundred years on either side of 500 BC, a period in which the great religious traditions had their origin – Zoroastrianism, Buddhism, Jainism, classical Hinduism, Confucianism and Judaism, leading to Christianity and Islam.

The Axial Period and the more recent advent of modernity are two transition periods which divide human cultural development into three main phases. These are further discussed in Chapter 7 (see Figure 2, page 107) but, since some references are made to them earlier, a brief description is provided here. The first cultural period may conveniently be called the Ethnic Phase, for during it the many independent cultures evolved from, and served to perpetuate, ethnic identity. The second may be called Transethnic, for in this phase ethnic identity was relegated to a secondary place. The prophets, seers and teachers who pioneered the Transethnic Phase refocused human attention on superhuman realities or goals which transcended the boundaries of ethnic identity. The three traditions which most successfully achieved their transethnic potential were Buddhism, Christianity and Islam, with the result that at the advent of modernity these three had practically divided up the globe among them into the Buddhist Orient, the Islamic Middle East and the Christian West.

The third phase of cultural development originated in the Christian West but has subsequently been transported all around the globe, and has already influenced the non-Christian world more deeply than traditional Christianity was ever able to do. At the same time, of course, this cultural phase has also undermined the traditional forms of Christianity. This third phase may be called Global, as it is global in its influence and horizon and is already creating aspects of human culture which are becoming universal to the planet. It could also be called the Secular Phase, in that it fastens attention on *this* world rather than on *other-worldly* goals as the Transethnic Phase of culture did. [1]

In this Global Phase of culture into which modernity has led us we have come to focus attention on the human species itself, as part of the planetary biosphere. We have become aware of what all humans have in common irrespective of class, race, religion, gender or age. We have developed a growing concern for humans' rights. We have come to see that what were regarded in the Transethnic Phase as divine or transcendent absolutes are actually of human origin.

But just at the point where we are coming to acknowledge how much of the world in which we live has been created through the millennia by the human species itself, the frightening truth is beginning to surface in our collective consciousness that it is also a very fragile world. What has taken millennia to construct can also be destroyed – and in a very short time. The human species has within it both the capacity to create and the capacity to destroy. We can destroy quite deliberately and often do so, as in warfare. But, even more serious, we can destroy through ignorance, by gross interference with the planetary ecology on which our life depends.

Part I of this book proceeds step by step to look at how the human species, slowly at first, created the various worlds in which we humans have lived both in the past and in the present. Every such world started with language, and it was this which enabled thought, story and culture to evolve, eventually producing rich, complex and sophisticated worlds.

Part II examines how the worlds we humans have constructed are the outcome of the search for meaning, and how religions evolved. Religions are elaborate systems of thought, constructed by humans out of the symbols to which the creative human imagination gave birth. But with the coming of the Global Phase of culture the traditional symbol systems are disintegrating, threatening us with a loss of meaning.

Part III discusses the transition from the world shared by Christendom to the emerging global world. In place of the former dualistic world, where humanly created symbols had become objectified into other-worldly entities, we are now seeing ourselves in a monistic psycho-physical universe. The future of humankind is inextricably tied to the future of the earth. We humans now find ourselves to be an essential part of the complex living earth and yet also responsible for its future. On us is the onus for creating a meaningful and worthwhile future.

PART I

How Human Worlds
Are Created

CHAPTER 1

In the Beginning
We Created Language

The world in which each of us lives as a thinking, planning, enquiring creature has been largely, if not quite wholly, created by human language. Without words we could not ask questions about the world, let alone attempt to answer them. Without words this book could not be written nor could you be reading it. Without words we could not communicate our thoughts to one another. Without words we could not even think the thoughts being expressed in this book. Without words we certainly could not speak about the world. Without words, it will be suggested later, we humans would not even possess the kind of consciousness in which we are aware that we are human selves, selves who have a past as well as a present and who live in a world to which we must relate. Can it be true that human self-consciousness depends on words? Let us explore further.

Words are the bearers of meaning in two different senses of the word 'bearer'. It is self-evident that words are the bearers of meaning in the sense of conveyance. Words are the means by which thoughts are conveyed from speaker to hearer. What is less self-evident, and has been all too little noticed, is that words also give birth to meaning. It is open to question just what level of thought we would be able to reach without access to words.

We may concede that the other higher animals appear to be capable of some level of thought, but do they think 'thoughts'? It is precisely because we cannot converse with them through language that we have no way of knowing. And in the absence of evidence to the contrary it seems probable that non-human animals, lacking verbal communication, have no capacity for abstract thought as we do, however much visual images of some kind may flit through their kind of consciousness. But having no capacity for abstract thought means that they live in a timeless present in which they remain unaware of past or future. They experience no consciousness of self and are unaware of any world of meaning. Meaningful thought, as we humans experience it, appears to depend on words.

Benjamin Lee Whorf (1897–1941), one of the pioneers of the modern study of language, wrote:

> Thinking is most mysterious, and by far the greatest light upon it that we have is thrown by the study of language ... the forms of a person's thoughts are controlled by inexorable laws of pattern of which he is unconscious ... thinking itself is in a language ... every language is a vast pattern-system, different from others, in which are culturally ordained the forms and categories by which the personality not only communicates, but also analyses nature, ... channels his reasoning, and builds the house of his consciousness. [1]

What words are, and how they perform their function as the bearers of meaning, will be discussed more fully later. It is sufficient here to say that words are the building blocks of human language, and without such language we cannot become human (as we normally experience the human condition) nor can we develop even the simplest form of human culture. The latter constitutes the social world in which we live. As John McCrone says in his illuminating book *The Ape that Spoke*, 'Language paved the way for all the special human abilities that we so value – abilities such as self-awareness, higher emotion and personal memories. Language provided the building material with which evolution could write revolutionary new software for the hardware of the ape brain.'[2]

Too often we take the existence of verbal language for granted. It has always been there, just like the air we breathe. By the time we have reached sufficient maturity to reflect on the nature of language and whence it came, language has long been an essential part of us and helped to make us what we are as humans. We may in fact never bother to reflect on our dependence on language, just as humans for thousands of years never reflected on the origin or quality of the air we breathe. Whorf went so far as to say, 'Natural man, whether simpleton or scientist, knows no more of the linguistic forces that bear upon him than the savage knows of gravitational forces.'[3]

As we take language for granted, so also did the ancients. If it is true that language is as old as humanity itself, on the ground that without language we could not be human, then it is understandable that the ancients should have assumed language to go back to the beginning and to be basic to creation itself. Both the ancients and we ourselves have been brought up in a cultural context where speech has been assumed. Therefore language was experienced as something inherited from the past, existing from time immemorial.

Even though language may appear to many moderns to be a mundane fact of life arousing neither excitement nor mystery, it was far from being so for the ancients. They may not have asked very penetrating questions about its origin but they did hold it in some awe. Moreover, as the biblical myth of the Tower of Babel exemplifies, they had some appreciation of how their welfare depended on being able to speak a common language. Without it they were thrown into division and confusion. It seemed to them to be self-evident that 'At first, the people of the whole world had only one language and used the same words'.[4]

Thus, in the biblical tradition, language was assumed to be as old as creation, and to have come from God. As we shall see, language was even thought to participate in the eternity of God, for God was conceived as one who spoke and uttered commands. But we can talk about language generically only because of particular languages. If language is as old as creation, what was the particular language which existed at the beginning? For Jews, and later for Christians, it was the language of Hebrew which was assumed to be, not only the language of Adam, the first man, but also the language of God. It is introduced into the story of Adam and Eve without any prior explanation, in contrast with such activities as agriculture, metallurgy and music, the human origin of which is specifically referred to. It was simply taken for granted that language was there from the beginning and that God was able to converse in it with humankind and deliver commandments (which are necessarily in verbal form).

Most people today would regard the assertion that God originally spoke Hebrew as an anthropomorphism of the quaintest kind. But in the pre-modern world it was common for Jews and Christians to believe just that; their convictions about the language God spoke would have been much closer to those which still obtain in Islam. Muslims regard Arabic to be the language of Allah; for that reason they believe the Qur'an should not be translated into any other (merely human) language since that would distort the absolute and perfect character of the revealed 'word of God'. The original Qur'an is believed to be in heaven, having been communicated to Muhammad, sura by sura, through the archangel Gabriel. Thus, in Islamic belief, Arabic is the language of heaven. Traditionally, therefore, Jew, Christian and Muslim all agreed that language originated with God and is as eternal as God; they simply disagreed about which particular language God originally spoke.

It also seemed self-evident to the ancients that language was a medium of power. Perhaps this was because words, being invisible and intangible, appeared to belong to the non-physical realm of spirit. (Spirit, that is breath or wind, also mystified the ancients and was associated with unseen power.) Words were thought to be powerful perhaps because of their association with authority. Someone uttered a command and others jumped into action. The belief that words embodied power caused the ancients to take with deadly seriousness the operation of blessings and curses. We need only think of how Isaac, having uttered his dying blessing over the wrong person, was powerless to retract what his words had set in motion.

Particular words assumed sacred significance in various cultures. In Hindu culture the Sanskrit word 'mantra' (literally 'instrument of thought') referred to a verbal formula which, when repeated in ritual, was thought to be instrumental in conjuring up and wielding supernatural power. Of special importance was the Vedic syllable 'Om', believed to contain the creative power of brahman. It became part of the most universal mantra of Tibetan

Buddhism, 'Om Mani Padme Hum', a formula which shows how the Hindu practice had left its deposit in Buddhism. In most religious traditions particular words, phrases and verbal formulae came to be treated in practice as mantras, that is, a set of sounds the repetition of which was thought to set in motion some form of transcendent power. It is exemplified in the Christian tradition by the practice of repeating the 'Hail Mary'.

In monotheistic cultures, the words spoken by God or having some association with God were naturally the most powerful of all. It was said that, when God spoke, his word would go forth from his mouth and not return to him empty but accomplish whatever he had intended. The phenomenon of prophecy became central to the Judaeo-Christian-Islamic tradition simply because the prophet was believed to be the mouthpiece for God. The oracle uttered by the prophet was quite literally 'the Word of God'. Prior to the rise of the prophets, people made physical representations of their gods. They used the visual medium for worship of the mysterious forces they believed they were encountering. The prophetic emphasis on language led to the iconoclastic destruction of idols and images. From then onwards speech became the exclusive medium through which humans were thought to make contact with God. Humans spoke to God in their prayers. God spoke to humans through the prophets. Words triumphed over the merely visual and the concrete.

Even though Christians came close to challenging the prophetic assertion that God was not to be seen by any person, when they developed the doctrine of the incarnation they continued nevertheless to affirm that it was the word which had become flesh, and that God had finally spoken through his son. In the course of time the whole heritage of the Christian cultural past came to be referred to as the 'Word of God'. To this day the Jew treasures the Tanach, the Christian treasures the Bible and the Muslim treasures the Qur'an, because each holy scripture respectively is believed to be the word of God. Thus language, whether it be the language of prayer or the revealed word of God to his people, remains the foundation and medium of traditional religion for Jew, Christian and Muslim.

Since language was held in awe by the ancients and was believed to go back to the time of origins, it is only to be expected that the Judaeo-Christian tradition, even in its earliest myths, should acknowledge the primacy of words. True, the English Bible opens with the words 'In the beginning God ...', as if implying that everything began with God. But if we explore the biblical story a little further, we find that the opening words of the Hebrew Bible may be better translated as follows: 'In the beginning of God's creation of the heavens and the earth, when the earth was yet without form or meaning, when darkness was over the face of the abyss, and the power of God was hovering over the surface of the waters, God said, "Let there be light" and there was light.' Put this way, the main verb in the long opening sentence is not 'created' but 'said'.

Thus even the Bible, in describing origins, unconsciously asserts that words came first. The initial act of creation consisted of speech, the uttering of words. As the biblical writers saw it, it was of course divine speech – but it was nevertheless speech. (The early Christian theologians reaffirmed this in their doctrine of *creatio ex nihilo*, declaring that God created the world out of nothing simply by uttering the divine *fiat* – let it be!)

It is probably this concern with the power of the spoken word in the original creation myth that came to be reflected by the evangelist in the Prologue of the Fourth Gospel. Its opening words may be literally translated as 'In the beginning was the word and the word was close to the Deity and *Deity was in fact the word*. It was in the beginning with the Deity. All things came into being through it [i.e. the word] and without it nothing came into being that has come to be. In it was life and the life was the light of humankind.'[5]

To both the ancient myth-teller of Genesis and the author of the Fourth Gospel it was self-evident that speech was so essential to the world that it went back to the beginning of things. It was as if speech participated in the divine reality, could not in fact be separated from that reality; it was speech which brought order out of chaos.

This is the very point where the theory of biological and cultural evolution begins to deliver to us a great shock, perhaps even greater than it caused in the nineteenth century. For if humanity has evolved biologically and culturally from pre-human creatures then the evolution of language is itself part of that evolution. Language, as the etymology of the word (from the Latin *lingua*, or tongue) indicates, is a form of communication peculiar to the human species. It consists of attributing symbolic significance to various standardised patterns of vocal sounds (in English there are about forty-five) which are produced by manipulation of the tongue. 'Speech, involving the use of symbols, must have been one of the first indications of humanity', wrote archaeologist Graham Clarke. 'Until hominids had developed words as symbols, the possibility of transmitting, and so accumulating, culture hardly existed.'[6] Language has to be recognised, therefore, as a corporate product of the human species. It is a human creation.

Language has been evolving for a very long time. We do not know precisely how, or for how long, it has evolved. Humans emerged in their present form no later than about 40,000 years ago and probably earlier. We can conclude with some confidence that just as the human species evolved biologically from pre-human species, so language in its diverse forms evolved from pre-linguistic forms of communication. Language did not suddenly appear on the scene from some superhuman or divine source, as traditionally assumed, any more than the human species itself suddenly appeared on this planet in the form we now know it.

Rather, language evolved as the human species evolved, for, without the capacity for language, we would not be fully human as we now understand the term. Because we are human we have the capacity for language; because we have the capacity for language, and have in fact developed language, we have been able to become human. Humanity and language, it seems reasonable to conclude, developed simultaneously, each assisting the development of the other. But if language evolved in tandem with the human condition itself, then we are faced with this paradoxical enigma: language is at one and the same time a human product and that which enabled our species to evolve into *Homo sapiens*. Of course language was not the product of an individual human but of humanity as an evolving species. No human individual is self-made; yet there is a sense in which the human species is self-made, or (better) humanity is a self-evolving species. Language is the collective product of the powers of human imagination and creativity and, as it develops, it further stimulates that same imagination and creativity.

Here we must distinguish between language and non-verbal forms of communication. Most living species have developed methods of communication, some vocal (such as bird calls) and some visual (such as display). Human language is unique in using sounds symbolically to create words. Words are arbitrary conventions, invented by humans, and that is why they differ so much from one particular language to another. Except for a few onomatopoeic words, there is no essential connection between the sound of a word and what it represents. That is why words for the same object can vary in sound so much from language to language. Words originated as arbitrary vocal symbols, first to name visible objects and events, and then to refer to imagined objects, abstract concepts and ideas. But words are something more than vocal sounds used symbolically; otherwise they could not be transformed into written form. The transition of words from speech to writing shows that verbal language is a non-physical human creation which transcends both its oral and written manifestations. It has proved to be of almost unbelievable importance in opening the door to a non-physical world (such as that discussed in Chapter 4).

Since there is a great deal about the origin of human language that we do not know, we can only make an intelligent guess as to the time-span over which it developed. It may well have taken a million years from its earliest beginnings. The question of why language developed is even more puzzling. But, considering both biological and cultural evolution, we are forced to conclude that language developed from within the potentially human species as the most effective way of responding to the challenges of its environment and of furthering its will to live. It may have been the one important advantage which the evolving *Homo sapiens* had over the Neanderthals, who eventually disappeared.

Language is a human product. It seems rather curious, therefore, that when the biblical myth of origins came to be questioned and to be replaced by the Darwinian theory of biological evolution in the nineteenth century, those who tried to reconcile the new view of origins with the Christian tradition did not pay more attention to the blatant anachronism now present in the myth. For the myth assumed the use of language. It even made the uttering of words the founding act of creation. Something which must thenceforth be acknowledged as a human product was being referred to as preceding the creation of humanity, and even as being the divine creative power itself!

During the nineteenth century, if not before, it was common to acknowledge that much of the biblical language used in reference to God was anthropomorphic. When people spoke of the 'the face of God' or 'the wrath of God', they were clearly using language symbolically, applying human features to a superhuman being. But little attention was paid to the association of language with God. If language is a human creation then it is just as much an anthropomorphism to speak of the 'word of God' as it is to speak of the 'face of God'. What this implies for the understanding of God is discussed later. At this stage let us pursue what it implies about the world in which we live.

In drawing attention to the primacy of words, the biblical myth was (no doubt unintentionally but perhaps intuitively) pointing to a basic truth. Words *do* go back to the very beginnings of the human condition. Words *were* the instrument which, more than anything else, enabled our particular species of hominid to become human. But words did not come on to the human scene from outside. Words were not of supernatural origin. Words emerged from within the evolving human condition. Words and the human condition evolved simultaneously.

Strangely enough, there are hints of this even in the biblical myths themselves, and this lends credence to the suggestion made above that the myth may express hidden intuitive depths. In the myth of the origin of humankind (Genesis 2:19–20) the story-teller relates how

> out of the ground the LORD God formed every beast of the field and every bird of the air, and brought them to the man to see what he would call them; and whatever man called every living creature, that was its name. The man gave names to all cattle, and to the birds of the air, and to every beast of the field; but for the man there was not found a helper fit for him.

The primary purpose of this myth of course was to explain the origin of humankind in general and of male and female in particular. But of special interest is something the story-teller betrays quite unconsciously: the acknowledgement that the names of the creatures came not from God but from humans. The myth attributed to humankind the prerogative of naming all the living creatures. The process of naming called for human imagination and was in itself a creative act. Thus the ancient story-teller was consciously acknowledging that language is, at least in part, a human creation.

This takes on greater significance when we realise just how important names were for the ancients. Names were not just for utilitarian use – a convenient identification tag. The name of a person or of a creature was thought to embody in some mysterious way the essence or spirit of that being. Hence the ancients were often reluctant to let their real name be known by any but their friends lest, for example, those whom they did not trust should insert their name in a curse formula with detrimental consequences. To know the name of someone was to be in a position to exercise power over that person. Fear of having one's name misused in those days is strikingly similar to our current concern to retain our personal privacy and not allow information of a personal kind to be too readily available to others, as through a computer network.

If one possesses power simply by being able to name, how much more power does one assume if one has the privilege of creating the name in the first place! Reflected in the myth, therefore, is the awareness that words embody creative power and that some words at least are of human origin. Although the myth makes specific mention only of the names of creatures, from our much later vantage point we are able to interpret that as a pointer to the fact that the whole of language is a human creation.

The reason why we do not know when, how or why language evolved is that it left absolutely no fossil deposits until the advent of writing, and that takes us back only some five thousand years. Anthropologist Richard Leakey believes, 'It is safe to assume that our ancestors had command of a sophisticated verbal system long before [that]'.[7] He sees the development of language to be roughly parallel to that of tool technology but this does not mean that either phenomenon depended wholly on the other. Leakey suggests that since language is so crucial for human culture its beginnings must go back at least to about 500,000 years ago. He concludes:

> Our ability to speak is just one aspect of the evolutionary drive to create a more accurate world in our heads. Just as making and using tools allows us some measure of control of our world, so too does the ability for creative thinking and the transmission of those thoughts. This is the heart of the cognitive advancement that created the human mind.[8]

According to Erich Harth, the Neanderthals could not have spoken as we do, for the fossil evidence suggests they did not possess the anatomical prerequisites to produce the required variety of sounds. Some think that speech may have first appeared about 150,000 years ago and that it came suddenly. The view represented by Noam Chomsky and his school of linguistics concludes that, 'Language descended upon the hominids like a gift from heaven, a *creation*, rather than a product of evolution.'[9] But once symbolic language began to develop, then, as Jacques Monod pointed out, it opened the way for another kind of evolution, one of ideas, knowledge and culture.[10]

Language begins with words, and probably the first words were those which named visible objects. 'Naming something makes it stand out more clearly from the surrounding background,' says McCrone. [11] He observes that, whereas animals respond in a general way to a familiar set of surroundings, humans, by virtue of being able to name the objects within view, can mentally lift any one of them out from its context and focus on it. What is more, anything which is so foreign that it cannot immediately be named is treated with suspicion, interest or fear, until it can be adequately named.

Words are so much a part of our life that we usually do not realise what extraordinary things they are. A word, as distinct from a cry of anguish or joy, is a particular set of sounds, which becomes a vocal symbol for something that is otherwise unrelated to it. The advent of the first words constituted a quantum leap in the evolution of our species. 'Once early man acquired the habit of using symbols instead of waiting for the real thing to come along, he started unlocking all his mental doors', says McCrone. [12] 'Language has been the tool with which humans have sculpted extraordinary new mental structures on top of the mind's natural foundations.' [13] We usually assume that it was the human mind which created words. That is only partly true. For it is also true that the creation of words led to the evolution of the human mind on the foundation of the former and more primitive animal mind.

Until the mid-nineteenth century we assumed that the human species was created just as we are now. We are becoming slowly adjusted to the overwhelming probability that we humans have become what we are only after an immensely long time of slow biological evolution. Evolution is often thought to apply only to the physical form of living organisms. But it applies equally to what we call, for want of a better term, the human mind. By 'mind' is meant our conscious awareness of our capacity to think, feel and deliberately exert a will. To our forebears it seemed self-evident that our minds (or souls) were spiritual entities (spiritual organs) which had been created by God in their mature and finished state in much the same way as our bodies were thought to have been. It now appears that our minds developed by slow evolution just as our physical bodies have done.

As McCrone explains in some detail, and rather convincingly, the key to the evolution of the human mind is language. 'Until our apemen ancestors developed language, they would have been as much creatures of the present as the rest of the animal kingdom.'[14] There is so much about human self-consciousness that we take for granted, such as an awareness of the passing of time, that we impute it to all conscious creatures. The probability is that animals have little or no sense of time but live in a kind of timeless present. Certainly they can respond to changing conditions. Their stomachs tell them when it is mealtime, if they are used to regular meals. But they have even less awareness of time past than young children, who are just beginning to develop some sense of time. McCrone concludes: 'Our apemen ancestors would have lived in the present tense and used memory only to broaden their under-standing of what was going on from moment to moment. Modern man's memory for his own personal history is an artificial addition to the mind, only made possible once he had developed speech.'[15]

The advent of words meant that the many tiny incidents of our past experience which are stored in our brains as memories could become linked together by nerve pathways in the brain. It is as if words opened up access to them by much faster routes than were previously available. (Indeed this is illustrated in part by the practice of 'word association' in depth psychology.) In this way words make it possible for a memory bank to be constructed, to which we have access by way of conscious recall.

Without a warehouse of memories to which we have instant access it would not be possible for us to develop an awareness of the passing of time and of the past. This in turn makes possible the development of human self-consciousness. As McCrone explains:

> Self-consciousness is clearly based on this artificial memory control which came with language. . . . We know who we are only because we have a stream of memories stretching back to our early childhood which can be recalled at will – or at least after a determined search. Control over our memory banks allows us to form the sense of personal identity that is the core of our feeling of self-awareness.[16]

Though at present we are unable (and indeed may never be able) to trace in any detail the origin of human language and the subsequent evolution of the human mind, we can observe the development of language and the growth of human self-consciousness in infants today. It is not exactly the same, of course, because today's human infant is born into a rich and sophisticated verbal environment and has the potential to develop in only a few years what took the human species as a whole several hundred thousand years to achieve.

Nevertheless, it enables us to learn much about the role and significance of language for the human condition. We have good reason to rejoice when our own children utter their first words. It constitutes a quantum leap in their own personal development, similar to that of the human species in the distant past. Here we must distinguish between merely copying a vocal sound in the way a parrot does and actually recognising mentally that the sound has a particular meaning. Only then does it function as a word. From only a few days old an infant can babble all kinds of sounds, but these remain meaningless. It is usually about six months to a year before a child can use its first meaningful word and sometimes a child's working vocabulary may remain restricted to only two or three words for quite some time. The first words a child learns to use are usually names, such as Dada and Mama. And the process does not just involve repeating and adopting the words heard from others. Once the child has grasped the idea and function of words, it may show remarkable ability for creating new names and words.

Dominant among the first words used are names for concrete, visible, identifiable objects. These words are not only the first steps in learning a language with which to communicate with others; they are also laying the foundations for the construction of yet another individual human mind. There is some evidence to suggest that where children are denied the opportunity to learn language, as in the extreme examples of being reared from infancy by animals, not only does the capacity to develop language atrophy, but they lead only a non-human, animal-like existence.

The importance of language for human existence can hardly be overemphasised. As Whorf said, 'Speech is the best show man puts on. It is his own "act" on the stage of evolution, in which he comes before the cosmic backdrop and really "does his stuff".'[17] Language and the human condition are inseparable. They have evolved together and are still evolving. Biologically we have evolved exceedingly slowly, for our genetic history is as old as life itself on this planet – perhaps three billion years. But, linguistically and culturally, our humanness is comparatively recent – perhaps a hundred thousand years – and it is evolving relatively much faster. Language is not something fixed and static. Language and culture in their many and diverse forms are ever changing and evolving. And with them we also change and develop.

The evolution of language is thus the key to human conscious-ness. We usually do not appreciate how much the quality or level of human consciousness we each experience as individuals depends on the human culture into which we are born. Language is the key to human culture and enables the emergence of what Leakey called a 'shared consciousness'. He observed:

> Perhaps the most pervasive element of language is that, through communicating with others, not just about practical affairs, but about feelings, desires and fears, a 'shared consciousness' is created. And the elaboration of a formal mythology produces a shared consciousness on the scale of the community. Language is without doubt an enormously powerful force holding together the intense social network that characterizes human existence.[18]

We enter this shared consciousness at birth and it in turn nurtures the development of our own individual consciousness.

As Don Cupitt has well said, 'Language is the medium in which we live and move and have our being. In it we act, we structure the world and order every aspect of our social life. Only Language stands between us and the Void. It shapes everything.'[19] We live in a world of language yet language is a human creation. In a very important sense the world in which we live is one which humans, as a species, have created.

Language and humanity evolved together. This fact is even

more far-reaching in its consequences than the theory of biological evolution as popularly understood. It means that everything dependent on language is also human in origin and form. It means that the Bible is a human product, that the Qur'an is a human product, that anything claiming to be the 'word of God' is a human product, for all such things are contingent on language, which is itself a human product. It means, further, that such basic concepts as truth, meaning, purpose, extremely important though they are, have been created by humans as part of the evolving phenomenon of language itself.

In Western culture it has been customary for us to assert that it was God who created the world in which we live and move and have our being, that it was God who brought order out of chaos, that it was God who brought all things into being. But how did the word 'God' come to us, and why? This is discussed in Chapter 9. It is sufficient to say here that even the word 'God' is of human origin, however much it may be regarded as the most important word in our cultural past. When we try to explain the meaning of 'God' we cannot avoid using words. Keith Ward asserted that, 'To believe in God is to believe that at the heart of all reality, of this very reality in which we exist, is Spirit, Consciousness, Value, Reason and Purpose.'[20] However we choose to interpret those words we are unable to disentangle ourselves from language; and even to associate consciousness with God is to impute to this term the experience of self-consciousness which we humans possess and which itself has been made possible by language.

In view of this, it is of fresh interest to observe that even the biblical tradition asserted that God created the world by uttering words. It is language (or uttering of words) which has created us as humans and it is language which forms the basis of the world we live in. Language, God and the human species can never be divorced from one another. The familiar words of the Fourth Gospel suddenly take on an entirely new meaning: 'In the beginning was the word, and the word was with God and the word was God and the word brought all things into being . . . and the word became flesh and made its dwelling in us.'

CHAPTER 2

With Language We Create Stories

A ll words, in all languages, are of human origin. We humans, collectively as a species, created them. That was only the first stage in human self-creativity. For words, unlike the signs and calls by which the other higher animals communicate messages to one another, open the door to a more complex level of human creativity. The next creative stage in human evolution was the creation of stories. We must now explore how this came about and what tremendous significance it was to have.

At first it may seem surprising to suggest that basic to the evolution of the human condition has been the phenomenon of story. This simple word, just like the human language which made it possible, holds the key to understanding the human condition. It is no accident that, as soon as we have taken our first steps into language, we are readily attracted to the telling of stories. The fascination which stories hold for children most probably reflects that long period in our cultural past when story-telling provided the growing edge for human culture. Moreover, the cultural heritage of a people is most clearly to be found in the cycle of stories it transmits from generation to generation. It is by means of stories that we interpret what is happening to us and come to understand who we are. When we say, 'That is the story of my life', we are recognising that human life unfolds as a story. So what is a story and how did it come to emerge?

The creation of words to name visible objects was only the beginning of language. Those are still usually the first words we acquire as infants. But along with them come words expressing feelings, words of description, words of command such as 'No!'. Words of action quickly follow. Only at the beginning, and mostly with naming words, are words acquired as isolated units. Thereafter, words are mostly acquired from the context of language in which they are heard. New words, especially abstract terms, are learned in context. As time goes on it is largely the context which enables the child to grasp the significance of each new word. In mastering a new word children try it out in different contexts until they get it about right. Words are used mainly in contextual relationships. Not only do they acquire their distinctive usage from the way they relate to others but they possess different shades of meaning in different contexts.

By far the most important aspect of the way in which words may be related together is the phenomenon by which they are synthetically constructed into sentences. The sentence consists wholly of words, yet it expresses a thought or idea which is not contained in the individual words, either singly or all together (if merely jumbled). The sentence is much more than the sum of its parts. Thus language develops synthetically. It evolves, in much the same way as life itself evolved, by the synthesis of simple components into more complex wholes. We call this the grammar, or syntax, of the language.

How did grammar come into being? It did not descend from a superhuman source any more than did the words it uses. No one invented it at any particular time. Grammar evolved, out of the potential already inherent in the relationship of words with one another. The idea that it evolved without any conscious effort on the part of humans is illustrated by the fact that, to this day, children learn basic grammar without ever being taught it. Indeed, the grammatical structure of a language may be so complex that only those who have fully mastered its use, as professional linguists, can then analyse it.

Thus the acquisition of language does not depend on conscious knowledge of its grammatical structure but usually precedes this. Young children can put new sentences together with such remarkable speed that their skill must derive from something more than the mere repetition of what is heard. It has been suggested that the human brain, in the course of evolution, has gradually become genetically prepared (programmed, we might say) for the acquisition of language. If this is so, the modern physiology of the human brain simply reflects the long evolutionary process of language development from the distant past. Jared Diamond notes that the gulf between human language and animal vocalisations is so great that most linguists now regard as unanswerable the question of how human language evolved from its animal precursors. [1]

Syntax, or the grammatical construction of sentences, was the necessary step between the creation of words and the creation of stories. Then, at some stage, there developed the ability to express the sequence of time; this was achieved through the creation of tenses in verbs. The achievement was not as straightforward as it may at first appear. Our English tenses of past, present and future are by no means found in all languages. Ancient Hebrew, for example, was more concerned to distinguish between an action which was completed and one which was uncompleted; this left some ambiguity as to whether one was speaking of the past, present or future.

This temporal ambiguity in some languages may reflect the long period in which early human consciousness was slowly becoming different from animal consciousness. So far as we can surmise, animals live in a timeless present. Humans, by contrast, live with an awareness of the passing of time. For us there is a past and future, as well as a present.

Did some glimmering awareness of the passing of time come to be reflected in verbal tenses, or did the evolution of language enable an awareness of time to develop? As so often in trying to understand the evolutionary process we have here an example of the chicken and egg conundrum. We are perhaps justified in concluding that any faint awareness of the passing of time was at least intensified by the advent of language, and for this reason. While the human memory retains mental images of experiences after they have passed, they remain internal and unique to a person unless, and until, they are communicated to others. One of the many great advantages which language provided for humans was the ability to share such experiences with others. This would have sharpened human ability to distinguish past experiences from present ones, and eventually it enabled humans to imagine future ones. In some such way human consciousness was extended to stretch back into the past and be projected into the future.

As soon as human consciousness had developed sufficiently, therefore, to retain memory of a past and to distinguish it from the present, the door was open for story-telling. Stories need not be very complex. In recent years the increasing number of storybooks published for the very young illustrate just how simple stories may be. When children today first begin to compose stories for themselves these often consist of only two or three sentences and are about some everyday event which they have observed or imagined. But what makes even three sentences into a story is some sense of sequence. And the sequence, like time itself, runs in only one direction.

The sequence of events so necessary for the construction of a story is not to be identified, however, with the experience of earthly time, even though there is an affinity between the two. Stories need not be related to any particular period of time; they may be timeless. Stories, like dreams, emanate from the human imagination. For our very ancient forebears, as for children today, this fact did not make them any the less real. Indeed the story may be experienced as more real than what is externally observed or experienced. This is why children often do not clearly distinguish between what they have only heard about or imagined and what they have actually seen. The story appears to have a reality of its own and frequently becomes the grid which is superimposed upon the sense-data of experience. This still happens whenever journalists' 'stories' reflect their own prior constructions of what they expected, or would like to have occurred.

The stories which have survived from ancient and pre-literate cultures are often very complex indeed. They evolved over a long time and were the means of perpetuating the character and identity of that culture. They constitute the focal point of the cultural heritage, interpreting, or giving meaning to, the patterns of behaviour, both ritual and moral, which structured the life of that society.

The corpus of traditional stories found in ancient societies is commonly referred to as its mythology. But we need to examine more closely just what is meant by 'myth'. Unfortunately this word has become very confusing, for in popular usage it has come to mean a narrative or belief which is both fictitious and false. Certainly myths are fictitious in the sense that they are stories created by human imagination but, wherever myths express the convictions of people, far from being false they actually constitute for them the ultimate truth. It is only for those who stand outside the culture that the myths are false.

Let us start from the beginning. Our word 'myth' is derived from the Greek *muthos*, which originally referred to anything mouthed or uttered in speech. It eventually came to mean a tale or story. In particular it was used in ancient Greece to refer to the many stories of the gods which formed the cultural heritage of the Greek people. These stories received their classical literary form in the epics of Homer.

Before discussing how these myths functioned in pre-literary Greece, let us note how the Greeks also pioneered the path by which the term 'myth' came to be degraded. In the flowering of the enquiring, analytical and philosophical Greek mind from the age of Pericles onwards, narratives which were purely imaginary or fictional came to be distinguished from those which referred to events in the empirical world. The Greek word *historia* (from which we derive both 'history' and 'story') referred to a form of knowledge or information which could be gained by critical enquiry (*historeo* meant 'to enquire into'). The myths which had been handed down by tradition came to be acknowledged as belonging to a different genre. As these were narratives about the gods, they could not have originated in the observation of events or by rational enquiry. Yet even at that stage the myths were not dismissed as worthless or untrue. Rather they were regarded as allegorical or symbolic accounts of reality, which had to be properly interpreted in order to understand their real significance.

It was at a later stage that the Greek word 'myth' came to be degraded. This is reflected in the New Testament where we read,

'Have nothing to do with godless and silly myths' (1 Timothy 4:7) and where 'wandering into myths' is contrasted with 'listening to the truth' (2 Timothy 4:4). We may note in passing that our word 'story', in spite of once being synonymous with history, has also manifested a fall. In journalistic usage it still claims to be a reliably attested narrative (an item of current history, in fact) but in other contexts it can mean just the opposite, as when a parent accuses a child of 'telling stories'.

So while in popular usage the word 'myth' today refers to a story, belief or notion that is false, in academic circles the word has become greatly upgraded. We have come to appreciate the significance and function of myth in human culture. It was the view of Mircea Eliade, a highly regarded historian of religion, that 'it seems unlikely that any society could completely dispense with myths', even though in modern times they often assert themselves in the form of political myths. He went so far as to predict that 'the understanding of the myth will one day be counted among the most useful discoveries of the 20th century'. [2]

Here are some of the ways in which myth is redefined in academic circles. Mark Schorer writes:

> Myths are the instruments by which we continually struggle to make our experience intelligible to ourselves. A myth is a large controlling image that gives philosophical meaning to the facts of ordinary life; that is, which has organizing value for experience. A mythology is a more or less articulated body of such images, a pantheon. Without such images, experience is chaotic, fragmentary and merely phenomenal. It is the chaos of experience that creates them and they are intended to rectify it. All real convictions involve a mythology. [3]

Similarly, Barbara Sproull writes:

> Myths proclaim basic attitudes towards reality. They organise the way we perceive facts and understand ourselves and the world ... there is no escaping our dependence on myth. Without it, we cannot determine what things are, what to do with them or how to be in relation to them. [4]

We are now in a better position to return to the Greek myths and examine their function in the Greek cultural tradition before the age of Homer. Myths are stories produced by human imagination, but they were not created for entertainment or even for information. The myths of ancient humankind are stories by which they interpreted their experience and by which they created an ordered world out of the chaos of irregular and often quite unexpected experiences they encountered. Myths were not mundane stories but sacred narratives. Mircea Eliade observed of the ancient myths:

> Myth tells how, through the deeds of Supernatural Beings, a reality came into existence, be it the whole of reality, or only a fragment of reality – an island, a species of plant, a particular kind of human behaviour, an institution. Myth, then, is always an account of a 'creation'; it relates how something was produced, began to *be* ... The actors in myths are Supernatural Beings. They are known primarily by what they did in the transcendent times of the 'beginnings'. Hence myths disclose their creative activity and reveal the sacredness of their works ... It is this sudden breakthrough of the sacred that really *establishes* the World and makes it what it is today.[5]

Myths of the kind Eliade is referring to are found in all preliterate societies, whether of the very ancient Greeks or the comparatively modern pre-European Maori and the Australian Aboriginals. The chief characters in these myths are gods, spirits or other creatures who, though superhuman, reflect the rational, emotional and volitional experience of humans. The stories told about these figures explain why things are as they are, and why events occur as they do, sometimes regularly, sometimes irregularly. The stories of the earth-mother and sky-father and their progeny (to take a very common example) encouraged people to relate to the world in a personal and trusting way. They explained why the various phenomena and events they observed were not disjointed, unrelated or haphazard. They gave reality a unity and some degree of reliability. They helped people to feel at home on the earth.

Today we are so far removed culturally from the ancient scene where the stories of the classical mythologies were told and heard with such conviction that it is difficult for us not to bring our own criteria of truth to bear upon them. It is grossly anachronistic to do so. The modern dependence on the scientific enterprise, the modern distinction between history and legend, and even the modern concern for logical consistency, meant little to the ancients. Although each of the myths usually had an inner consistency, within the total corpus they were very often inconsistent with one another.

This is why myths should be associated with poetry and not with history or science. Myth is the language of faith.[6] Myth, or the telling of imaginative stories, is how the human species has been able to relate to, unify and feel confident in its environment. Myth was the method by which the primitive human mind first structured the environment, providing it with cohesion and meaning. Thus, as is discussed more specifically in the next chapter, the creation and retelling of stories is the process by which the developing human consciousness creates for itself a world, or as Eliade said above 'establishes the World'.

This can be usefully illustrated by the way in which the Babylonian creation myth, known as *Enuma Elish*, functioned at the great Babylonian New Festival (*Akitu*). This association of myth and ritual arose out of the annual round of seasons and the Babylonians' accompanying observation that at the onset of winter all life was departing from around them. They came to feel that it would not return in spring unless the appropriate rituals were performed. These consisted of an eleven-day festival during which the story of the original creation by the god Marduk was solemnly recited while the Babylonian king acted out the leading role in the accompanying drama. As a result, the Babylonians could look with confidence to the coming of another spring. Hence the creation story not only structured their world by explaining how it came into being but the re-telling of the myth was instrumental in re-creating it.

The culture of the ancient Middle East was agricultural and depended for its livelihood on the cycle of the seasons and favourable weather conditions. This led to a predominantly cyclic view of time in which, on a daily, monthly and annual basis, the ancients felt they were continually returning to the point where they had been before. For us the seasons still structure time, but we are more aware that the daily and annual cycles are contained within irreversible linear time, thus leading to a kind of temporal spiral.

The changing phenomena of nature observed in the seasonal cycle – sprouting, growing, flowering, fruiting, harvesting, dying – pointed to mysterious forces and powers. It was around these powers that the chief myths evolved. They enabled the ancients to interpret reality in a constructive and positive way. The gods personified not only the destructive forces of nature with which the ancients had to struggle, such as storms, droughts and pestilences, but also the beneficent powers on which they depended for life, such as the sun, the moon and the return of growth. The stories they told about these gods had the effect of personalising reality, of humanising it and making it appear reasonably friendly to humans.

Although the myths of ancient times were chiefly about the gods, there was no clear dividing line between the divine and the human spheres. Supernatural figures, who (in our view) were wholly the product of creative human imagination, mingled freely with humans. Sometimes the myth focused on human figures, as with the now-famous Epic of Gilgamesh, where the hero of the story was conceived as two parts god and one part man. Gilgamesh inherited from his goddess mother great beauty, strength and restlessness but from his human father he inherited mortality. This sets the scene for one of the many fascinating themes in the myth, the human search for the immortality enjoyed by the gods. Human imagination had (unconsciously) created the gods as a way of understanding natural phenomena and ordering the environment. The ancients conceived of the gods in such a way as to embody their own values and aspirations. The gods were immortal, as they aspired to be, for death is a phenomenon which humans, even to this day, find difficult to accept.

All the ancient mythologies appear to have been polytheistic. The only pure relic of polytheistic myth to be found in the Bible is the little narrative in Genesis 6: 'When humankind began to multiply over the face of the earth and daughters were born to them, the sons of the gods observed that the daughters of human-kind were beautiful; so they took as their own wives whomsoever they chose from them all.' This marital union gave rise to a hybrid race, half-human and half-divine. The biblical narrator used this story to explain the reason for the Flood, by which God intended to make a new start with humanity, confining it to the descendants of the righteous Noah.

This story marks the beginning of the transition from one phase of culture to another, the Axial Period described in the Intro-duction. It is only to be expected that a radical transition in culture would be reflected in the myths or stories which embodied it. The Bible not only manifests the new type of myth which was to characterise the second phase of cultural development but also clearly illustrates the transition. The myths of Phase One (or Eth-nic) culture were stories about the gods. The myths of Phase Two (Transethnic) culture, by contrast, are stories about humans, but humans inspired by divine or some other transcendent sources. In the transition from Phase One to Phase Two, myth left the realm of pure fantasy and became grounded in human history. In narrating exploits of the gods, the creative human imagination enjoyed almost complete freedom. The myth-makers of Phase Two were considerably more limited in that their story had to be reasonably consistent with known earthly conditions.

This is exemplified in some of the most powerful cultural traditions which emerged out of the Axial Period. The Buddhist myth focused on the historical figure of Gautama, his experience of enlightenment and the dharma (or teaching) which resulted from it. The Jewish myth fastened on Moses, the deliverer and law-giver, who led a group of Hebrew slaves to freedom and nationhood. The Christian myth fastened on Jesus of Nazareth, whose life, death and resurrection were interpreted as the key to human salva-tion and the centre of human history. The Islamic myth fastened on a set of writings, the Qur'an, known to have been uttered by the historical figure Muhammad but believed to have originated from a divine source. In each case the myth was historically grounded.

Certainly, over time, there was a strong tendency for the myth to be embellished with other-worldly (i.e. non-earthly and non-historical) components. Indeed it was largely because of this phenomenon that the evolving myth gathered increasing power to convince. While Theravada Buddhism continued to focus on the historical figure of the Buddha, greatly magnified in religious stature, Mahayana Buddhism so fastened on the nature of Buddha-hood that the original historical figure became almost irrelevant. Although the ancient Fathers of the Church tried hard to preserve the humanity of Jesus in balance with the divinity which had quickly been imputed to him, it was the latter which became dominant through most of Christian history. Jesus was affirmed to be the one and only Son of God and, as such, was incorporated into the Holy Trinity. The myth of the incarnation of God in an historical human being, as expressed in the mythical narratives of a virginal conception, a resurrection from death and an ascension into heaven, largely obscured from view the original first-century Jew. Only in modern times has the full humanity of Jesus been rediscovered. While the full humanity of Muhammad has always been retained in Islam, he has come increasingly to be honoured so that any apparent disrespect to him can lead to violent reaction, as in the Salman Rushdie affair.

The transition from the Phase One type of myth to the histori-cally grounded myth of Phase Two is thus documented in the Bible. The Israelite prophets fought vigorously against the gods of nature whose stories or myths permeated the cultures of the ancient Middle East. They finally laughed those gods out of court. The gods of the nations were declared to be idols, human creations which had neither power nor existence. In their place the prophets affirmed the God of Israel as the only true divinity. But the story or myth which ancient Israel told about its God turns out to be the story of the people of Israel themselves. The only exploits which can be told about this God, after his act of creation, are those which have to do with the fortunes of Israel. Whereas the now-displaced gods of old had been associated with natural phenomena, this God was the one who controlled human events, or what we now call history. Thus the Bible, more than any other set of holy scriptures, focuses attention on humans and human events. There is a great deal of historical material in it. From Genesis 12 on, the Bible is the story of a people. For Jews, and later for Christians and Muslims, the story of Israel was also the story of God.

Judaism, Christianity and Islam eventually diverged because their respective stories (or myths) began to unfold differently even though they acknowledged a common origin. From our modern vantage point it has been easy for us to see the difference between their kind of story (which is chiefly about humans and contains genuine historical content, whether it is about the people of Israel, the figure of Jesus of Nazareth or a holy book) and the stories of ancient mythology (which were about the gods and may be judged to be wholly the products of poetic imagination).

What has been less obvious until quite recently is that, in both the pre-Axial and the post-Axial cultures, the reality of human existence was being interpreted through a story or cycle of stories. Indeed, no distinction was made between reality and the story. Reality was the story and the story was reality. And this was as true for the cultures who worshipped the earth-mother as it was for the Jew, Christian and Muslim, who each lived by their own story. In the case of Christendom, for example, the story told by Christianity was a description of reality. Jesus Christ was the key to understanding the universe; he was the Saviour and Judge, to whom all human existence should be directed.

It is only in modern times that we are coming to see that Christianity is based on a story in the same way as Judaism and Islam are based on stories, and in a similar way to how the ancient cultures were based on stories. Moreover, in all cases the stories were humanly created, not so much by any one individual as collectively by communities. They were stories which evolved. Only in modern times are we able to appreciate how these stories evolved. With Christianity, for example, the Christian story began to evolve around the memory and influence of a first-century Jew from soon after his tragic death at the hands of the Romans. Christians firmly believed (and many still do) that they were in a living personal relationship with a divine spiritual being. The power of the evolving Christian story had taken them over, and they continued to respond to it through the ages. It was the Christian story which became their understanding of reality and which they accepted as the model for their own life-story.

The history of Christian civilisation itself is striking testimony to the power and significance of story, as is the history of Islamic civilisation. But perhaps most striking of all is the history of the Jewish people, who have retained their identity through 3000 years all because of their commitment to the story which constituted their identity.

But the very fact that in modern times we can talk about story or myth in this way is an indication that we have been passing through a further cultural transition of a radical kind. And it is this fact which explains why the traditional myths of post-Axial cultures have been losing their appeal. Increasing numbers of modern people appear to have outgrown them in much the same way as a child who has loved to hear the same story again and again suddenly reaches a point of personal growth where the story has lost its spell.

The application of the scientific method to historical research has led us to draw a sharp distinction between myth and history. Just as the historically grounded myths of Phase Two culture rendered obsolete the non-historical or purely imaginary myths of Phase One culture, so modern historiography has undermined the emotional and intellectual power of the historically grounded myths of Phase Two. We have been moving, in stages, from pure myth to historically grounded myth to history. In the case of the Christian myth, this has necessitated the attempt to disentangle the 'historical Jesus' from the 'Christ of Faith', the image of devotion in which Christians have long imagined him. Historical research, we now find, is able to recover all too little knowledge of the original historical Jesus and this has served to bring home to us that what Christians have lived by all through the centuries is in fact a story – a very powerful story, but one which evolved as human imagination and devotion reflected on a specific set of experiences.

In the initial process of shock which this transition has brought to the Christian West there has been a strong tendency, on the one hand to dismiss story or myth as unreal and irrelevant, and on the other hand to assume that historiography has a finality which it does not possess. In fact what we commonly call history is also a story, and the historian is also a story-teller. It is no accident that 'story' and 'history', as noted earlier, are derived from the same Greek word.

Just as the post-Axial myths were historically grounded and did not allow the creativity of human imagination quite as much free rein as in pre-Axial times, so in modern times the scope of the historian is even more limited. Historians have to weave their stories out of the extant evidence of the past, and every element of the story should be consistent with, and based upon, that evidence. Even so, much in the writing of history is still left to the imagination of the historian and to subjective selection, from the evidence, of what is deemed significant. History is not the careful assembling of unrelated chronicles but the telling of a story. The historian is like a detective attempting to reconstruct the crime, always a difficult task and sometimes impossible.

The history of our family, of our nation or of humankind itself, on which we draw for the understanding of our place in the universe, is still a story, a human and fallible construction; it is never final and is always open to review. Each generation has to write history afresh for itself. We are always having to revise the way we tell the story by which we live.

The modern way of telling stories, that is, by using the so-called historical method, not only undermined convictions about the traditional stories (or myths) by which people lived hitherto but also served to bring home to us the relative character of all cultural products, including story-telling, history writing, religion and philosophy. In particular it has made it clear that no story is ever final and no empirical 'truth' is ever absolute and unchangeable. This applies also to people. However much we may admire the saints, holy men and women, sages and inspired leaders of the past we have to acknowledge that none of them was perfect. They were products of particular cultures. They cannot be divorced from their time and place and set on a timeless pedestal. The moment we do so we are replacing them with an image and story of our own making. There may be a legitimate reason for doing so, but only if we acknowledge what we are doing.

Does this mean that the time for telling stories is over? Not at all! Even modern historiography is a new way of telling stories. We still depend on stories. What is new is that we now have to acknowledge that they are stories. Moreover, there is no longer one simple story which we all share. We are in the midst of a bewildering medley of stories. As Don Cupitt has said:

> Our world has now become so complex and fast-changing that people can no longer live lives that are governed by stable customs and religious imperatives. The body of stories that people live by cannot be held within a single fixed canon. Instead we have now a whole living literature which is being continuously added to and modified as values change.[7]

We still live by stories, for from ancient times right down to the present we humans have used stories or myths to structure the world in which we live. We cannot really get away from the telling of stories. Our whole life is lived within them and by them. By stories we reach back to our roots in the past and by stories we try to look into the future. The daily news comes to us in the form of stories told by journalists. In each day of our life we are weaving the story which constitutes our very identity. Because stories shape our lives and because, collectively, we have created the stories in the first place, it is legitimate to conclude that by means of stories we create the world we live in. We must now turn to exploring just how we do this.

CHAPTER 3

With Stories We Create Worlds

'Man has language because he has a world, and he has a world because he has language', wrote Paul Tillich.[1] Similarly Don Cupitt asserted that 'it is by telling stories upon stories we build up our world, ourselves and our history as language and in language'.[2] Why is our world related to language? Do we realise how dependent upon language is the world we see ourselves living in? As fish live in an ocean of water, so we humans live in an ocean of language. But whereas there was an ocean of water before it brought forth fish, the ocean of language is a human creation.

For as long as any of us can remember we have been aware of living within a world. But what is a world? A world may be defined as a cohesive whole. It may be analysed into component parts, but it is only in relation to all the others that these parts constitute a world. A world is more than the sum of its parts. It is the whole that is created when the parts are seen in mutual relationship. As Paul Tillich said, a world 'is a structure or a unity of manifoldness'.[3] There may be many worlds, as we shall presently see. But when we speak of '*the* world' we mean that which constitutes the world for us. In other words we mean *our* world. As we see and feel this world, it is for us one world and not a collection of unrelated parts. This is why, when we want to refer to the whole of reality in our world, we often call it the *universe*.

But how did we come to have this notion of a world which is a cohesive whole? It is not because we have ever actually seen it. What we see with the naked eye at any one time is only an infinitesimal part of what we are referring to when we speak of 'the world'. Within the narrow horizon of our vision we are confined to what we can see from our own particular viewing point, and this even excludes the viewer. We see ourselves only by means of a mirror. What we mean by 'the world' is something we have mentally constructed in the course of experience. As the coherent whole which the word 'world' implies, it exists primarily in the mind. Much of what we take to be the world, we have in fact never seen at all; it has been constructed by us from what we have learned from others. When we talk about 'the world' we are referring to something which we see, as it were, only with the mind's eye, even though we do not doubt its external existence for one moment.

One of the first philosophers to realise that what we refer to as 'the world' is a mental image was Giovanni Vico (1688–1744). He drew a clear distinction between the 'world as it really is' and 'the world we create out of experience and scientific investigation'. The world we create and perceive is never free of subjectivism. Indeed the reason why the world often seems to be intelligible and coherent to us is that our own minds have constructed it in the first place.

Vico was a forerunner of Immanuel Kant (1724–1804). Kant drew a similar distinction between the world of objects in themselves (these he called 'noumena') and the world of objects as we know them, or as they appear to us to be (these he called 'phenomena'). What is for us 'the world' is a unity we ourselves have constructed in our own mind out of the phenomena of our experience and out of what we have been told by others. Each of us has been unconsciously constructing it from birth and we are continually modifying and extending it throughout life in the light of new experiences and information. Indeed if we go back to what memories survive from our childhood we may be surprised to realise just how much our 'world' has in fact changed and expanded in the course of our lifetime.

But our actual mental construction of this world started even before the time of which we retain any memory. A newly born child sees or feels no 'world' as such but mainly exists in a state of undifferentiated unity with its surroundings, just as it did in the womb, and not unlike the state to which some mystics seek to return as a desirable goal. From birth onwards the infant receives an increasing host of sense impressions – sound, sight, touch, smell, taste – which originate externally. As adults we take these for granted and they may appear simple and easy to grasp. But this is because, when we receive these sense impressions, we immediately and unconsciously relate them to the world we have already constructed, and where we find for them the most appropriate place to contribute to the coherent whole. There it constitutes new information for us about what is external to us. Further, the very existence of the world we have constructed sometimes causes us to screen out from these external messages what does not interest us. For the infant, however, no such world as yet exists; the sense impressions are probably quite unrelated and present themselves as a meaningless chaos.

The brain is the physical organ which performs the task of bringing order out of this chaos. It acts as the initial creator of our world. The computer-like human brain has the capacity to synthesise into a coherent unified whole all the impressions mediated through the five independent senses; it appears to be already programmed to do so at birth. More, in the first few months of life the infant's brain has to work with the skill and speed of a modern computer in order just to begin to construct its emerging world, simple though that may be when compared with the world of a mature adult.

These first steps in the construction of our personal world we humans probably share with the other higher animals, though we can only make a judgement about it by observing their behaviour. As animals explore and become familiar with the territory of their habitat, they are probably establishing mental images which they will continue to recognise thereafter and which will give them confidence within that territory. For example, when a domestic cat is removed to a new home it needs some time to become familiar with its new surroundings before it settles and appears to be at ease. It often begins by exploring every aspect of its immediate environment; it appears to be mentally marking out a space, that is, creating a world to which it can relate as its own.

The world we humans construct for ourselves probably starts in much the same way. Memories established by visual and other sensory experiences begin to be related together. Yet, at first, it is not so much one complete mental picture which constitutes our world as a cluster of visual impressions, which we retain in a mental reservoir and from which we select for the purposes of recognition. Visual impressions are extremely powerful in constructing our world and are the reason we have come to speak of ourselves as having a world-view. Yet the world we see in our minds is usually very fuzzy around the edges, owing to our increasing ignorance the further we move from the small well-known patch in which we move about each day.

Although this world exists primarily in our heads we normally identify it absolutely with reality. This is because, insofar as its foundations are formed out of sense data, our convictions are continually reconfirmed by appeal to the same sense data. So we need to reach quite a high degree of sophistication before, with Kant, we can begin to draw a distinction between what we see in our heads (or mind's eye) and the 'thing in itself'. If this distinction is valid it means that we are always one stage removed from the inferred world, the 'thing in itself'. The world we see ourselves living in, and to which we make our conscious responses, is our own mental construction, rather than the external reality itself.

This distinction becomes clearer when we move to the next stage of constructing our world. The appeal to sense data is only the beginning of *our* world, as distinct from the inferred external world. Leakey observed: 'The realness of the world in your head depends both on the quality of the information collected and on the way in which it is integrated into a coherent form.'[4] Before the sense data can be adequately integrated into the kind of coherent worlds we humans construct, it has to be interpreted. Similar sense data can be interpreted very differently. That is why artists, for example, often depict the world in ways we have not seen.

Each of us constructs a world slightly different from those of all others. For one thing, each of us is at the centre of our own world. This is unavoidable, as we construct our worlds from what we see with our own eyes and from what we individually experience. No two people view reality from exactly the same point in space. No two have exactly the same experiences nor do they interpret them in exactly the same way. This means there are as many different ways of constructing a world as there are people.

In the more extreme cases we have recognised this for some time. It is the reason why we sometimes say we are worlds apart in our thinking. A child and a parent have different worlds and consequently respond differently. An Australian Aboriginal and a European live in very different worlds (this was particularly marked in the period before they had any mutual contact). An orthodox Muslim and an orthodox Christian live in different worlds. A fundamentalist Christian responds to a world very different from that inhabited by a secular humanist. To the extent that we come from differing family backgrounds, differing localities, differing cultures or from differing periods in history, the worlds which we have constructed and to which we respond may vary considerably.

If our worlds were completely different, however, human existence as we know it would be impossible. It is only because our worlds have much in common, overlapping at many points, that we can relate to one another. Conversely, the more our worlds differ, the more difficult we find it to converse with one another or even to establish real personal contact with one another.

Paradoxically, the things which so clearly illustrate how different our worlds may be – language and culture – are also the things which deliver us from the danger of solipsism and which, further, enable us to construct worlds that have a substantial amount in common. Because we are shaped by a common language and culture, our many individual worlds are grouped together in closely related cultural families. People nurtured in the same culture are clearly likely to construct worlds which are much closer to one another than those being constructed in quite different cultures, because they are drawing so much of their world from that culture.

In any culture which manifests strong cohesion, we can even

speak of the many common elements of the individual worlds as constituting the 'shared consciousness' of that culture (as referred to in Chapter 1). It is this common or shared world which gives identity to the culture. But this points to the fact that, for much of the content of the personal world each of us constructs, we are dependent on culture and hence on language. That is the significance of the assertions of Tillich and Cupitt quoted above.

If the human brain plays an essential role in laying the foundations of our world by synthesising all the messages conveyed to us by the senses from external reality, language has a similarly important role. Benjamin Whorf's linguistic studies led him to two cardinal hypotheses: first, that all higher levels of thinking are dependent on language, and second, that the structure of the language one habitually uses influences the manner in which one understands one's environment.[5] With the latter process, 'A change in language can transform our appreciation of the Cosmos'.[6]

Language leads us to higher levels of thought by enabling us to interpret the world we have begun to construct and to give it some meaning or significance. We have long tended to assume that thought precedes language and that language has simply been invented, or has evolved of necessity, as a way of communicating thought. It is partly true that thought of a kind precedes language because the higher animals appear to be capable of thought and yet they possess no verbal language. But it is only *partly* true, because the phenomenon of thinking remains severely restricted without verbal language. Whorf maintained that the much higher levels of thinking which we humans can reach have been made possible only by the advent of such language. That is, once verbal language began to evolve, it made possible the creation of internal human worlds which previously did not exist. These internal human worlds constitute the character of human consciousness. They contain much more than visual images; they interpret the basic sense data by evaluating it and giving it meaning. But meanings and values depend on the existence of language.

The process by which language has enabled us to construct an internal human world had three main stages. The first was through the creation of naming words. As seen in Chapter 1, assigning names to specific objects is itself a creative act, which makes a start at bringing order out of chaos. Just as the domestic cat, set down in a strange environment, may be thought of as mapping out a new world for itself as it explores the new habitat and builds up a store of mental images which it may thereafter readily re-cognise, so too, but at a much more sophisticated level, we humans use words to construct for ourselves a world which is thereafter known or re-cognisable. With words we order our environment and over-come chaos. To be able to name is to know. To know is to feel that we possess some mastery. We feel much more comfortable, more at home, surrounded by what can be named. That is why children learning to speak are for ever asking 'What is that?' To be able to name something is to be brought into a stable and safe relationship with it.

A good practical analogy for this is the work of the pioneer botanists as they identified the different species of plants and created names for them. Their work set the science of botany on an orderly footing. Once botanists have named the objects of their study they have transformed an apparently uncharted chaos into an ordered and known world. Indeed each new science quickly develops its own highly specialised vocabulary, partly for this pur-pose. By the same token, however, it makes us realise how human in origin and character the science of botany is (as indeed is the whole scientific enterprise). Plants do not come already fitted with name-tags; humans supply the tags. What the botanist does, in establishing some order in the study of plants, is analogous to what a little child is doing when continually wanting to know the name of each new object and phenomenon encountered. The child is instinctively learning how to order its environment so as to create a world in which it feels at home. To be able to name is to develop some mastery over external reality. It is the first step in creating a known world.

The unnameable, on the other hand, leaves us uncertain and afraid. It remains a dangerous intruder in our world. We acknow-ledge the importance of being able to name when we experience an illness. We are much happier if the doctor, in diagnosing our malady, can actually give it a name (even if he or she is not sure of the cure!). Being able to name the disease seems to us, psychologically, to be already halfway towards curing it. Our ability to name the unknown gives us an advantage and to some degree places the object at our disposal.

But the naming of tangible objects by the creation of words is only the first stage of constructing a world. The second stage involves interpretation of what is viewed as the world, an interpretation which expresses the significance of this world for us. Language is absolutely essential for this, for only through language can human consciousness understand, explore and create the phenomenon of meaning (this will be examined more closely in Chapter 6) and, in doing so, bring a new and significant dimension to the world we are constructing.

The process of interpreting our growing world not only involves an extension to our working vocabulary but requires words which function differently from naming words. These express our emotional response to the people and things around us. Out of these there quickly develops a rich vocabulary of words expressing value, such as nice, nasty, good, bad, pretty, ugly, loud, soft, and so on. All words of value, however sophisticated they eventually become, possess an essentially subjective component. We are expressing through them what is attractive or repugnant, supportive or dangerous, to us personally. The only values we ever know are human values. With such words we are interpreting our world on the basis of its value to us.

Then comes the third stage in the construction of our world, the stage by which we attempt to link up the various parts into a coherent and meaningful whole. A common phenomenon is that, whereas a two–year–old is always asking 'What is that?', a four–year–old is beginning to turn to another set of questions, such as 'Why does that happen?' and 'Where does that come from?'. These questions are answered by the telling of stories or myths, as discussed in the previous chapter. Asking questions about the origin of things now known by name, and about the causal connections which link the various aspects of the world, is of course an extension of our human need to gain mastery over it. The naming process simply provided the first step. The creation of words or concepts to express our relation to external reality marks the second step. The creation of stories, which have the effect of establishing the causal links and which possess explanatory power, marks the third step.

The further we progress from naming words to value words, and then on to stories, the more deeply involved we become with language. The world we are constructing increasingly depends on language. Without language we cannot even ask the questions, let alone attempt to answer them. Although external reality (the inferred 'real world') is not dependent on language, what we know as 'our world' certainly is. When we use the term 'world-view' we are implying a great deal more about our subjective contribution to our world than we usually realise. We are referring to a world we have ourselves constructed, and largely through the medium of language.

Words, language, stories, accompanied by established patterns of behaviour, constitute the core of a particular human culture. Into such a culture we are born. Parallel to the physical maternal womb from which each of us emerges at birth as a physical organism, there is what may be called a cultural womb, into which we are plunged at birth, and by means of which we develop into human beings. Language is the medium by which we are nurtured in the cultural womb to ever higher levels of self-consciousness. In the early years of life children are remarkably receptive to the culture being transmitted and can absorb it very quickly. In constructing their personal worlds children are being conditioned by the shared consciousness of their culture. As Benjamin Whorf observed, the kind of consciousness we develop, and the way we construct our world, are shaped by the language and culture into which we are born.

To illustrate the nature of a shared world, and the way it is created and grows to maturity out of a convincing myth, let us look briefly at the three cultures of Middle Eastern origin which, though acknowledging a common ancestry, have developed quite distinctive versions of what they inherited. A shared world depends at first on a common language. The Jewish world has never lost its dependence on Hebrew nor the Islamic world on Arabic. For a long time Christianity depended on either Greek or Latin. But even more important than common language is a common story or myth. It is this which integrates a culture and provides a common world within which to live.

We should note that, in each of the Jewish, Christian and Islamic myths, historical event is fused with mythical interpretation. Even in modern times it has been difficult to separate event from myth, and the attempt to do so has led to tension and debate within each tradition. Because of this fusion, as discussed in the previous chapter, these may be called historically grounded myths, in contrast with the nature myths of the Phase One cultures.

The foundation myth which remains basic to the Jewish, Christian and Islamic worlds began to emerge in the latter part of the second millennium BC. It forms the earliest stratum of the biblical Pentateuch; it is commonly referred to by biblical scholars as the 'J Source' and probably dates from around 950–900 BC.[7] This drew upon earlier tribal memories and legends to create an epic story, explaining the origin of the Israelite people and relating them to world history. It stretched from creation to the entry into the Promised Land and made the Exodus from Egypt the focal point.

This epic story constructed for the Israelites a meaningful world; it had many important components, which have tended to be assumed ever since by Jew, Christian and Muslim. It is a world which is meaningful because it was created by a divine designer. It is a world in which historical events are meaningful, and not accidental, because they fit into a divine plan. It is a world through which one can walk with the confident assurance that righteousness will ultimately triumph. It is a world in which a particular people have been chosen by God for a special mission and they are joined to God by an eternal covenant.

The myth of being the chosen people of God has structured the

Jewish world for nearly 3000 years. The Jewish world, according to their scriptures, was created 5754 years ago (this being 1994 in the Christian calendar). Time for them is structured around the weekly sabbath which commemorates the creation of the world. On that day Jews gather together ('synagogue' means a gathering) to rehearse their myth by reading the Torah, which chiefly narrates how they came to be delivered from slavery, constituted as the people of God by a covenant, and led to the Promised Land.

In the course of the Jewish year Jews celebrate the foundation events of their historically grounded myth. The festivals of Pesah-Matzot (Passover-Unleavened Bread), Shavuot (Weeks or Pentecost) and Sukkot (Tabernacles) probably originated as nature festivals from pre-Israelite times, but they were transformed by ancient Israel into annual celebrations of the founding events of their basic story. This in itself is an interesting reminder of the transition from Phase One to Phase Two culture.

The centre of the Jewish world has been the holy city of Jerusalem. Through the centuries of living in the Diaspora, Jews have continued to look forward to their return to this centre at the coming of the Messiah and, with this in mind, they end each Passover with the words 'Next year, Jerusalem'. In these ways the Jewish myth has created a world of structured time and space within which to live from generation to generation. Today even ardent Zionists, who are not at all religious in the traditional sense, continue to draw support from this myth.

The equivalent Christian myth was not a wholly new and original one; rather it claimed to be the legitimate completion of the Jewish myth, which was thereby extended and transformed. The Messiah whom the Jews still await was affirmed by Christians to have come. The old order from Adam to David had now been succeeded by a new order, with Christ as the new Adam and the Blessed Virgin as the new Eve. The Christian community or church claimed to be the new people of God, thus supplanting the Jews as the chosen people.

On the foundation of this Christian myth a new world was created in which time, space and history were structured differently.

The original world had begun at the same time and in the same way as the Jewish world but it was replaced by a new world, which began with the birth of Christ. This event, interpreted as the incarnation, now became the central point in history, dividing historical time into two eras, to be known as BC and AD.[8]

The first day of the week, the day of Christ's resurrection, became the new Christian sabbath. The chief annual Jewish festivals, Passover and Weeks, were christianised to become Easter and Pentecost. Jerusalem remained the holy city, eventually being seen as the symbol of the heavenly city. But the centre of the Christian world was Bethlehem, the birthplace of Jesus, which became the goal for Christian pilgrimage, along with many sites in Galilee and Jerusalem made holy by the events of Jesus' life and death. By making the birth of Christ the central point of history, Bethlehem the centre of earthly space and the mental image of Christ on the heavenly throne the focal point of the universe, Christians had constructed the Christian world on the basis of their myth.

As Islam suddenly erupted in Arabia some six centuries after the rise of Christianity it proceeded to develop its own distinctive myth. This differed markedly from the Jewish and Christian myths, even though it also drew heavily from them both. As has been well said, 'Christianity may be described as Judaism *transformed*, but Islam is Judaism *transplanted*.' Many aspects of Islam make it appear to be Judaism transplanted into Arab soil, and its myth remains closer to the Jewish one than the Christian one. In contrast to Christianity Islam reasserted the pure, imageless monotheism of Judaism and gave it an intense, even militant, missionary zeal. Muhammad, the last of the prophets, confirmed the words of the prophets before him from Abraham to Jesus, and came to be honoured as the personal instrument through whom God had chosen to deliver his final and absolute message to humankind, as now preserved in the Qur'an.

On the foundation of this myth the Islamic world was constructed remarkably quickly. The new people of God were the Umma Muslima, starting with the Arabs but soon incorporating other ethnic groups. Arabic replaced Hebrew as the language of

God. Mecca took precedence over Jerusalem as the holy city. Friday replaced the Jewish sabbath as the weekly day of prayer. Immediately following the Hijrah (or flight) of Muhammad from Mecca to Medina, there was established the first Islamic society. The Islamic calendar starts from this point and is calculated by the lunar rather than the solar year. Thus the Islamic world measures and structures time differently. Similarly, in the Islamic world, space radiates out concentrically from Mecca. Muslims turn to it regularly every day for prayer. Moreover, the more ancient Arab ritual of the annual Hajj (or pilgrimage to Mecca) received divine authorisation through Muhammad. All Muslims try at least once in their lifetime to travel to this centre of their world.

The Islamic story, in its time and place, was as powerful and convincing as the Christian story and became the basis of an equally impressive civilisation. As one moved from Christendom to Islam and vice versa, one was left in no doubt from the sounds one heard, the buildings and art one saw, the rituals one observed and the way people lived and thought, that one was moving from one world to another.

Each such shared world (and there have been many others in the course of human history) has its own unity and cohesion, supplied by the basic story. The story explains, in each case, the origin and nature of reality and the purpose of human existence. It provides the framework for the world which is substantially shared by all within it. Until the modern era, the shared world of each culture was identified with reality itself; to those within the culture it was 'the real world'. For those who embrace any of the traditional cultures, such as Judaism, Christianity or Islam, in anything close to the pre-modern commitment, this is still the case.

Only with the advent of modernity has it become possible to step, at least partially, out of the world of one's mother culture and see it as relative to time and place. This is also to acknowledge that this world has evolved in the course of time out of the collective experience and thinking of our forebears and is to be judged a world which has been humanly created. In the pre-modern era, however, the shared world of one's culture had the capacity to perpetuate itself from generation to generation with very little change, not only because of its inherent power to win conviction, but also because it was backed up by the authority of social pressure, to say nothing of the civil and religious dignitaries who wielded such power in the highly authoritarian societies of the past. Any threat to, or deviation from, the world-view shared by society as a whole was given no encouragement, and often quickly crushed.

Yet in spite of the greater willingness of people in times past to embrace without question, and adopt as their own, the world shared by their culture, they appropriated it in their own way, integrating it with their own personal experience. This normally went on quite unconsciously. There has usually been little awareness in the past of the fact that we each view reality a little differently and thus construct in our heads our own internal world.

Even so, there were occasionally in the past, as there are more commonly in the present, sudden or dramatic experiences which today we would describe by saying, 'My world fell to pieces!' The recorded experience of Paul on the road to Damascus is a particularly revealing example. The world of Pharisaic Judaism in which he had lived and felt so secure was suddenly shaken, as if by an earthquake. The Jewish myth upon which that world was based, and which had empowered him to persecute Christians in the interests of righteousness, for him suddenly cracked. A new myth – the Christian myth – began to replace it as he believed himself to be encountering the voice of the risen Christ. It left him not only blind but shattered. He needed time to construct a new world in which to live.

But if one's world is shattered, not because of its displacement by another, but because of some serious fault within it or some tragic event, then it may lead to grief and even despair. When people say that they have lost their faith, it is this to which they refer. They have lost the world in which they felt secure and in which they put their trust. A person's world may be shattered by the sudden loss of employment, or by the loss of a close personal friend or relative upon whom they have depended emotionally and who constituted an important pillar in their world. It may also be shattered because the controlling myth by which they had ordered their life has cracked.

In today's social and intellectual climate we are much more aware of our subjective role in constructing our world. We are much more aware of how our understanding of reality changes in the course of a lifetime. Social change has so accelerated during this century that we are becoming increasingly aware of the need to keep re-appraising the way we understand the context in which we live. This means that we face the need continually to reconstruct our world or to move from one world to another. It is with words and stories that we construct these worlds, an observation unexpectedly reflected in an ancient text, 'By faith we understand *the worlds to have been fashioned by the word* of God, so what had not yet come to light became visible.'[9]

But is there some more permanent reality out there, of which our world is but a personal interpretation, or do we live wholly in a world of our construction? That issue is explored in the next chapter. In the meantime it is important to see that what we have usually taken to be the ultimate reality is in fact a world of human construction. Josef Popper-Lynkeus once said, 'Every time a man dies, a whole universe is destroyed.'[10] There is an important sense in which, when a person dies, their world dies with them. We can equally say that, when a culture dies, it marks the death of a whole shared world. (This is examined in Part III.)

Inside the head of each of us there is a whole world. For us it is reality itself. Yet it is a world which we personally, along with others collectively, have actually constructed. It is through the tinted glass of this world that we respond to reality, for better or for worse. More than 2000 years ago the anonymous author we call Ecclesiastes seemed to stumble across this remarkable insight but, agnostic questioner though he was, he had no other recourse but to attribute to God the world to be found inside each of us. So he wrote, 'God has put *the world into the human mind*, yet in such a way that a person cannot find out what God has done from the beginning to the end.'[11]

CHAPTER 4

The Composition of Our Worlds

What common sense keeps confirming for us as the 'world out there' has turned out to be our own mental construction of the inferred reality. It is a mental image within our heads. We are one step removed from the total universe of which we assume we are a tiny fragment. Whatever is to be understood as the genuinely 'real world' is more elusive than we usually think. It has become necessary to distinguish between, on the one hand, the personal and shared worlds (which we humans have constructed) and, on the other, the inferred or real world which, in practice, we assume our world to be.

This distinction has been strikingly expressed by a physicist, Bruce Gregory, in a book with the challenging title of *Inventing Reality*. He writes:

> There is a sense in which no one, including philosophers, doubts the existence of a real objective world. The stubbornly physical nature of the world we encounter every day is obvious. *The minute we begin to talk about this world, however, it somehow becomes transformed into another world, an interpreted world, a world delimited by language.*[1]

In other words, the only world we 'know' with our minds, and talk about with one another, is different from the reality we infer by our senses, in that it is a world already interpreted by us. Our world, the world to which we respond in the way we live, is not simply reality itself (whatever that might be) but reality understood and interpreted through the grid of language and of our myth-based culture.

It is pertinent that this assertion was made by a modern

scientist, for it is the growth of modern science which, more than anything else, has been responsible for undermining much of the shared worlds of the pre-modern societies. The advent of empirical science (as outlined in the Introduction) has forced us to see that what our forebears took to be the real world was at best a partial view only. It was a world which had been evolving in each culture, constructed collectively out of experience and creative human imagination.

The modern scientific enterprise, as exemplified in the burgeoning number of sciences, has been particularly successful in bringing us into closer touch with the presumed objective universe. It has done so by challenging us to doubt every aspect of the shared world being transmitted in the cultural tradition. To express it over-simply to make the point quickly, we may say that those components of the shared world which could be confirmed by empirical testing were retained, or in some cases modified, while those components which had been created solely by human imagination (e.g. fairies, goblins, angels) were eliminated, or seen to belong to a different order and to function differently. As a result of the whole scientific enterprise, the shared world of the Christian West has been going through a radical transformation during the last 400 years. (This will be explored further in Part III.)

This change has not been confined to the West. The scientific enterprise is a human activity open to all races and cultures to employ. Because of its obvious benefits it has spread out from the West, where it largely originated, until today it is almost universal to humankind. It has become the basis of a new and global form of shared consciousness, one which transcends ethnic, cultural, national and religious boundaries. It has been building up a common body of reasonably reliable knowledge about the supposed real world, the objective world (see Chapter 12 for amplification of this).

The apparent success of the scientific enterprise, as evidenced by the complex technology to which it has given rise, brought to the scientific community the confident conviction that the world being revealed by science was in fact the real world and that at last humans were in complete touch with it. In the popular mind this confidence in the power of science sometimes reached the level of adulation. It was widely thought that, whereas the pre-modern world had been exposed as false, it had now been replaced by a scientific world as the true world. Thus the gap between reality and the world in the human mind (as discussed in the last chapter) could be deemed to be effectively closed.

Now that the first flush of success is over in the scientific enterprise, and there is time to reflect on what has been achieved, we are coming to realise that, in spite of all we owe to science, we still need to distinguish between reality itself and the world created by the scientific mind. Even though our scientifically based culture gives us confidence that we know more about the inferred reality than did our pre-modern forebears, we are still looking at it through a grid of our own making. It is still a world we have constructed. That was the point of Bruce Gregory's assertion quoted above.

We have substituted scientific laws for what was cultural tradition and folklore, and we feel much more confident with scientific laws because we can keep testing their validity. But even scientific laws remain human formulations. They are not to be observed in the external world. We humans have created the laws as a way of *interpreting* what we have observed. And we have had to use language, another human creation, to enunciate the laws. We may have replaced fairies and angels with quarks and leptons but we are still using words and language which we have created, in order to understand reality. The shared world being created by the scientific enterprise is just as much a humanly constructed one as those it has been displacing. It is still a world which we have constructed and which exists primarily in human minds. As Bruce Gregory bluntly puts it, it is a world invented by us humans. That is why scientists are making less extravagant claims than they used to. It is common for scientists now to refer to their theories as models rather than laws, thus acknowledging that these are not absolute structures which are built into the fabric of reality but human instruments created for the purpose of understanding it better. Any particular model will continue to be used so long as it proves useful to the on-going scientific enterprise. When it no longer proves useful it is discarded. The model must never be absolutely identified with the reality being investigated.

Once again we are brought back to the acknowledgement that we depend on language. There is no way for us to understand reality except through the medium of language. Even to refer to 'reality' (or 'the real world'), and to ask questions about it, we depend on language. Language shapes the way we ask the questions and this in turn helps to determine what will be deemed acceptable as an adequate answer. Thus Bruce Gregory says:

> Language tells us what the world is made of, not because language somehow accurately captures a world independent of language, but because it is the heart of our way of dealing with the world. When we create a new way of talking about the world, we virtually create a new world . . . Explanations, no matter how wonderful, are stories about how we got from where we were to where we are.[2]

The shared world which is emerging as a result of the scientific enterprise, therefore, is just as much a human construction as were the shared worlds being transmitted in the traditional cultures. It should not be identified with reality itself and hence fixed and final; it should be treated as a model open to continual change and adaptation. For this very reason, however, it differs significantly from the pre-scientific models. It is continually being tested for its inner consistency and its ability to make reliable predictions; from time to time it undergoes paradigm shifts, as Thomas Kuhn has clearly explained.[3] This process enables the scientific model of reality to win conviction on a global scale and to displace those confined to particular cultures.

There is one aspect in particular of the shared world being created by science which not only has caused it largely to displace the traditional one that used to be shared in the West, but also makes clear how much of our human worlds depend on language. The shared consciousness of traditional Western Christendom, like most of the societies representative of Phase Two culture, can be called dualistic. The Christian dualistic world was made up of two worlds, this-world and the other-world (the world-to-come). This-world consisted of the tangible, visible, physical world as popularly understood. It was thought to have had a beginning (some 6000 years ago) and it was expected to come to an end. The other-world was a spiritual world which, being outside space and time, had neither beginning nor end. It was intangible, largely invisible and virtually changeless or eternal. Humans were conceived as having a foot in both worlds. By virtue of our physical bodies we were thought currently to exist in this world. But by virtue of our immortal and non-physical souls we were thought really to belong to the spiritual world; that was where our ultimate destiny was believed to lie.

The other-world was not wholly invisible for it included the starry heavens above, this-world being confined to the basically flat earth of plains, mountains and seas here below. Consequently, on a clear night one could, as it were, view the other-world from afar, stand in awe of its grandeur and imagine the streets of gold, angelic choirs and life of bliss said to be found in that heavenly spiritual sphere. The reality of that other-world seemed for so many to be beyond dispute. The spires of the great cathedrals ever pointed to it, the cultural tradition affirmed it, and the most able intellects of the land were as convinced of it as the simplest peasants.

The cosmology of the new scientific world has gradually caused the other-world to dissolve by incorporating the starry heavens into this-world of space and time. The vertical dimension, which once appeared so convincingly to divide reality into two worlds, has itself become a dimension of this modern space-time world. The dualistic model of reality has been fading from human consciousness and replaced by a vast, more complex one-world model. This is why, as noted in the Introduction, modernity has often been described as the process of secularisation (the triumph of *this*-worldliness). The reason why the other-world could fade from modern human consciousness is that not only was it a human creation (as are all worlds), but it existed only in the corporate human mind and was constructed with the help of language.

The gradual disappearance of the other-world from modern consciousness appeared to leave only the physical or material world as the sum total of reality. The traditional dualistic view of reality had apparently been reduced to, or replaced by, a monistic, materialistic reality. Indeed, the rapid expansion of modern science has taken place within an intellectual climate where the philosophy of materialism was assumed, sometimes with very little critical examination. The behavioural school of psychology, for example, studies the behaviour of the human organism in a way which completely ignores the internal exercise of the will, the process of human thought and the reality of anything corresponding to such terms as mind or psyche.

More recently, the inadequacies of the purely materialistic view of reality have come to be felt even by some scientists. For it left us with a problem. How are we to understand and explain, on a purely materialistic base, the cognitive capacity of the human being, to say nothing of what (for want of a better term) we have been accustomed to call our spiritual dimension? An interesting and fruitful attempt to answer these questions is found in a book entitled *The Self and Its Brain*. Its joint authors are two scholars, both of whom have been knighted for their high achievements in their respective fields. John Eccles (born 1903) is a brain scientist and Karl Popper (born 1902) is a philosopher of science.

Popper agrees that the philosophy of materialism has been a great inspiration to the advance of science both in physics and in biology but he believes that materialism must transcend itself. The reason is that, as soon as one replaces the myth of the divine creation of the universe with the theory of biological evolution, one has to explain how an inanimate, material universe apparently has the potential to produce the 'human brain, the human mind, the human consciousness of self and the human awareness of the universe'. Popper shares with the materialists their 'emphasis on material objects as the paradigms of reality' but finds himself parting company with them 'when evolution produces minds, and human language ... [and] when human minds produce stories, explanatory myths, tools and works of art and science'. [4]

On a purely materialist basis the world can be analysed into its simplest components. These were long thought to be atoms but have now been further reduced to the sub-atomic particles of energy. If the universe consists of no more than inanimate particles of energy, what does this energy have which has enabled it, indeed motivated it, not only to form ever more complex patterns, but eventually to produce sentient, conscious beings who in turn have created works of art, philosophy and science itself?

The philosophy of materialism was forced to regard the universe as a very complex machine, the internal structures of which determine all that occurs. Such a view rules out any internal creativity; there can be nothing really new. This led Popper to the view that the universe, by virtue of its evolutionary nature, is creative, and 'that the evolution of sentient animals with conscious experiences has brought about something new. These experiences were first of a more rudimentary and later of a higher kind; and in the end that kind of consciousness of self and that kind of creativity emerged which we find in man.' [5]

Since the traditional model of reality as a dualism of matter and spirit is no longer very convincing, and since the model of reality as a materialistic monism has no place for human thought and experience, nor even for the scientist and the scientific enterprise, Popper looked for a new model. He has proposed a model of the universe consisting not of two worlds but of three; these three interdependent worlds he called World 1, World 2 and World 3. (To avoid confusion, the term 'world' will continue to mean any human construction of the whole of reality, and the terms World 1, World 2 and World 3 will refer to Popper's model. Popper's three Worlds may be regarded as a useful way of analysing any particular human world. Figure 1 overleaf is based on Popper's model but has been adapted to illustrate the themes of this book.)

World 1 is the presumed physical universe. It contains all physical objects and processes, whether on this planet, within our galaxy or within the universe as a whole. It encompasses both organic and inorganic substances. It contains all living organisms,

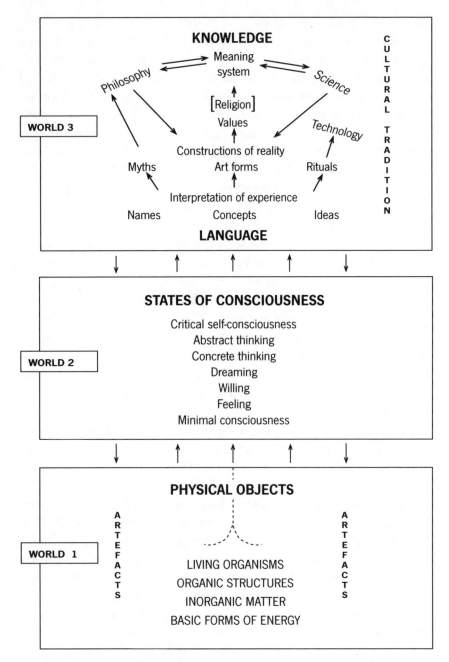

Figure 1: *Three World model of reality*

including the human species. It contains all living organs, including the human brain. In World 1 also are the artefacts fashioned by humans or other creatures.

Popper referred to his World 2 as the world of subjective experiences. It consists of states of consciousness and includes all levels of consciousness from that present in the most lowly forms of life right up to human self-consciousness. While it is only our own personal consciousness that we know first-hand, we can empathetically understand that of other humans without too much difficulty. The consciousness experienced by the higher animals is obviously more difficult to appreciate; we can only attempt an intelligent guess at how an animal experiences its particular state of consciousness, but there is good reason to affirm that it exists. Human consciousness consists of a set of subjective processes, such as recognising, remembering, thinking, feeling, deciding, willing and perhaps even dreaming (and it may be conjectured that all living organisms share in some or all of these, even if at the most minimal level). Each of these processes is very private and is not readily accessible to the external observer. That is why we know almost nothing of animal consciousness from the inside. It is only through the medium of language, as we shall see, that we know anything about the consciousness present within other humans and, as a consequence, reach a clearer understanding of our own consciousness. World 2 is a sphere of intense activity.

Humans have the potential to reach a level of consciousness which non-humans do not reach. The latter do not experience self-consciousness in the way humans do. Animals, it would appear, have no awareness of their own inner world. Before such awareness can develop, a language comparable to human language is needed. Certainly there are various forms of communication among non-human organisms, but the quality of the human mode of communication through language gives rise to a whole new world – World 3. And it is by encounter with World 3 that self-consciousness is reached.

World 3 is what makes Popper's model of reality so distinctive. He refers to it as the 'products of the human mind' (yet in a way these products and the human mind itself evolve in tandem). These products are very real objects but they are quite non-physical. The key which effectively opened up World 3 was the advent of language. So initially World 3 consisted largely of names, descriptive terms and concepts, but then quickly built up into such things as stories, poetry and explanatory theories (both true and false). These led to works of art – visual, dramatic and musical. Also to be found in World 3 are patterns of behaviour, codes of ethics, and social institutions. As cognition and human reflection became more abstract through the increasingly symbolic use of language it led to religion, philosophy and science.

We need to distinguish between the non-physical objects of World 3 and their physical embodiment in World 1, for the two can readily be confused. Let us take some examples. A marble statue belongs, of course, to World 1. But the really important feature of the statue, what reveals the sculptor's creativity, is not the quality of the marble but the statue's form or shape; that belongs to World 3. A Beethoven symphony may be written as a manuscript of music. The manuscript exists in World 1. Even the sound waves we hear when it is being played come to us in World 1. But the pattern of the musical notes belongs to World 3. The symphony cannot even be identified with any one performance of it, for performances may be disappointing; the symphony is a non-physical creation, which enables it to be interpreted in performances. As Popper says, 'The World 3 object is a real ideal object which exists, but exists nowhere, and whose existence is somehow the potentiality of its being reinterpreted by human minds.'[6] Thus the symphony, once composed, continues to exist as a human product whether it is being played or not. Indeed it came to birth in World 2, in the creative consciousness of Beethoven, before it was ever written down or even heard in World 1.

A book, including both its pages and printed type, belongs to World 1, but the story belongs to World 3 and, once it has been composed, continues to be a World 3 object. Before the advent of writing, all stories, myths, proverbs and folk wisdom were objects in World 3 without being embodied in World 1 at all and they came to birth through the activity of World 2. The Qur'an, for example, was virtually complete before it was ever committed to writing. As it issued forth sura by sura from the mouth of Muhammad it was immediately committed to memory by his followers, who were consequently known as the Qur'an bearers.

Admittedly, most objects of World 3 do come to be embodied in World 1 but this is not necessarily the case, as the original Qur'an exemplifies. Through the very long period of pre-literate humankind none of the verbal content of World 3 was embodied in World 1 except insofar as it was encoded in the brains of humans. Other examples include all material which circulates, even to this day, only in oral form, such as jokes, gossip and closely guarded secrets.

Then there are examples like the whole enterprise of mathematics. Mathematics is largely a human creation; the decimal system of counting, for example, did not exist until it was humanly invented (starting probably from the practice of counting on ten fingers) and when it was invented it added nothing to the physical content of World 1. Mathematics may be regarded as an art form, using a whole new language of its own; it is an art form which has been particularly useful for the advance of the scientific enterprise.

For mathematics illustrates something else about World 3. After humans have created certain World 3 objects they proceed to use them to make various discoveries, not only about objects in World 1 but also about other objects in World 3. For example, it was discovered that the ratio of the circumference of a circle to its diameter remained constant at what is called Pi. Of course the ratio now known as Pi existed before humans became aware of it because it is integral to the concept of the circle. What we often fail to realise, however, is that the very notion of the circle is also a humanly created concept. Pure circles, like pure straight lines, exist only in abstraction; it is approximations to them which we observe with our eyes and which may prompt us to create the appropriate concepts to interpret what we see, and then to create further concepts which we do not see! Thus, as soon as World 3 comes into existence with its own particular kind of objectivity, its substance forms the building blocks for further human construction.

World 1 is the purely physical world of whose existence we are convinced by virtue of sense data, while Worlds 2 and 3 are non-physical. This does not mean that Worlds 2 and 3 are any less real than World 1. Certainly without World 1 there could be no Worlds 2 and 3; and just as World 1 has the capacity to give rise to World 2, so World 2 has the capacity to give rise to World 3. Without World 2, therefore, there could be no World 3. And without Worlds 2 and 3, there could be no human awareness of World 1. Moreover, without Worlds 2 and 3 we would not and could not be human.

Human consciousness was originally confined to responding to World 1 only; this was the time when it was still much closer to animal consciousness. From the time World 3 began to be created human consciousness has been responding to both Worlds 1 and 3 and, as a result, there has been increasing interplay between Worlds 2 and 3. In the highly complex cultures which exist today we often spend more time giving our attention to, and responding to, World 3 than to World 1. The proverbial bookworm, for example, seems hardly aware of World 1, for it is not the quality of the paper or print that the reader is primarily interested in but the story or content conveyed by the words. The child glued to the television is not interested in the 'box' itself, but in the World 3 content being transmitted by medium of the screen.

The increasing interplay between Worlds 2 and 3 has had the effect of raising the level of human consciousness in World 2. We are referring to this when we speak of an educated or cultured mind, and when we compare the sensitivity of the latter with the boorishness of the philistine. During a normal lifetime, the human subject rises from lower levels of consciousness (including the unconscious) to the highest level we know, that of critical self-consciousness. The creation of language, a foundation component of World 3, had the bootstrap effect of raising the level of self-consciousness in World 2. ('Bootstrap' commonly refers to the process of positive feedback by which natural forces reinforce themselves, and so appear to lift themselves up by their own bootstrap.)

We humans have long been aware of the distinction between World 1 and World 2 and it was this experience which led first to Plato's dualism of body and soul and later to Descartes' dualism of mind and body. It is also the reason why many still find the traditional dualistic universe so convincing that they continue to embrace it and make it the model for their personal world.

It is important to remember that Popper's three Worlds constitute only a humanly created model, and we are faced with the paradoxical fact that the model itself belongs to World 3, even though it purports to be a mental construction for describing the whole. But this is no different from the position we humans are always in; we try to hold the universe in our minds, even though our mind itself is only the tiniest fragment of the whole. Popper's model does not rate as a scientific theory. Models are justified simply on their ability to provide useful insights and should be discarded when their usefulness declines or when they can be replaced by a more useful model.

This particular model may be called a metaphysical model, and it is particularly useful for the way in which it acknowledges the reality of consciousness. Any philosophy or scientific investigation which is exclusively materialistic can find no place for consciousness and simply ignores it. Quite recently scholars at the growing edge of science have been turning more attention to the phenomenon of consciousness, and it is partly quantum physics which has caused them to do so. Popper's model further helps us to understand the essential difference between the universe (or at least planet earth) in its pre-human state and the ever accumulating products of the human mind; for it is the latter, both physical (in the form of artefacts) and non-physical (in the form of knowledge), which are changing the character of the planet.

Let us then look more closely at World 3. We are now in a position to appreciate more fully the nature of what was discussed in the first three chapters: words, language, stories and worlds (or human apprehensions of reality). All these belong to World 3.

They have been produced collectively by the human species and they have been accumulating as they have been passed on from generation to generation. Although much gets lost from human sight, perhaps passing into eternal oblivion, more has been created to take its place. In modern times the content of World 3 has been accumulating at an accelerating rate, as instanced by the rapid expansion of libraries, which now contain not only books, but musical recordings, magnetic tapes and even electronic databases.

Basic to World 3 is language. Popper himself asserted that the first product of the human mind was language, and 'that the human brain and the human mind evolved in interaction with language'.[7] So language is the *sine qua non* of World 3. As we have already seen, human language originated a very long time ago and has slowly evolved. Much more recently, there have been three significant inventions which greatly accelerated the growth of the content of World 3. The first was the invention of writing some 4000–5000 years ago. Then came the invention of printing some 400 years ago. Recently came the invention of the computer, which not only greatly multiplies our capacity to store data but, even more important, has opened up a new avenue for creating objective knowledge.

The content in World 3 today is overwhelming, and we spend a great deal of our time engrossed within it. Even just a few hundred years ago most people had to focus their attention on producing, with their own hands, the basic commodities of life such as food, clothing and shelter. The proportion of people involved in those activities today is much less and even those who are, being far better educated, can draw on the great body of new knowledge which has been built up in modern times. Most of the population in the so-called developed nations are caught up in a world of ideas, planning, negotiations, professional skills, sport, entertainment and so on, all of which draw very heavily and sometimes exclusively on World 3 content.

The content of World 3 makes up a great deal of the personal world which each of us constructs and in which we each live. Eccles thought of World 3 as 'the story of the cultural evolution of man'. He went further, saying:

... man has developed as a result of two interacting but quite different evolutions. One is the biological evolution by the ordinary chance and necessity with mutations and survival on the terms of natural selection; and the second way is with his development of the thought processes leading to creativity in a wide range of cultural performance; artistic, literary, critical, scientific, technological and so on. Finally we come up to the level at which man is trying to struggle with the immense problems of the meaning of life: what is it all for? What is the nature of my existence? How can I face up not only to self-awareness but to death-awareness?[8]

It is only because of the degree of self-consciousness humans have reached through the growth of World 3 that these questions surfaced (this is discussed further in Chapter 6); however, it is only within World 3 also that answers can be given. All human ideas and philosophies belong to World 3.

Popper's model now enables us to appreciate why the dualistic view of reality evolved as it did, why it seemed so self-evidently true and why some people still find it convincing. The power of the other-world was that it appeared to give meaning to life, to explain the nature of human existence and to supply a satisfying answer to death-awareness. The beliefs, myths, stories and visual images through which the nature of the other-world was transmitted from generation to generation did have a certain reality, but it was a World 3 order of reality, a non-physical reality. This will be explored further in Chapters 7–10.

Further, Popper's model helps us to understand how the worlds we construct are different from, yet closely related to, the physical reality which exists independent of human thought. World 1 of his model affirms the existence of physical reality and saves us from solipsism. But World 1 exists only as uninterpreted reality. Our worlds are reality interpreted as meaningful; they, including Popper's model, belong to World 3. The key to how our worlds relate to the physical universe is World 2, where human consciousness is located. The totality of human consciousness, past and present, has been remarkably creative; we must now turn to this creative source of our worlds.

CHAPTER 5

The Creative Source
of Our Worlds

All living organisms may be assumed to experience at least some minimal level of consciousness. Indeed some physicists are now suggesting that consciousness begins at the sub-atomic level. Only in the higher animals, however, do we recognise signs of consciousness similar to our own and even here we must make a distinction. It is important to distinguish between consciousness which is experienced without awareness of it (this we share with all conscious, sentient beings) and what we may call critical self-consciousness (this appears to be unique to the human species, though other members of the ape family may be not far from it).

The consciousness which we share with animals, and which manifests itself to the external observer, we experience from the time of our birth onwards. It is what we are referring to when we say of a person recovering from a coma that they have regained consciousness. But self-consciousness is much more than that. Even human infants display no signs of self-consciousness. It begins to develop only some time after our birth, and takes time to grow in depth, often reaching a quite dramatic moment of self-revelation around the age of puberty.

The pioneering depth psychologist Carl Jung (1875–1961) described the emergence of his own self-consciousness as occurring quite suddenly one day when he was about eleven years old. It seemed to him that he suddenly emerged as out of a mist and he realised 'that I was I'. Many others can testify that it has been an inner experience which came to them quite unexpectedly. Previously they had been aware of an external world and responded to it without wholly realising they were doing so. Only from a particular point of self-revelation onwards were they able, with the mind's eye, to see not only the world but also themselves within that world.

Just when our human ancestors first experienced the glimmerings of self-consciousness there is no way of telling. It was certainly a very long time ago. The first manifestation of self-consciousness must have proved a great mystery to our earliest human ancestors. As they began to reflect on their new level of awareness, what were they to make of it? To get some idea of that we may explore the way it came to be reflected in the earliest surviving myths which attempt to describe the nature and origin of humankind.

Let us take the biblical myth of Adam and Eve. It can be read at different levels. It contains a remarkable number of insights, some of which have been lost sight of or ignored because of the way traditional Christian doctrine interpreted the myth as the Fall. It has been too little noticed, for example, that it depicts God as telling an untruth. The myth relates how God solemnly warned the couple not to eat of the tree of the knowledge of good and evil because on the day they did so they would die. It was the wily serpent who revealed the truth. He said they would not die but their eyes would be opened and they would 'be like God, knowing good and evil'. As the story proceeds, we are left to realise for ourselves that it was not God but the serpent who was speaking the truth. They did not die on the day they ate the fruit – and their eyes were certainly opened! The serpent implied that it was out of divine self-interest that God had placed the prohibition, not wishing his human creatures to become like himself. This implication is even confirmed by the narrator who, at the end of the story, rather surprisingly interprets the divine plan as unfolding something like this. It was bad enough for humans to have become like God by having gained the knowledge of good and evil; it would be even worse if they were to eat from the tree of life and become immortal like God. So God found it necessary to expel them from the Garden of Eden to protect the uniqueness of his own immortality!

The myth links the status of being God-like with the possession of a moral sense – that is, with being sufficiently self-aware to know when one has to take full responsibility for a decision. That is why the philosopher Georg Wilhelm Hegel (1770–1831) referred to this story as the 'Myth of Man'. For him it was the myth which described the evolutionary transition from the animal state to the human state. He thought it should be referred to as the 'Rise' rather than the 'Fall'. Before our hominid ancestors became human they had no self-awareness, no sense of time and no moral sense. Their eyes had to be opened before they could become human, i.e. open to self-awareness, open to the awareness of good and evil and the moral responsibility which accompanies it. Of course this was to involve humankind in suffering, guilt and mental anguish. This is both the tragedy and the greatness of the human condition. 'The greatness of man', wrote Hegel, 'just consists in the fact that he eats his bread in the sweat of his brow ... The sorrow of the natural life is essentially connected with the greatness of the character and destiny of man.'[1]

So much for the ancient way of explaining the origin of human self-consciousness. According to the modern view of biological evolution the human condition was not suddenly created in its present form but slowly evolved. So how did human self-consciousness arise? What is the scientifically based equivalent of the biblical myth?

While there is no way of answering this question with any exactness there is a growing consensus of opinion which relates self-consciousness to the advent of language. For example, in his study of human consciousness in *The Death of Forever*, Darryl Reanney, a distinguished authority on the origins of life, writes:

> While it cannot be rigorously proven, I believe I am justified in adopting, as a provisional working hypothesis, the view that the role of language and other symbolic codes is the pivotal feature in the creation and maintenance of our sense of self. We create self-consciousness by giving unrealised mental options a concrete symbolic structure.[2]

Similarly, McCrone points out in *The Ape that Spoke* that

psychologists have been wrong to attempt to divide the mind into the rational and the irrational. He asserts:

> ... the real split is between the raw and naked abilities of the animal brain and the artificially or culturally extended abilities of the human mind ... Self-consciousness is a language-driven extension built on top of the natural foundations of awareness ... The story of man's rise is not that he has steadily become more rational but rather that he has become increasingly a creature of his culture. As civilisations have flourished over the past 3,000 years, man has become richer in his supposedly irrational emotions as well as in his intellectual powers. [3]

Consequently it was that branch of the ape family that invented speech which raced away to develop human self-consciousness.

This is also the conclusion reached by Popper:

> As to the *self*-consciousness of man, I am inclined to think that the most adequate metaphysical hypothesis is that it only rises with World 3; indeed my suggestion is that it arises together with World 3, and in interaction with World 3. It seems to me that self-consciousness, or the self-conscious mind, has a definite biological function, namely to build up World 3, to understand World 3, and to anchor our selves in World 3. [4]

We are able to testify to the correlation between language, memory and self-consciousness from our own personal experiences in childhood. Most of us learned to speak between eighteen and thirty months of age. Only after we had some basic vocabulary did we capture the significance of the word 'I'; and many of us trace our earliest memories from this period. In other words our own earliest sense of self-identity is associated with learning the language of our cultural womb.

Since the gradual growth from consciousness to self-consciousness can lead to a sudden revelation in individual experience even to this day, it must have been just as epoch-making for our species in the distant past, though it may have occurred in a succession of tiny leaps over a long period of time rather than at one decisive point. It is this transition in the evolution of humankind for which Pierre Teilhard de Chardin (1881–1955)[5] coined the term noogenesis – the coming into being of thought or reflection. He was referring not to the thought processes in animal consciousness but to the reflective thought which takes place in human self-consciousness. Animals, he conceded, may be said to know, but they do not know that they know. Only humans experience self-awareness and are capable of reflection. Teilhard defined reflection as the power of consciousness 'to take possession of itself *as of an object* endowed with its own particular consistence and value: no longer merely to know oneself; no longer merely to know, but to know that one knows'.[6]

It was the birth of self-reflective thought, said Teilhard, which opened up a great chasm between humankind and the other animals. He regarded the leap from consciousness to self-consciousness to be as epoch-making within the total picture of planetary evolution as the transition that occurred when life emerged from non-life. Only with growing self-consciousness do we become aware of ourselves as decision-makers. Only with this awareness can we develop a sense of responsibility for our decisions. This in turn opens the door to moral awareness and the experience of guilt. Animals, by contrast, live in a state of innocence. They are not aware that they are making decisions; thus questions of right and wrong behaviour have no relevance to them.

Thus the Bible contains a myth which, with only minimal reinterpretation, describes the very transition which Teilhard referred to as noogenesis. Geneticist Theodosius Dobzhansky referred to the critical events in evolutionary history as 'evolutionary transcendence'. In the process of cosmic evolution non-living matter transcended itself when it produced life. The immense diversity of living creatures transcended itself when it produced humankind; in the advent of self-consciousness, humankind came to transcend the animal state from which it evolved.

At this point depth psychology throws fascinating new light on our understanding of human consciousness and its creative potential. Previously when people had abnormal experiences, such as seeing visions which no one else saw or hearing voices which no one else heard, it seemed logical to conclude that the visions or voices had come to them from an external source. This fitted the dualist view of reality that was so dominant in the post-Axial phase and appeared to give it empirical confirmation. The visions and voices were taken to be the manifestations of the unseen spiritual world. Even dreams were interpreted as journeys of the soul into strange domains which took place during sleep.

The recognition of the subconscious depths of the psyche opened the way to an entirely different explanation. The voices and visions came not from an external but from an internal source. Of course, in one sense, this merely replaced a supposed awesome external domain with an equally mysterious inner domain. Freud was not the first to discover this inner domain, for the term 'subconscious' was actually coined by that strange but able scholar of medieval Basel, Paracelsus (1493–1541).

Certainly, though, Freud pioneered modern depth psychology and showed fairly convincingly that the human psyche is much vaster and more complex than the stream of consciousness we are aware of during our waking hours. The latter is but the tip of the psychic iceberg, most of which is beneath the surface of consciousness; the subconscious is an area of psychic activity which carries on even while we are asleep, as our dreams show so plainly.

Although Freud contributed much to our understanding of the human psyche with his technique of psychoanalysis, he was chiefly concerned with developing a therapy for healing psychic illness. It fell to Carl Jung to draw attention to the outstanding creative capacity of the large subconscious base of the human psyche. Jung approached the subconscious with much the same awe and wonder as people in the past approached the holy places and phenomena celebrated in religious traditions. Here in the human subconscious Jung felt he had drawn close to the source of all human creativity. It was the origin of all that had come to be most distinctive in the human species. It was the source of all that humans had created, in art, poetry, religion and all the various components of culture, including today the scientific enterprise itself. Everything that Popper has placed in World 3 of his model is the totality of products created by all the psyches of the human species.

Because World 3 products cannot be attributed to individual humans (except in relatively small areas) but have evolved with the species itself, it is not surprising that Jung reflected this in his model of the psyche. Jung never claimed that he knew what the psyche is. He confessed quite late in life that all he could be sure of was that there is within the human being a psychic realm in which certain manifestations have their beginning.

The most distinctive aspect of Jung's model of the psyche was his division of the unconscious into two. There is what he called the personal unconscious, which is the depository of all experiences that have left some permanent mark on a person. Some of this, which lies still close to the surface, can be recalled to consciousness as we search our memory for something. But much of it can no longer be recalled, perhaps because it has been repressed on account of unpleasant associations. But this psychic content is not necessarily frozen into inactivity and may indeed be very active, influencing the decisions of the conscious ego without our realising it.

The personal unconscious in Jung's model is almost identical with the whole of the unconscious in Freud's model. But Jung believed he had found evidence of an even deeper layer of the unconscious. This he called the 'collective unconscious' because it is substantially the same in all people today and it has been slowly evolving within the human species over a very long time. 'The collective unconscious', he wrote, 'contains the whole spiritual heritage of mankind's evolution born anew in the brain structure of every individual'.[7] If this is so it means that the human psyche of every person today is composed of operating levels which vary quite significantly in their age. Our self-consciousness, as we have seen, is actually younger than our physical age. Our personal unconscious dates from at least the time of our birth, and perhaps even includes the pre-natal period of the foetus. But our collective unconscious is as old as the human species itself.

What is in the collective unconscious? Jung never suggested that it contains anything like memories, as found in the personal unconscious. Nor is there any way of penetrating the collective unconscious, as there is (to a limited degree) with the personal unconscious by means of dreams and such techniques as hypnosis. What constitutes the collective unconscious, according to Jung, are propensities which have slowly evolved over the long history of humankind. These propensities form the embryonic structure of the psyche and have the capacity to shape the psychic material descending into the personal unconscious in the course of our experience.

Jung called these propensities 'archetypes', a term he borrowed from the mystical theologian Dionysius the Areopagite (c. 500 AD). The original Greek word, *archetupos*, means a primordial pattern or even an originating model. Jung found the same concept in the Latin term used by Augustine, *ideae principales*, to refer to the basic ideas believed to exist in the mind of God, from whom humans receive the ultimate truth by revelation. This notion of eternal ideas Augustine had taken over from Plato. But what Plato had attributed to the mind of God, Jung placed in the collective unconscious of the human psyche.

Just as the genes contain the blueprint, as it were, for the structure of the human physical organism and motivate its growth from the fertilised ovum through to adult maturity, so the archetypes contain the blueprint for the structure of the human psyche and motivate its development. Just as the human body, particularly in the pre-natal period, shows signs of recapitulating the many stages of past biological evolution, so too the growth of the individual human psyche reflects these stages. That is why we may regard the mature human psyche as being composed of operating levels of differing ages.

The archetypes perform two roles. The first is to provide the structure for the developing psyche. As consciousness begins to manifest itself as a layer above the unconscious it needs to be directed and provided with a unifying point. The centre of consciousness is the ego and we are each born with a psychic propensity or archetype to develop an ego. The ego plays an important role in psychic health, as it has a mediating function between the

signals coming from the outer world and the continuing motivation rising from the unconscious. The ego acts as a kind of
controller, selecting from the wealth of data being presented to it
that on which it wishes to focus attention. As time goes on and
consciousness develops into self-consciousness, the ego assumes
an increasingly responsible role in decision-making.

The ego, being an internal spiritual entity, is fragile and vulnerable and can be easily wounded. A shield of protection is raised
around it to guard it from the external world. This is what Jung
called the persona, using the Latin term for the mask worn by the
actor on stage to make clear which role he was playing. The
persona is the face one chooses to show to the world. It is reflected
in the clothes one wears, one's general appearance, one's general
stance. It is when the ego is reaching self-consciousness that the
possession of an adequate persona becomes most important. Part
of the trauma of puberty and growth to adulthood is finding the
most comfortable persona. It is an archetype which prompts the
creation of the persona.

As these archetypes structure consciousness, so others structure
the unconscious. The function of the ego is to develop an ever
clearer conscious identity in relation to the world outside. But the
external cultural world makes certain demands to which the ego
cannot respond without coming into conflict with the pre-human
and animal-like urges still present in the unconscious. These latter
Jung referred to as the shadow. There is tension between the ego
and the shadow; since the shadow is in the unconscious, hidden
from consciousness, the ego often finds itself puzzled by this
internal struggle.

One of the best examples of it is found in some well-known
words of St. Paul (Romans 7:15–20):

> I do not understand my own actions. For I do the very thing I hate
> ... So then it is no longer I [ego] that do it, but sin [shadow] which
> dwells within me, that is in my flesh [unconscious]. I can will what
> is right but I cannot do it. For I do not do the good I want, but the
> evil I do not want is what I do. Now if I do what I do not want, it
> is no longer I [ego] that do it, but sin [shadow] which dwells in me.

The shadow is not necessarily evil; rather it is amoral or (even better) pre-moral. It is the residue of the pre-human animal psyche which has not yet been adapted to the restraints of culture. If ignored, or repressed, the libido of the shadow may burst out in outrageous behaviour. It is common for a repressed shadow to be unconsciously projected on to somebody else. We project our shadow on to someone displaying the urges which we refuse to acknowledge in ourselves.

In medieval Christendom the collective shadow of the human species was projected on to the mythical figure of Satan (or the devil). By blaming his influence for the wicked things one did, one was able to escape full responsibility for one's actions. Shifting blame for one's own misdeeds on to the shoulders of another is such a common human practice that it is not surprising it is reflected in the biblical myth of the human condition. The man, Adam, when challenged by God, shifted the blame on to the woman, Eve, and the woman shifted the blame on to the serpent; hence in medieval times the serpent became identified with Satan.

The most important archetype of all for structuring the psyche is the archetype of the self. This is not to be confused with the ego. Whereas the ego is the centre of consciousness, the self is the centre of the whole psyche, including both consciousness and the unconscious. This is why we sometimes conclude that we know a person better than they know themselves (i.e. their ego has an inadequate understanding of their self). The archetype of the self has the function of promoting psychic unity, harmonising the many psychic components and developing the psyche to its full potential or maturity. The full realisation of the self (or mature self-understanding) is what Jung called the process of individuation.

This process takes place in two successive stages. In the first half of life, roughly up to the age of forty, the main task of the psyche is to become harmoniously adjusted to the external world, particularly from childhood to early adulthood. This involves the growth of a firm ego identity and the establishment of an adequate persona, one with which the ego feels comfortable and which is not hypocritical. In the second half of life the main task of the psyche is to understand and come to harmonious terms with one's own inner reality. This is the growth to mature self-understanding (it may also be called growth in God-consciousness).

The other function of the archetypes is to give some structure and form to the psychic material which is more or less continuously active in the unconscious. This material, as memories exemplify, has descended into the unconscious from consciousness, having originated in the person's experience of the external world. But the ways in which this material is reshaped and used for creative purposes depend on psychic structures inherited from our racial past, even though retained in only the barest of outlines. Thus in the personal unconscious the descending external material meets the rising archetypes of the collective unconscious and together they form a whirlpool of activity, only a portion of which makes itself evident to us in our dreams.

The reason why dreams can take the weirdest forms is that, during sleep, the unconscious is temporarily freed from the hampering restrictions of the conscious ego. The nearest we ever get in conscious life to this degree of freedom is in day-dreaming or during our very young years. Just as the young (and this is also true of all the higher animals) gambol and play with great friskiness and abandon, so does the psyche in the unconscious. Imagination can run riot. The psyche engages in a rapid succession of vivid experiences which often appear to have no consistency or logic, at least on the surface. The operations of the psyche do not depend on language; on the contrary, the psyche is the ultimate source of language. The currency used in the psyche consists of sounds, visual pictures and symbols, often picturesque, bizarre and colourful. Some of them are wholly imaginary and some recapture images encountered in conscious experience.

The psyche is so creative that it produces a great deal more than the conscious ego can ever make use of. Indeed a lot of what the psyche comes up with may in fact be judged useless by the ego. Just as biological evolution, once started, in the course of time threw up an unbelievable number of variant and diverse species, so the psyche swarms with fast-moving dramas, images, concepts and ideas.

The most creative work ever produced by the human psyche is language. It was produced collectively and over a long period. As noted earlier, language consists of using vocal sounds symbolically. Language was the first symbol system created by human-kind. Although, as noted above, we do not know exactly how and when language was created, we can say that it was the creation, collectively, of the human psyche, for the latter is the only part of the human organism that could have created it. Moreover, as already demonstrated, we cannot adequately speak of the human mind without language. Language and the human mind evolved in tandem.

We can go further. Language, human self-consciousness and world-consciousness (that is, awareness of existing in a world) all evolved together, each assisting the others to develop. Paul Tillich put it this way:

> Without its world the self would be an empty form. Self-consciousness would have no content ... There is no self-consciousness without world-consciousness, but the converse is also true. World-consciousness is possible only on the basis of a fully developed self-consciousness.[8]

The psyche (whatever it may be) is the key to the human condition and the creative source of all the human species has produced. It is the psyche which has enabled humans to create the worlds in which they live, and to which they are continually relating. As humans we find ourselves living in a world which we have collectively created; and, within that world of shared consciousness, each of us has created our own particular version of it.

The human psyche has also evolved to the point where we each have the potential to experience critical self-consciousness. This is the potential to examine critically our own thinking and the culture which has shaped us. It may be described as a process of human self-transcendence, and it has enabled the human species to become what it has become. We are forever becoming dissatisfied with what we have achieved to date and being prompted to reach out for what we have not yet achieved; and it is this which currently transcends us. What we see in competitive sports, and in athletes' strenuous efforts to surpass previous records, may be taken as pointers to what we are doing in every aspect of human culture. That is how human self–transcendence operates.

To achieve this, the psyche has further shown its creativity by leading us to create a second level of symbols over and above the primary level of language. This is examined in Chapter 8. The psyche is indeed a remarkable source of creativity: it is a veritable symbol–making factory. But to do justice to it we must first explore the human drive to find meaning.

PART II

Why Human Worlds Are Created

CHAPTER 6

The Human Quest for Meaning

In the evolution of human culture the human species has played a dual role: it has been both creaturely and creative. The human species has gradually developed self-consciousness, largely through the creation and subsequent refinement of language. Through innumerable generations, our species has virtally lifted itself on to a higher than animal plane of existence. Even the worlds we live in (either collectively or individually) turn out to be largely our own construction.

It is understandable that, for such a long time in our cultural tradition, the human condition in its contemporary form, along with the worlds we live in, were attributed to the creativity of a power transcendent to the species and quite independent of it. Transcendence of a kind there has certainly been; but it may be better referred to as self-transcendence. Human self-transcendence has come about through the operation of that extraordinary human entity we call the psyche; this has proved to be such a source of creativity that we must still hold it in awe.

But how did the human psyche come to have this creative power? If it is true that all forms of planetary life evolved in the far distant past out of that which was non-living, then the inanimate universe must have had the potential for life from the beginning. Further, the universe itself must have had not only the potential for life but also the potential for human self-consciousness (this will be discussed more fully in Chapter 13). In the same way, we must conclude, the creativity present in the human psyche is simply a manifestation of the creativity potentially present in the universe itself.

But the creativity permeating the universe took a unique form within the human species, in that it provided us with an entity, the psyche, which can reflect on the universe of which it is a tiny part. It can even ask questions about the emergent universe which has brought it about. Should we not wonder in amazement how the helpless day-old infant we may be holding in our arms can be asking us only four years later, 'Where did I come from? How did I come to be here?'

As human self-consciousness continually developed to higher levels, in tandem with language, the questions became even more penetrating. People were clearly not content to see events as unconnected and inexplicable. They looked for some kind of order in the world they had constructed. They not only asked the 'how' questions; they also asked the 'why' questions. But questions of this deeper kind can be asked only within the medium of language such as we humans possess. Thus we humans can ask questions which no other planetary animals can possibly ask.

Just when, in the distant past, the first questions came to be enunciated we have no way of telling. By the time the first human civilisations left some records of what they were thinking, questioning had been going on for a long time and what came to be regarded as authoritative answers were being handed down in the various cultural traditions that were evolving.

The first questions asked were probably quite childlike, such as: What makes that noise? Where has the sun gone? Why does it rise in a different place from where it disappeared? We have only to think of how the process repeats itself in each new generation and of how children, on learning to speak, are forever asking questions. Some of their questions are very simple and easy to answer. But out of 'the mouths of babes and sucklings' can also come some surprisingly penetrating and basic questions. So it was with the human race. The capacity to ask questions opened the way for people eventually to ask what have been called the big questions: Why are we here? Why do we grow? Why do we die? What is life for? What is the meaning of human existence?

Such questioning arises out of the creative and enquiring capacity of the human psyche and is the beginning of the human quest for meaning. It is the next logical step after the evolution of language and of human consciousness, simply because meaning is intrinsic to language. This is why Benjamin Lee Whorf, the pioneer in linguistics, said that 'Linguistics is essentially the quest for MEANING.' Because meaning is intrinsic to language, and we humans are creatures of language, the quest for meaning is basic to the human condition.

Now, however, we must ask the question: What is meaning? What is the meaning of meaning? In posing such a question, we find ourselves forced to beg the question even to discuss it, because there appears to be nothing simpler to which we can reduce the notion of meaning. 'Meaning' is very difficult to define and there are several levels at which it may be understood. Perhaps the nearest synonyms we have for 'meaning' are 'purpose' and 'significance'. Even then the particular nuance depends on the context in which the word is used. When we ask, 'What is the meaning of this?', for example, we may be asking mischievous children to explain their outrageous behaviour, or we may be wondering if some strange portent in the sky has some special significance that we ignore at our peril.

The first chapter outlined the two ways in which words and sentences may be described as the 'bearers' of meaning. On the one hand, some words, such as proper names and concrete nouns, carry meaning simply by the way they point to or signify specific visual objects which are readily identifiable. Those are the easiest words by which to understand the nature of meaning and, as was noted earlier, they were probably the first words of human language to emerge. Once human language had begun to develop, however, it apparently manifested a genius for growth and creativity not unlike that found in the evolutionary process itself. Language began to spawn an increasing number of words which have no external referents at all. For example, there are the many abstract words such as justice, duty, involvement. The meaning of such words is contained wholly within the word itself. We learn the meaning of the word as we learn how to use it. The usage of the word and its meaning are almost one and the same.

On the other hand, meaning may be regarded as prior to words. For example, when we cannot find the right words to express what we want to say we create new words. Thus human language came to be created in the first place out of the human urge towards meaning. It is a case of 'Meaning will out!', and words become the bearer of it. Yet we have to ask ourselves whether the meaning was completely clear in our minds before we found the words to express it, or whether we reached clarity of meaning only when we found the right words to express it. To the degree that the latter is true, then what is prior to language is not so much meaning as the drift towards meaning.[1] Thus it seems to be the case that meaning and language developed in tandem. In this case words were the midwife enabling meaning to come to birth. Language gave clarity to meaning but it was the drift towards meaning that created language.

Since we have been so long used to assuming that language was somehow given to us in primeval times, it was natural for our forebears to assume that meaning in all its completeness has also existed from before creation, in some kind of Platonic world, awaiting its expression in human language. It may seem strange at first to suggest that meaning is only now in the process of being created, and that we humans play a dominant role in that process. But when we explore the nature of meaning a little further we may find out why it is so.

While words may be treated as the very building blocks of language, they are not the constants we often take them to be. This is why one needs to know a language very well indeed in order to appreciate all that a speaker may be intending to convey. This is part of the tantalising mystery of language. It is not a wholly precise tool for the expression and communication of meaning. Even more enigmatic is the fact that, though meaning is embodied in words and dependent on words for expression, it is not wholly to be identified with them. Meaning seems almost to be fluttering through the words like a will-o'-the-wisp in such a way as to be easily lost.

That is why a person can hear the words spoken and understand the meaning of the particular words used, yet fail to grasp the meaning of the whole which the speaker is intending to convey. This may bring forth the response, 'What you say does not make any sense to me. I find that statement meaningless.' After further discussion the response may change to, 'Ah! I see what you're getting at. Now I've got your meaning.' Meaning can possess all the elusiveness of a joke we are being told. Either we see it or we don't. Words have the potential both to convey meaning and to bring meaning to birth; yet even then they may fail. The use of words to convey meaning also depends on our ability to receive and understand meaning, an ability which strengthens as we mature.

This becomes a little clearer as we move from words to sentences. Another set of words which language spawned are connecting terms such as 'and', 'if', 'at', whose function is to connect other words together into a sentence. These words do not convey meaning in isolation. Their meaning depends on the way they are used in sentences. Meaning becomes more complex in sentences than in words, and that is why the meaning of a sentence cannot be contained, let alone conveyed, in only one word. Moreover, such meanings as the particular words of a sentence have in themselves may give little indication of the meaning conveyed in the sentence as a whole, even though they have contributed to it. Thus, whenever we construct a new sentence, we are in fact creating meaning. It is a more complex expression of meaning than that by which a name signifies an object. On rare occasions we create meaning of such value that our utterance may become a proverb or a quotation.

It was the drift towards meaning which brought each word into being. It is the drift towards meaning which gives each sentence its reason for being expressed. It is the drift towards meaning which lies behind the composition of every story. It is the drift towards meaning which has prompted us humans to create from our sense data a world in which to live. The reason we construct a world is our quest for meaning. Words, sentences, stories, worlds – the phenomena unique to the human animal – have all resulted from this mysterious urge to meaning which has surfaced in human existence.

The first chapter drew attention to the Prologue of the Fourth Gospel in attempting to show how much of what we have come to value depends on the creation of language. We are now ready to develop that a little further. Prior even to language was what we have called the drift towards meaning. This too is reflected in the Prologue.

The term *logos*, commonly translated as 'word', came to be rarely used, even by the Greeks, simply to refer to words as such; Greek already had *epos*, *onoma* and *rhema* to refer to words. *Logos* came to mean something more than a word, something like 'reason', 'thought', 'reflection'. For the Stoics *logos* was the ultimate principle of purpose and design believed to permeate reality; it provided the regularity to be observed in the cosmos. Because of the special significance attached to *logos*, it later appeared in so many English derivatives, such as 'logic' and all the areas of disciplined study whose names end in '-ology'.

John Macquarrie in *Thinking about God*[2] suggested that *logos* could be rendered as 'meaning' and then went on to paraphrase the Prologue to the Fourth Gospel accordingly. Following his lead, but making a fresh paraphrase, I suggest that in today's cultural context the Prologue could be rendered as follows:

> In the beginning was the potential for meaning. 'Meaning' and 'God' are so close to each other that they are virtually the same. To say that God was at the beginning is to say that the drift towards meaning has been there from the beginning. Everything created has been meaningful and nothing was made to be meaningless. The emergence of life was the drift toward meaning and from life emerged human enlightenment. The light of meaning dispelled the darkness of absurdity and meaningless chaos has not been able to overcome it ... Every person may share in the enlightening truth which meaning brings into the world it has made. The world always remains potentially meaningful even though many fail to recognise it. But those who have found meaning, and who entrust themselves to it, have been enabled to become the children of God.

It was the drift towards meaning which we find at work in the human psyche. It is the reason the psyche has been the creative source, in succession, of language, of human self-consciousness and of the world we construct for ourselves out of the mass of sense data we encounter. The drift towards meaning is the reason why the psyche is being continually motivated towards harmonious unity with external phenomena and towards the unity of personal integrity within, or what Jung called 'individuation'.

One who has illustrated very strikingly the close relationship between meaning, language and the psyche is the psychiatrist Viktor Frankl. In his book *Man's Search for Meaning* (1962), he described how he was led to this insight out of his own experiences as a prisoner in the Nazi concentration camps of Auschwitz and Dachau. First he had to learn how to cope with the indescribable conditions of the death camps. This he did in part by drawing upon his inner world of thought and imagining various future goals, such as the completion of his psychiatric training, impossible though it seemed at the time. Then he began to ask himself what it was about his fellow prisoners which enabled some to survive while others perished. The answer he stumbled upon had already been succinctly expressed in a dictum of Nietzsche, which Frankl thereafter loved to quote: 'He who has a *why* to live for can bear with almost any *how*.' The conviction of having a purpose for which to live, of finding a meaning in continued existence, could make all the difference between life and death.

Frankl found this confirmed in his own experience. At the time he was taken to Auschwitz a manuscript he had ready for publication was confiscated. When he fell ill with typhus he jotted down on little scraps of paper many notes intended to help him rewrite the lost manuscript should he live to be liberated. He later became convinced that this deep concern enabled him to survive the ordeal.

Perhaps it was the cosmic drift towards meaning which originally led to life in geological time. Teilhard de Chardin would have said so, though many today are inclined to assign the advent of planetary life more to chance than to design. With more confidence we can say that, once life had emerged and the human species had evolved biologically, it has been the human quest for meaning which has prompted us to construct, and to retain intact, the personal world in which we live. This is why we say that a person's world has fallen apart if they feel they have nothing more to live for. Where meaning is lost, our world disintegrates and life ebbs away.

The new insights into the human condition which Frankl believed he had reached led him after the war to pioneer a new method of promoting the health of the psyche, parallel to but different from Freud's psychoanalysis. Whereas the latter was retrospective, leading the patient to look back into the past to find the causes of his or her psychic disturbance, Frankl encouraged his patient to look forwards into the future and focus on the possible goals, achievements and sense of fulfilment which could be contemplated.

Frankl named his method 'logotherapy', which may be construed as healing by the creation of meaning. Whereas Freud concentrated on *the will to pleasure* and Adler on *the will to power*, Frankl became convinced that the primary motivation of humankind, and hence the basis of psychic health, is *the will to meaning*. Logotherapy simply attempts to assist the patient to find or create meaning in his or her life. Frankl believes it is a mistake to assume that psychic health is achieved by delivering a patient from all tension; rather, what we need for psychic wholeness is the striving for a meaningful goal, and this may quite properly involve us in some tension.

No individual human is self-made; we depend for our humanity on the vast genetic and cultural heritage built up in the past. Similarly, no individual engages in the quest for meaning on their own. It is true that rare individuals from time to time make epoch-making contributions to the total heritage. But most people in any one age simply adopt as the meaning of their existence what is the prevailing form of it in the culture to which they belong.

Moreover there is a parallel between the individual and society in the importance of meaning. Just as an individual can suffer spiritually and mentally where there are no motivating goals and aspirations, so society at large, in order to be healthy and vibrant,

depends on a unifying sense of identity and some common convictions about the worthwhileness of life. Where these are deficient
society suffers, and the individuals dependent on that society suffer
in turn. Frankl thought that widespread in the twentieth century is
what he called an 'existential vacuum'. He pointed out that, because we do not have instincts to tell us what to do (as animals
have), and because we are losing hold of the cultural traditions
which in the past have told us what we ought to do, we are too
often left floundering and uncertain, not knowing either what we
want to do or why.

A similar observation was made in 1952 by theologian Paul
Tillich in his widely read book *The Courage to Be*. He started by
drawing a clear distinction between pathological anxiety (such as a
neurosis) and existential anxiety (which is normal to the human
condition). He then distinguished three types of existential anxiety
which we humans experience. One he called ontic anxiety; it is
occasioned by the knowledge of our mortality. All through life,
and particularly from adulthood onwards, we live perpetually
under the threat of the death which will ultimately bring our life to
an end. The second he called moral anxiety; it is occasioned by the
guilt we feel over our moral failures to make the right decisions, or
to live up to the standards which others expect of us and, even
more, which we have set for ourselves. The third he called spiritual
anxiety; this is occasioned by the loss of a spiritual centre which
gives meaning and significance to life. The threat of meaninglessness can drain us of motivation because it makes us feel that
nothing, not even our own life, has any value; it results in a
spiritual death which is ultimately more devastating than physical
death.

Tillich contended that these three types of anxiety normally
exist in close association in human life, but one of them may
become predominant, either in an individual person or as the
character of a particular period of culture. He suggested that in the
history of Western civilisation each of the three had become predominant in turn. What prevailed in the ancient world was ontic
anxiety, the fear that death entailed a complete end to existence,

thus giving the final victory to non-being. 'Farewell for ever!' an ancient Roman proclaimed on his tombstone. Death was viewed, therefore, as 'the last enemy to be rendered inactive' (1 Corinthians 15:26). It prompted many to ask, 'What must I do to gain eternal life?' The Christian gospel was proclaimed as the answer to ontic anxiety in that it claimed victory over death by showing the path to life everlasting.

By the Middle Ages, however, it was no longer ontic anxiety which prevailed but moral anxiety. Paradoxically, this was partly because the ancient form of the Christian message had performed its task so well. Few, if any, in the Middle Ages had any doubt they would survive death. The basic question was not *whether* life would continue after death, but *where* it would continue – in heaven or in hell? The moral guilt by which they felt themselves condemned before the God of righteousness troubled them a good deal more than their mortality. Suicides were rare, not only because it was deemed sinful but because death was no escape from life's problems. So the good news which Christianity proclaimed was that the divine sacrifice made by Christ on the cross enabled the faithful to be saved from the hell they deserved. All this was reflected in the way the crucifix became the central Christian symbol, in the way the eucharist became the re-presentation of the divine sacrifice on the altar, and in the way no one dared to die out of communion with the church.

In modern times, said Tillich, the predominant anxiety has changed once again. The kind of world most of us find ourselves living in is very different from that which medieval Christendom had created; as the reality of hell has receded from modern consciousness so also has the intensity of moral anxiety. For some people it has entailed the resurgence of ontic anxiety; for them, human mortality has returned as the chief enemy to be overcome. Even in traditional Christian circles there has been a certain shift of emphasis away from the fear of hell to the hope that Christian allegiance is the way to ensure for oneself some form of spiritual existence after death. It is for this reason that the bodily resurrection of Jesus has become such a focal point for conservative

Christians, as a way of demonstrating that 'because Christ lives, we shall live also'.

Many other moderns, however, have come to accept their mortality. This is partly due to the recognition that the phenomenon of death is not wholly negative but offers some unexpected benefits. There are times when it comes as a welcome relief. Acceptance of human mortality is also due to the great increase in the average life expectancy. It is thus not the phenomenon of death itself which concerns us moderns but premature death, death which comes before one has had the normal opportunities for life. When death comes at the end of a long life, when one is losing one's accustomed vigour and mental faculties, we find that death may even be welcomed, in the spirit of the words of St. Francis, 'And thou, most kind and gentle death, waiting to hush our latest breath, O praise him, Alleluia'. In modern times, then, as Tillich saw it, what is predominant in our existential anxiety is neither ontic anxiety nor moral anxiety but spiritual anxiety. This arises from the fear that our existence has no ultimate meaning or significance, the fear that we have not achieved anything of worth, the fear that we have not found any sense of fulfilment or the fear that, when we are dead and gone, it will make no difference whether we have lived at all. Such fears of meaninglessness are associated also with the growing possibility that neither history nor the cosmos manifests any obvious purpose. There is the fear that the universe is a great cosmic accident, brought about by a mixture of chance and necessity, and that our existence is simply lived out amid a meaningless chaos. Tillich suggested that this predominant form of existential anxiety today comes to visible expression in the arts.

The spiritual anxiety of which Tillich wrote is not, of course, an exclusively modern phenomenon. It has always been a strand of our total existential anxiety, perhaps ever since humankind arrived on the planetary scene in something like our present physical form and cultural state. If it is only in modern times that spiritual anxiety has come to predominate over the ontic and moral strands of existential anxiety, that may be because our greatly increased knowledge of ourselves, and of the planet we inhabit, has removed some of the reasons which accentuated the other two modes.

But, as Viktor Frankl pointed out, the rising anxiety about meaninglessness is due to the breakdown in the traditional cultures. Many feel that they have been left stranded in an unthinking, unfeeling cosmos which operates more by chance than by design, and in which they find themselves trapped as in a meaningless, cosmic maze. Those who still embrace one of the traditional cultures have been protected from this sense of meaninglessness.

Some, apparently seeking spiritual comfort and reassurance in order to avoid the nihilistic abyss of meaninglessness, are returning to the cultural womb, even if it means they must close their minds to any difficulties that may pose in today's intellectual climate. This explains the widespread resurgence of fundamentalism in both Christendom and Islam. Back in the warm safety of the cultural womb they feel assured of meaning.

Others look elsewhere. Never has the spawning of new religions been so prolific as now. There are thousands of them, emerging out of Christian, Buddhist, Islamic, Hindu and even primal cultures. Aware that the more traditional faiths have lost their power to win conviction, people eagerly try something new, as a drowning person clutches at a straw. They are looking for certainty. They seek the one true and eternal answer to the meaning of life. Often, when they feel they have found it, they proclaim it vigorously to others and claim that theirs alone is the only true one. They reject all others as false, inadequate, man-made.

Each of the great cultures of the past evolved to provide a comprehensive set of answers to the human quest for meaning. Just how traditional cultures provided individuals with their sense of meaning we shall consider in later chapters, just as we shall also look for newer goals for the modern age.

But one final point needs to be made. The human quest for meaning does not necessarily mean that hidden somewhere in the cosmos is the final answer to the quest, waiting for us to discover it. Frankl said that to ask in general terms 'What is the meaning of life?' is rather like going to the world's champion chess player and asking him, 'What is the best chess move one can ever make?' The question is nonsensical. What is a good move depends on where all the chess pieces are on the board. So it is in life. It is vain to search in general for the meaning of life. Life's meaning depends on whose life it is, on who a person is and what their circumstances are.

Even then, the question involves not so much finding something which is already there but rather creating meaning out of the raw material with which one has been provided. The meaning of life has to be custom-built, tailored to individual circumstances, relative to time and place. There is no need to dismiss the various answers which people of the past have found satisfying, simply because they are so clearly human and not absolute. All answers to the big questions are humanly created, and none the worse for that.

Once we grasp that, we are then free to study the various answers which have been given in the past and to appreciate them for what they were. It also helps us to understand why various answers, which may no longer satisfy us, nevertheless did provide a real sense of meaning to others, both in the past and in the present. No answer, however satisfying it is at the time, can ever become final or last forever.

We shall now turn back to look at some of the worlds of meaning which have evolved in the past. We shall try to see how and why people came to create meaning in the context in which they lived. Whatever we may learn from them we cannot simply take over and use as our own, unless it still has the intrinsic power to become meaningful in the different cultural context in which we live. There is no value at all in simply repeating, like a ventriloquist's dummy, the meaning which has come out of somebody else's life. The meaning of a person's life is very personal, custom-built and unique to that person.

It is true that our forebears were usually not aware that they themselves were the creators of meaning. They were creating meaning quite unconsciously. It often seemed to them that meaning, like language itself, was being divinely revealed to them from a transcendent source, where it had existed from the beginning of time. The difference between them and us is that we are aware that meaning is a human creation. What people once used to construct unconsciously we have to learn to do consciously.

As we look back through the long periods of evolution – first biological evolution, then anthropological evolution and finally language-based cultural evolution – we can sense that it has been the cosmic drift which has brought us to this moment. As a result, we humans find ourselves to be creatures whose very *raison d'etre* is to be creators. We are creatures who find ourselves thrust into existence, and motivated by the cosmic drift towards meaning. Human existence is the quest for meaning – meaning for ourselves, meaning for human society, meaning for the cosmos. It is the quest for meaning, and not the possession of final answers, which is the key to human existence.

Until modern times, and particularly since the Axial Period, our forebears were fairly confident they did possess the final answers to the quest for ultimate meaning. We must now turn to those answers and explore just how they arose.

CHAPTER 7

Religion as the Creation of Meaning

The quest for meaning lies behind all religious aspirations and phenomena. Albert Einstein put it simply thus: 'To be religious is to have found an answer to the question of what is the meaning of life.' Einstein was not himself religious in the traditional sense of that term, yet, in a nutshell, he penetrated to the underlying significance of all religion. Even before Einstein, Feuerbach had asserted, 'He who has an aim in life, an aim which is in itself true and essential, has *eo ipso* a religion.'[1]

Because we live in a time of radical cultural and religious change, however, this broad use of the term 'religion' may not be readily understood or even universally acceptable; indeed the word has come to mean quite different things to different people. Those who enthusiastically embrace one of the well-known religious faiths usually use 'religion' positively; those who have rejected traditional forms of religion often treat the word negatively and even speak of themselves as non-religious. So before going further it would be useful to clarify what is meant here by 'religious' and 'religion'.

It is tempting to interpret 'religion' in terms of the traditional religion of one's culture. Fielding in his novel *Tom Jones* has Parson Thwackum say, 'When I mention religion, I mean the Christian religion; and not only the Christian religion, but the Protestant religion; and not only the Protestant religion, but the Church of England.'[2] We all see the absurdity of such chauvinism but sometimes fail to realise that, if we define religion in terms of belief in God and life after death, we exclude such a well-known path of faith as Buddhism.

In today's religious pluralism, which includes stances described as anti-religion and unbelief, we must avoid all definitions which interpret religion by reference to the particular forms which one either embraces or rejects; otherwise, what is religion to one person is simply superstition or non-belief to another. Derived as it is from the Latin *religio*, 'religion' did not originally refer to any particular set of beliefs at all, but to the degree of commitment or devotion which people displayed towards their most important interests. *Religio*, and hence 'religion', basically meant conscientiousness, and could be extended to mean 'a conscientious concern for what really matters'. This is what Paul Tillich was recovering for the word when he defined religion as 'the state of being grasped by an ultimate concern, a concern which qualifies all other concerns as preliminary and which itself *contains the answer to the question of the meaning of life*' (italics added). [3] Carlo Della Casa, an Italian scholar of the modern study of religion, put it even more simply: 'Religion is a total mode for the interpreting and living of life.'[4]

W. Cantwell Smith, in his seminal book *The Meaning and End of Religion*, has shown that the popular use of the noun 'religion' to refer to a specific set of beliefs and practices, particularly with a supernatural dimension, is quite modern. For example, the word never used to be used in the plural, as we do today when we talk about 'the religions of the world'. Smith urged us to stop talking about 'religions' and to fasten attention rather on the capacity of people to be religious. In this sense the atheist who is sincerely and passionately protesting against traditional theism out of a concern for truth may be more religious than the nominal Christian who has only a half-hearted commitment to the faith he or she claims to profess.

Through most of human history, including even Christian history, people did not think of themselves as 'having a religion'. This is well illustrated by Chinese culture. Western scholars sometimes discuss whether Confucianism is a religion. It is a question that not only has the West found difficult to answer, but the Chinese are not even able to ask, since there is no word in the Chinese language for 'religion', in the sense of a set of beliefs to be embraced.

So Smith asserted that we should stop thinking of religion as a 'thing', made up of beliefs, rituals, holy scriptures, moral codes and institutional structures. These are simply products of the religious dimension of human existence. These products come and go and are subject to change. He called them the 'cumulative tradition' of each particular religious path and asserted that it is much more important to ask how and why these cumulative traditions evolved in the first place.

What Smith called a cumulative tradition is more or less equivalent to what is known today, following the lead of the anthropologists, as a culture. E.B. Tylor, in 1871, defined culture as 'that complex whole which includes knowledge, belief, art, morals, law, custom and any other capabilities and habits acquired by man as a member of society'. Religion finds no mention in this definition because it is a dimension of the complex whole rather than a component part; pre-Axial societies were clearly religious, yet they were not aware of embracing a thing called religion (see below). Religion is not a thing in itself, as W. Cantwell Smith rightly observed, and therefore cannot find expression except within culture.

Religion and culture are so closely interwoven that they are distinguishable but not separable; neither can exist without the other. 'Morality, culture, and religion interpenetrate one another', wrote Paul Tillich. 'The religious element in culture is the inexhaustible depth of a genuine creation. One may call it the substance or ground from which culture lives. It is the element of ultimacy which culture lacks in itself but to which it points.'[5] But without the element of ultimacy then, according to Tillich, a culture has no depth, no staying power, and no clear identity. Since religion has to do with the quest for meaning we may say that it constitutes the motivation, the unifying energy, the life force of a culture (or what Tillich called its substance). Thus culture manifests in visible or concrete forms the products of the religious quest, namely, the quest for meaning.

Every known human society has had what may be called a religious dimension to its culture. That is because every human culture is a coherent structure, unified and held together by its own particular set of answers to the quest for meaning. This does not mean that there existed anything like a complete, and clearly enunciated, set of answers right from the beginning, as there might have done if religion were a set of absolute truths which could exist independently of humans and their culture. It is, rather, that answers to the quest for meaning developed in the course of the evolving culture, in response to whatever was experienced as the most pressing concerns at any particular time.

In the earliest stages of human evolution the most pressing needs were very basic and were largely the same as those we humans share with the other animals: the need for air, drink, food, shelter, survival and the regeneration of the species. Built into each individual animal of each species is the instinct to procreate, on which the survival of the species depends. From such basic needs and animal instincts our primitive human ancestors started. What was described in the last chapter as the drive for meaning may be embryonically present in all forms of life, but only in the human species has it surfaced in such a way as to be recognisable. It was able so to manifest itself only after humans had created language, for it is language which has given birth to meaning.

As already noted, we know all too little about this early period in which the human species developed a language-based culture and slowly opened up the great gulf which now exists between humans and other animals. During this long period of development human culture as we know it began to evolve. We look back to that time through minds shaped by a highly sophisticated culture dependent on what then took place. As a result, we humans no longer simply exist in a timeless present devoid of apparent meaning in the way other animals do. As individuals, we begin to manifest the drive for meaning from a very early age after our helpless infancy. We are prompted to interpret our lives within the context of the world in which we find ourselves. We try to enunciate the meaning of our lives.

Most people, of course, do not do this in any systematic or academic way, specifically asking themselves, 'What is the meaning of my life?' What happens in practice is that before we reach the maturity needed in order to pose the question in that form, we have already absorbed from our cultural womb the traditional answers to it, the answers which underlie our culture and give it its particular identity.

If most people, even today, do not specifically pose the question, 'What is the meaning of life?', how much less did they do so in primitive times. It would be naively anachronistic for us to put such questions back into their minds. Indeed it would appear, rather, that not until the Axial Period was there any analytical questioning of that kind (and this we shall presently turn to). In the pre-Axial Period human culture evolved more unconsciously than consciously. As we look back, we may try to interpret what was going on but we must guard against imposing our analysis on the consciousness of those people.

In the earliest cultures we know – those which existed before the Axial Period and which were referred to in the Introduction as Ethnic cultures – there was no conscious awareness of possessing a religion. That is why, even to this day, we have no name for the religious dimension of their culture and have simply to speak of, say, the 'religion of the Babylonians', or 'the religion of the ancient Romans'. If we enquire about their religion, our attention probably turns to the various gods and spirits in which they believed and in the various rituals, such as sacrifices, by which they sought to placate them.

Just how the concepts of gods arose and functioned is dealt with in the next two chapters. At this point we need to guard against the temptation to separate out these beliefs and practices from the rest of the culture and speak of it as their religion. The people themselves did not do this. Their gods and spirits were all part of the furniture of the world they lived in, the world which they had (unconsciously) constructed and which, for them, was reality. We need to remember that, on the basis of the above definition of religion, *it was not their belief in the existence of gods which determined how religious they were but the quality of reverence they displayed towards what concerned them ultimately in the world they had constructed*. The fact that they saw the world inhabited by gods was a feature just as much of their primitive 'science' as it was of their primitive 'religion'. The rituals (judged by us to be magical) that they used to influence the gods and ensure a continuing supply of food and other commodities necessary for life was a part just as much of their primitive 'technology' as of their religious practice. It is misleading to separate out specific beliefs and practices and label them religion. Religion is not a segment of life but a dimension which applies to the whole. It has to do with attitudes (such as awe and wonder), with qualities (such as love, loyalty and integrity) and with ultimate goals.

To enquire about the religion of the earliest human cultures, we must ask what grasped them as their ultimate concern. As already noted, their chief concern was to secure the basic commodities on which their survival depended. They found themselves living in a mysterious world which appeared to be permeated by unseen forces, both dangerous and friendly. Their livelihood depended on these forces, and yet they also felt threatened by them. Perhaps the chief ultimate goal was simply the survival of the tribe. Primitive human culture evolved out of the need to preserve the social group in its encounter with the forces of nature. Because of the latter, the religious dimension of their culture came to be expressed in what we may call 'nature religion'. Because of the need to preserve the social group, all pre-Axial religion may legitimately be called ethnic; the religious imperative which demanded their obedient response was experienced by virtue of their birth into a particular tribe or people, whose culture had shaped them (see Figure 2).

In the Ethnic Phase of religious experience, group or tribal identity overshadowed individual identity. The human species is essentially gregarious and could never have evolved its present state if the emphasis had not been on group identity and survival. The group was often thought to be embodied in its most authoritarian figure, such as the chief, patriarch or king. We need to remember that the value we today place on the freedom and rights of each individual is a modern phenomenon.

Chief among the ceremonies which manifested a religious dimension were those in which adults were initiated into full

I **ETHNIC** (tribal)	1. Authority vested in the past and transmitted by elders. 2. Golden age was in the past. 3. Natural world is highly respected. 4. Change is abhorrent. 5. Personal fulfilment is obtained by identification with one's 'tribe'.
AXIAL PERIOD 800–200 BC Prophets – seers – philosophers	
II **TRANS-** **ETHNIC** (religious)	[Buddhist, Christian, Muslim worlds] 1. Authority vested in transcendent order and trans-mitted by revelation. 2. Golden age is awaited in the future. 3. Natural world is down-graded. 4. Change is earnestly desired. 5. Personal fulfilment is obtained by identification with the trans-ethnic 'other-worldly' community.
ENLIGHTENMENT 1650–1850 Transition to modernity	
III **GLOBAL** (secular)	1. Authority internalised and relativised, to be tested by experience. 2. Golden age is elusive [past or future?]. 3. Heightened respect for natural world. 4. Change is both feared and hoped for. 5. Personal fulfilment is obtained by identification with our common humanity in responsible, collective caring for planet.

Figure 2: *Three phases of human culture*

membership of the tribe or group. Such personal identity as any individual might possess was dependent on, and closely inter-twined with, tribal identity. Opportunities for personal initiative were quite minimal. The elders of the tribe jealously guarded the preservation of the tradition, tolerated no change and discouraged all questioning of it. It was transmitted with absolute authority and meticulous exactness.

It was in the Axial Period that the religious dimension of human existence manifested itself more clearly as the quest for meaning. Whereas the pre-Axial cultures had evolved over a very long period in response to the basic human needs for food, survival and reproduction, in the Axial Period there emerged people who began to ask questions about the traditions. This was a daring thing to do, as exemplified by the fate of Socrates, and the proverbial 'stoning of the prophets'.

The questioning took various forms. The recorded words of the Israelite prophets, from 750 to 450 BC, were devastatingly iconoclastic with regard to such well-established rituals as animal sacrifice. The philosophers of Greece were more reflective, sub-jecting their culture to critical analysis and attempting to penetrate to the centre of what constituted reality. Others like Zarathustra of Iran and Confucius of China attempted, in their different ways, to reform their tradition so as to bring to the surface the importance of some specific human values. Zarathustra, for example, sought the final victory of the good in what he saw as a cosmic struggle between good and evil, and to this end he apotheosised such values as truth, good thought and holy spirit. Confucius promoted an ideal model of humanity, which he called 'man at his best', who displayed such virtues as propriety, human-heartedness and filial piety. The ancient Indian seers show clearly by the Upanishads they wrote between 800 and 400 BC that, in the complex culture which had emerged from the fusion of the incoming Aryans with the indigenous Dravidians, they were searching for the ultimately real. It was only after Gautama the Buddha had expressed dis-satisfaction with all the known forms of spirituality that he reached enlightenment; he proceeded to share his discovery with others in a way which led his followers to abandon the caste social system and the way of the Brahmins and to follow his new Eightfold Path.

Just what led to this questioning of tradition and the search for something new is not clear. The phenomenon occurred at several places on the continent of Eurasia, quite independently of one another, and in a relatively short space, say 800 to 300 BC. Karl Jaspers regarded it as an axis which cut human history in two. Viktor von Strauss in 1870 referred to it as a 'strange movement of the spirit [which] passed through all civilised peoples'.[6]

It may be useful to see this Axial divide as a very special threshold of change in the longer period of transition which Teilhard de Chardin referred to as noogenesis (as noted in Chapters 5 and 12). It is not possible to suggest a time when the process of noogenesis actually began because, by its very nature, the dawning of human self-consciousness must have proceeded very slowly at first. But, just as after a long morning twilight the tip of the sun suddenly appears over the horizon, so the Axial Period may be understood as that moment in geological time when humans at last became aware of their potential for self-reflection and for critical thought.

The pre-Axial cultures had developed more or less unconsciously; that is, they had arisen of their own accord out of the collective unconscious of the human species. Those individuals who pioneered the Axial Period manifested a greater degree of personal self-awareness than appears to have been the case hitherto. They were developing an awareness of time, history and human mortality. They began quite openly to criticise past tradition. They were critical of the world they lived in and, in varying degrees, distanced themselves from it, looking for salvation in some other realm of reality. The prophets, seers and philosophers were consciously seeking meaningful answers to their questions.

There was, of course, nothing like a complete break with the past at the Axial Period. Human history does not divide into neat segments. There is always continuity, even in times of pronounced discontinuity. At this distance in time, however, it is possible for us to recognise that a distinct cultural shift was taking place at the

Axial Period, which had the effect of creating a new cultural layer over what remained from the past. This new layer transcended the preceding ethnic traditions and can be appropriately termed Transethnic. Although it engulfed and incorporated the Ethnic traditions, rather than destroying them, it nevertheless relativised them in to a secondary place. This new cultural layer is found today in what are commonly called the 'world religions', such as Zoroastrianism, Judaism, Christianity and Islam from the Middle East and Hinduism, Buddhism, Jainism and Confucianism from the Orient.

Unlike the Ethnic religions, which could be named only by reference to an ethnic group, the Transethnic religions were nameable because each consisted of a set of ideas, beliefs and practices which were no longer permanently tied to any one ethnic group. They could even be termed ideologies, though this term is usually reserved for systems of political ideas, in deference to the conviction that religious ideas were not of human origin. The Transethnic traditions took their name either from a founder (as in Buddhism, Christianity, Confucianism) or from a key concept (as in Islam). Because they resulted from critical assessment of past culture or reflection on the human condition, or a mixture of both, they were able to loosen their ties with the cultural tradition within which they emerged.

Judaism, Hinduism and Confucianism never quite escaped from their ethnic origins, though there are signs that they had the potential to do so; they have remained largely ethnic to this day. Buddhism, Christianity and Islam, by contrast, successfully disengaged themselves from their ethnic base and jumped over ethnic boundaries. Buddhism was able to exploit to the full the transethnic potential of Hinduism; Christianity and Islam were similarly placed in relation to Judaism. Christianity and Islam each made such absolute and exclusive claims that they developed a religious imperialism and became the foundations of extensive civilisations; Buddhism peacefully permeated all the cultures of the Orient and was more content to live in association with alternative paths of faith.

The three main Transethnic traditions of the post-Axial period had several features in common. They were no longer primarily concerned with this world and its basic needs of food, survival and reproduction, as the Ethnic religions had been. They no longer focused attention on the preservation of ethnic identity. Indeed, they often devalued the things of this world in favour of a transcendent realm of reality more lasting than this, to which they looked for the eternal destiny of the essential human being.

Whereas our ancestors in pre-Axial times accommodated themselves as fully as possible to the conditions of this world, so that even death was assumed to lead into a vague continuation of the same, the post-Axial traditions developed a dualistic conception of reality. They had different ways of describing the other-world which transcended this visible and mundane existence. But people's sights were redirected to a form of reality, other than the here and now, which could be found widely attractive and convincing. It seemed that human consciousness had reached a spiritual state which no longer found satisfaction in the things of this-world. For the first time in human history the central religious preoccupation was with other-worldly goals which transcended this-world and were to be reached by such various methods as enlightenment, divine salvation, ascetic renunciation and so on.

Each of the three dominant post-Axial traditions had the capacity to become universal to humankind and might have done so by now if it had not been for the other two. By the year 1900 these three had practically divided the world among them. The Christian West extended from Russia to the Americas. The Islamic Middle East stretched from Algeria to Indonesia. Buddhism permeated the whole of the Orient, including Tibet, China, Indo-China and Japan; in India it had been reabsorbed back into Hinduism.

At the centre of each of these cultural movements was a set of ideas, concepts and beliefs (hence the validity of the term ideology). These were succinctly expressed in the Four Noble Truths of Buddhism, the Creeds of Christendom and the Shahada of Islam. Of course it is only from the outside of these that we can recognise the basic 'truths' of each to consist of ideas which are of human origin; from the inside they were believed to be of divine or cosmic origin. Surrounding the central truths, in each case, was a complex of related ideas expressed in holy scriptures, authoritative teaching and appropriate rituals. Each tradition formed a coherent and consistent whole, with its own internal logic. Each provided a shared world of meaning in which to live and find personal fulfilment.

In the Ethnic Phase of culture, personal identity and fulfilment were drawn from the identity of one's tribe or race. The Transethnic Phase offered an enlargement of one's world and awakened the sense of one's common humanity. This was achieved, not (as one might have thought) by focusing attention on humanity, but by turning attention away from this world altogether to fasten on other-worldly goals. (As a simple analogy, one might imagine how, if we humans suddenly found ourselves invaded from outer space, we would suddenly be drawn together and all international hostility would temporarily cease.)

The dualistic view of reality which characterised Transethnic religions was reflected in social organisation. To join the Sangha (Buddhist order of monks), the Christian church or the Umma Muslima (people of God) was to separate oneself from this-world, in part at least, to prepare oneself more adequately for the other-world.

Another feature common to the Transethnic traditions is that they were deeply embedded in historical events. The Ethnic religions had no known beginning and were timeless. The Transethnic traditions had an historical beginning, which they regularly celebrated. Whatever has a beginning also has a history. Change and development were intrinsic to the Transethnic traditions. Though each of them was anchored to a fairly permanent system of ideas, they were by no means static. They manifested conflict, division and diversification. Buddhism, Christianity and Islam exist today in a remarkable variety of forms; each can be described as a family of religions in itself.

Since they had a beginning, will they also have an end? An

historian of religion, Robert Ellwood, in his book *The History and Future of Faith*,[7] has proposed a model for describing the lifecycle of the Transethnic traditions, which he refers to as the great religions. In his model a great religion passes through five consecutive stages of varying length: the first is Apostolic; the second Wisdom and Imperial; the third Devotional; the fourth Reformation; the last Folk Religion. By applying this model, Ellwood comes to the general conclusion that during the twentieth and twenty-first centuries Confucianism and Buddhism are experiencing their demise, Christianity and Hinduism are reaching their Folk Religion stage, and Islam is just entering the Reformation stage (comparable to Christianity in the times of Luther, Calvin and Loyola). As Ellwood concedes, the titles he has chosen for the first four stages reflect the history of Christianity rather more than the other traditions. That may be a weakness in the theory in trying to apply it universally, yet it enables Western readers to follow his model more readily.

The Apostolic stage covers both the time of the founder and the fluid yet formative period which follows. It is exemplified by the struggle of Confucianism in the era of the 'Hundred Schools', the slow spread of Buddhism in Gautama's own lifetime and that of his immediate successors, the spread of Christianity in the first three centuries, the establishment of Islam in the lifetime of Muhammad.

The Wisdom and Imperial stage was entered by Christianity when Constantine made it the state religion of the Roman Empire and Ecumenical Councils gave to Christianity its definitive shape. This was comparable to the official adoption of Confucianism by the Han Dynasty, and to the Buddhist India of King Ashoka (which was followed by the rise of the Mahayana Schools of thought with their emphasis on the universality of Buddhahood). In Islam it is represented by the rapid expansion and consolidation which took place under the Caliphs; it lasted through the Ommayyad rule from Damascus and the Abbasid rule from Baghdad.

What Ellwood calls the Devotional stage occurred when the imperial unity of the second stage had given way to the rise of provincial or feudal states and some degree of religious diversity.

The universality of the original vision was being lost. The outer framework remained but no longer brought spiritual satisfaction. In the spiritual vacuum opening up people began to turn inwards. In Christendom this period stretched roughly from 1000 to 1500 AD, is represented by St. Francis and St. Bernard, and is manifested in the friars, the monastic institutions and the growing devotion to Mary. In Buddhism it was the period 500 to 1000 AD, which saw increasing devotion offered to the bodhisattvas and the rise of Pure Land Buddhism in China and Japan. The equivalent period in Islam ran from the decline of the Abbasid Caliphate and the fall of Baghdad in 1258 on to the beginning of the twentieth century; it was the age when Sufism flourished.

It was this devotionalism which provided the spiritual roots of the Reformation stage. In Christianity, it is illustrated by Luther's intense search for the certain conviction of his salvation. According to Ellwood, the Christian Reformation stage stretches from John Calvin to Karl Barth, with Vatican II bringing even Roman Catholicism into it. The Reformation period for Islam has begun only during this century and is manifested in what the West calls 'the resurgence of Islam'. Ellwood sees a parallel between Calvin's Geneva and Khomeini's Iran. In Buddhism, the Reformation was begun in the Kamakura period (1192–1338) with such spiritual leaders as Honen, Shinran and Nichiren, from whom developed a kind of Buddhist denominationalism, parallel to that in Protestantism.

What, then, is the Folk Religion stage which, according to Ellwood, Buddhism has now been in for some time, and which Christianity is now entering? It refers to a stage in which the great religion is no longer overtly observed in the official organs of society, is no longer dominant in the intellectual leadership, and is no longer providing the chief motivation of the on-going culture. In this stage Buddhism and Christianity, within their traditional geographical areas, continue to live at a popular level. Folk Religion is passed on through personal and family networks and is revived from time to time by charismatic preachers and teachers. But it has become a privatised and personal religion. Social manifestation of the traditional religion is confined to voluntary groups, often looking inwards to their own personal satisfaction rather than outwards to the needs of the wider community, which becomes secular and religiously neutral.

Ellwood's model of the lifecycle of the Transethnic religious traditions should not be pressed too far, but is well worth pondering as we try to understand the current religious situation of humankind. It suggests that the end is in sight for all of the religious traditions to which the Axial Period gave rise. It does not mean that they will disappear without trace. Very few cultural elements do that; they tend to be submerged and appear in other forms. Cultural traditions which have been as powerful and widespread as these have already left tremendous deposits in current cultures around the world. What the model does imply is that classical forms of these traditions, rather than their substance, are slowly becoming obsolete.

Perhaps the factor most responsible for the slow demise of the great religions in their classical form is the dualistic view of reality they developed. Such a suggestion finds confirmation in the fact that the word which best sums up the kind of global culture currently succeeding the post-Axial cultures is 'secular', in the sense of meaning 'this-worldly'. In none of the great religions was the dualism more pronounced than in Christianity. It is probably no accident that it was also in the Christian culture of the West that the dualistic view of reality first began to disintegrate, as if it had been pressed to the limit, only to collapse thereafter.

The dualistic world-view had both strengths and weaknesses. One great strength of the Christian dualism was that the other-world provided a standpoint from which to look critically at this-world and to treat it objectively as something humans could manipulate for their own ends, since the sacred elements originally thought to be there had been transferred to the other-world. (Some have seen this as one of the reasons that modern empirical science came to birth in the Christian West.) An even greater strength of Christian dualism is that the other-world provided the meaning for this-world. It not only explained why this-world is finite, having a beginning and an end, but it gave meaning to everything which occurs within this-world, including human existence itself.

The weakness of Christian dualism was that it devalued this-world, as people were encouraged to fasten attention more and more on the other-world. This-world was declared to be a fallen world, destined for final destruction. Humans were taught to see themselves as sinful, worthless creatures, who could achieve nothing of value without the grace of God. Nothing could be expected from this world or from the human species who domi-nated it. The only lasting reality was to be found in the other-world.

Over the last 500 years the reality of that other-world has been fading from human consciousness, at least in the West. Coper-nicus, Galileo and their successors have brought the heavens (the visible space occupied by the other-world) into this-world. The Protestant reformers in one fell swoop abolished purgatory, which in the late Middle Ages had become a section of the other-world of central and urgent interest for personal human destiny. From the Enlightenment onwards the concept of God, around whose throne the other-world had been devoutly visualised, was coming in-creasingly under question. The holy scriptures and ecclesiastical tradition, on whose authority the other-world had long been proclaimed, were being increasingly recognised as human in origin and content.

The result of these and related factors has been that by the late twentieth century human attention had switched from the other-world to this-world. This has been clearly evident, not only in science, politics and economics, but even in religious thought and Christian preaching, though not of course to the same degree. It is widely assumed that the physical world is the real world and the other-world has been allowed to fade into non-existence.

It has already been noted in Chapter 4 that the complete identification of reality with the physical world is open to ques-tion. We are now able to pursue Popper's Three World model a little further. The supposed other-world of the great religions in general, and of Christianity in particular, belongs to World 3. It does have a reality but that should not be confused with the order of reality to which World 1 belongs. Consequently it should never have been allowed to usurp the reality of World 1. The other-world was a human creation, as is all of World 3. It evolved out of human devotion and imagination in an attempt to supply meaning to this-world and, in particular, meaning to human existence in this world.

It is not surprising that, as Christian dualism faded from Western consciousness, a loss of ultimate meaning began to be experienced. Nietzsche saw it coming as he announced the 'Death of God' in his famous Parable of the Madman. It was reflected in the rise of existentialism. Owen Barfield echoed Tillich when he wrote, 'Amid all the menacing signs that surround us in the middle of this twentieth century, perhaps the one which fills thoughtful people with the greatest foreboding is the growing sense of mean-inglessness.'[8]

In the primal cultures our human ancestors were hardly yet aware of asking about the meaning of life, for the religious dimension of their existence had to do with survival in this-world. In the post-Axial cultures people became more aware of the quest for ultimate meaning and, in seeking it consciously, they unconsciously created it, constructing a whole new world to contain it. The other-world served as the meaning of existence in this-world. So convincing was the world of meaning that it began to be treated as having a reality of its own in a way which made this-world dispensable. That was more than it could bear. The humanly constructed world of meaning began to collapse like a house of cards.

We have reached a critical turning-point in human history. We humans are creatures of meaning. We do 'not live by bread alone but every word that proceeds from the mouth of God',[9] which is simply another way of saying that we live by meaning. If the house of meaning constructed in the past is no longer adequate, we shall have to create meaning afresh. But this time we shall be aware of what we are doing; we shall have to create meaning consciously and deliberately. That will be the great difference between our task and the achievement of our forebears.

But how shall we create meaning? That is the challenge we shall turn to in Part III. In particular we shall explore what can be salvaged from the traditional house of meaning. Before we are ready to do this, however, we must examine more carefully just what it was the traditional meaning system consisted of. This brings us to the role of symbols, the topic of the next chapter.

CHAPTER 8

Symbols as
the Bearers of Meaning

The post-Axial religious traditions evolved out of a more intense and self-conscious quest for meaning than had ever been made before. In each of them we find a coherent system of ideas, beliefs and rituals which provided meaning for their respective adherents and made possible a sense of personal fulfilment. Each system established a shared world within which to live. We can legitimately speak of a Christian world, an Islamic world, a Jewish world and, though perhaps a little more indefinitely, a Buddhist world. For any person living wholly within any of these worlds that was all that needed to be said. The basic questions about human existence seemed to have been adequately answered. For those who are still firmly anchored in any one of those traditions, the answers it provides remain satisfying and appear to be self-evidently true.

But how can there be such different meaning systems? And why do they seem more or less equally convincing? The answer that has usually been given from within any of these traditions is that it alone is the true one and all the others are false or misleading. The Christian tradition, with Islam a close second, has been particularly judgemental of all the attempts to find meaning outside the Christian doctrinal system. 'Outside the Church there is no salvation', it proudly proclaimed. Christianity and Islam each claimed their traditions to be of divine, superhuman origin. All others were seen by them to be no more than human in origin and were to be dismissed as superstition, heathenism, spiritual darkness, works of idolaters and infidels.

Since the advent of the modern global village in the post-Enlightenment era, such religious chauvinism has been shown up for what it is. The absolute claims made by the Christian tradition have had to be increasingly modified, and the non–Christian traditions have come to be acknowledged as possessing some genuine spiritual value. In this situation another reason must be sought to explain why quite different meaning systems have evolved and why, without necessarily being judged entirely equal, they have nevertheless had the power to convince, and to bring satisfaction to, their adherents.

The reason is to be found in the composition of the meaning systems. They are basically symbol systems which have slowly evolved to provide answers to the human quest for meaning. The symbol systems are *all* of human origin. That does not mean that they should now be dispensed with, though many have reached such a conclusion. But it does mean that we have to learn to appreciate the significance of symbols in the human quest for meaning. (Indeed, we need to acknowledge how much the human condition depends on the use of symbols in all sorts of ways.) Carl Jung shrewdly observed that 'religions are the world's great psycho-therapeutic symbol systems'; that is, they have brought health or wholeness to the human psyche. All the religious traditions have resorted to, and relied heavily on, the use of symbol. Robert Bellah even defined religion in terms of symbols, saying, 'Religion is a set of symbolic forms and acts that relate humankind to the ultimate conditions of their existence.'[1]

The use of symbols extends far beyond religion. We all have a general acquaintance with the use of symbols in everyday life. The wedding–ring is the symbol of the marriage union. The flag is a symbol of national unity and loyalty. Because of what they represent people can feel strong emotional attachment to symbolic objects. The distress caused by the loss of a wedding–ring is not due solely to its monetary value, and people have been known to die rather than see their national flag desecrated. It is with this general understanding of symbolism that incidental references to it have already been made in this book, for example, that language itself is a system of auditory symbols. We must now examine the character of symbols more closely.

Rarely have we humans appreciated just how much our very humanity is dependent on, and permeated by, the use of symbols. Thomas Carlyle observed that 'it is in and through symbols that man, consciously or unconsciously, lives, works and has his being'.[2] Symbols are so basic to human culture that anthropologists have sometimes described the human species as *Homo symbolicus*, the symbol-using creature. Their use by humans is older than language. Even some animals appear to use symbolic objects and symbolic gestures, so it may not be quite as exclusively human as sometimes claimed.

What is the essence of a symbol? Let us start with the etymology of the word. 'Symbol' is derived from the Greek *sumballein,* which means 'to throw together'. What is thrown together in a symbol is a visible, audible or tangible object and something which is invisible, inaudible or intangible which the former represents, mediates or transmits.

In modern language 'symbol' has come to be used very widely, covering signs and tokens of all kinds. Yet it is useful to distinguish between a symbol and a sign, particularly with religious symbols. A sign (such as a direction post or an advertisement) points to something quite other than itself. There is no essential connection between the sign and what it points to. If the sign disappears what it points to remains unaffected. But a symbol in some way participates in that to which it points. Damage to the symbol is regarded as also damaging that to which it points.

This may be illustrated with reference to a country's currency. Money consists of the symbols of value, which we use for trade. A coin or banknote has both an intrinsic value and an extrinsic value. In the early days of coinage, and even while we adhered to the gold standard, the two values were approximately the same. Today the intrinsic value of a banknote, and even of a coin, is very little indeed. The importance of these symbolic objects of exchange lies in the extrinsic value which they mediate. Even though the banknote remains unchanged its extrinsic value may vary considerably, depending on inflation, the state of the currency and the context in which it is tendered for trade. These symbols of value are more than signs. If they are destroyed, their extrinsic value is also lost. If a country decides to change its currency the extrinsic value of the banknote may become worthless. Conversely, as with a gold sovereign, the intrinsic value may eventually greatly exceed the extrinsic value. In short, with these everyday trading symbols of value we need to distinguish clearly between two values which, though different, cannot be divorced from each other. A symbol binds or 'throws together' two things or values in such a way that the intangible is represented, mediated or transmitted by the tangible.

There are many types of symbol and this simple definition admittedly suits some more than others. The line between sign and symbol is sometimes ambiguous and some things may be acknowledged as symbolic by some people and not by others. Such ambiguities arise from the nature of symbol itself. Symbolism is resorted to precisely because what the symbol is intended to mediate is itself intangible and difficult to define; if this were not so, there would have been no need to use symbols in the first place.

These ambiguities have led to much misunderstanding of and debate about religious symbols, as we shall later observe. In an age dominated by empirical science there has been a tendency to dismiss symbols unless they can be exactly defined (in which case they may be better classed as signs). Just as the word 'myth' has come to be used somewhat derogatorily, so there is a popular tendency to conclude that if something can be categorised as a symbol, then it may be regarded as dispensable or of secondary value. We rarely do this with our banknotes; we should be cautious about abandoning our religious symbols unless they have gone out of currency.

It was observed at the close of Chapter 5 that the human psyche, in view of its remarkable creative capacity, may be regarded as a veritable symbol-making factory. Perhaps the most important manifestation of this remains human language. That was where we started in Chapter 1 and it may be useful to return briefly to the point that human speech makes symbolic use of vocal sounds. Human languages are symbol systems. Since our very humanity has been made possible by language, that is an indication of how dependent on the use of symbols we humans have become.

But language, important though it was, was only the first great jump forward for *Homo symbolicus*. Language, in turn, greatly multiplied the possibilities for the human use of symbols. Words make symbolic use of vocal sounds. Myths, particularly the central myths of the great religions, make symbolic use of words. With such words and myths, as we have seen, humans build for themselves a meaningful world. Thus the worlds we construct have been made possible largely by the initial creation of symbols.

Perhaps the earliest symbols in human use are the visual images which appear in our dreams. If there is some substance to Jung's theory of the collective unconscious and his interpretation of dreams, then the collective unconscious is by far the oldest area of the human psyche, and the visual images and sequences we experience in dreams constitute a symbolic code by which the unconscious is communicating with consciousness. Some of these images reflect what has been actually witnessed and some of them are completely imaginary – that is, pure creations of the unconscious.

Then came human speech, the symbolic use of vocal sound. This was later followed (as recently as about 5000 years ago) by the invention of writing. Writing is not so much the creation of new symbols as the transcription of one mode of symbolism, audible symbols, into another mode, visible symbols. The written symbol system had the great advantage of enabling any one generation to establish something close to first-hand contact with generations both past and future. (From now on this contact will take place even more effectively through the medium of sound and sight preserved on magnetic tape.)

As well as creating verbal language for communication, the collective mental efforts of humankind have created other 'languages' for different purposes. Mathematics is a symbolic language, created to solve problems by measuring, calculating and computing. Mathematical symbols began as an extension of the alphabetical symbols, as is still the case with simple algebra. Then, beginning with arabic numerals, mathematicians created their own distinctive symbol systems. The skill of the mathematician is displayed in the art of manipulating the mathematical symbol system.

Through mathematics we have been led to another great advance in the use of symbols, the full consequences of which cannot yet be envisaged for it is still developing. We are now living in the age of the modern computer, which is a mechanical extension of the human psyche in much the same way as the hammer and other manual tools are the extensions of our hands. As the human psyche is a manipulator of symbols, starting with visual images and extending to words and other humanly created symbols, so the computer greatly multiplies its manipulating capacity. The computer may be described as a symbol-manipulator. It is not surprising that an analogy is commonly drawn between the computer and the human brain, leading us to speak of the computer as having a memory and using various languages.

Thus the visual images of our dreams, the words of language, the myths with which we construct our worlds, the languages we use for calculating and computing – all are examples of our dependence on symbols. We swim, as it were, in an ocean of symbols. Within this immense ocean there are symbols we use specifically in the quest for meaning. These may be called the religious symbols. As the very nature of the symbol is to 'throw together' a tangible object with something intangible, it can readily be grasped why symbols have become so valuable, even indispensable, in the search for meaning. For if the ultimate meaning of human existence is to be sought while still unknown, it is natural to attempt to reach out to it by grasping something tangible in the expectation that it will mediate to us what we seek.

In an evolving culture a whole host of potential symbols may be thrown up and tried. Symbols are not consciously created by humans but arise out of the circumstances of life. What, in the long run, have become the standard or classical religious symbols are those which have proved their worth in being able to mediate some intangible value, to nurture trust and confidence, to raise hope, or to give birth to an inspiring vision. The most precious and evocative symbols have invariably enabled people to respond to ultimate issues in a meaningful and satisfying way.

Even in today's secular surroundings we humans tend to fasten on particular objects and attribute to them a value far beyond their intrinsic worth. This may be for a great variety of reasons. When we speak of something as having sentimental value, it is often because that object has been associated with some person or event or place which has meant much to us. The object has become for us a symbol of something beyond itself. When a child lacking confidence becomes attached to a well-worn toy or bit of blanket, it is because the object brings comfort and a sense of security; it has become associated with the warm, comfortable, familiar surroundings where the child feels safe. The object has become a symbol and wields for the child symbolic power.

These everyday examples are survivals of what was much more widespread in primitive times. Almost any object, in appropriate circumstances, could become a fetish, a talisman, an amulet or charm. These are all words for an object which, in earlier times, was valued and even reverenced because it was believed to possess hidden magical powers, particularly for healing. Such symbolic objects were powerful because they were thought to mediate power from a source beyond themselves. They mostly gained their supposed power through force of circumstances, by being associated with special people, places or events.

There was another class of objects deliberately manufactured to be the medium of power. Chief in this class were what came to be called idols or images. These were designed to be visual representations of hidden powers and spiritual beings. They became focal points for worship. To them people brought their offerings in gratitude for favours received, or their entreaties for favours hoped for. Later iconoclasts (idol-smashers) often assumed that people worshipped the object itself. Of course, there was always the danger that the worshipper would identify the object with the spiritual power whose help they sought, but even the so-called primitive mind mostly drew a distinction between the image, idol or icon and the spiritual power thought to reside in it or to be associated with it. In other words, the idol was, as its name implies, a likeness, a representation, rather than the intangible source of power it was intended to mediate. The genuine acknowledgement of a religious symbol is to be clearly distinguished from crass idolatry.

Religious symbols frequently performed their full role within the context of a ritual. Ritual is a symbolic drama in which objects, gestures, movements and words all unite in a meaningful way. By way of illustration, let us look at the two central rituals in the Christian tradition, commonly referred to as the sacraments of baptism and holy communion. These employ such common objects as water and bread, which in the respective rituals perform roles far exceeding their normal use. Nevertheless there is a clear connection, in each case, between their normal use and their ritualistic purpose. Water, so frequently used to cleanse and renew the body, is used in baptism symbolically as the means of spiritual cleansing and renewal. Bread and wine, the most common ingredients of a daily meal in the Middle East, are used in holy communion as the instrument of spiritual food to nourish the soul.

These examples clearly show how a symbol 'throws together' two things: a visible, temporal object and a non–physical attribute, which, in the case of religious symbols, is thought to be of ultimate value. In the pre–modern cultural context where the hidden, unseen world seemed even more real than the tangible world, there was little difficulty in appreciating just what that non–physical attribute was. It was a spiritual, other–worldly power. In a universe viewed and experienced as dualistic, one was fully attuned to see and experience religious symbols for what one had been conditioned to expect of them. There was such a simplicity, transparency and consistency about the whole ritual that it was inappropriate to ask questions about its nature or even to speak of such holy objects as the sanctified bread and wine as symbols. Certainly there was the danger of idolatry – that is, of identifying the tangible with the intangible; we shall explore that later. But now we must turn to the symbolic character of religious language.

We have seen that human language is itself a symbol system,

which enabled the drive towards meaning to find some clarity of expression. Language in its earliest form was mainly used as an aid to better communication by naming, describing, warning and so on. Since language is already a system of symbols, we may, for convenience, speak of its face-value use as first level symbolism. But language opened the door for other forms of language. The language of mathematics has been mentioned; it could be termed a second level of symbolism. Similarly, when we use language in metaphor, poetry, allegory, parable and myth, what chiefly concerns us is no longer the ordinary, face-value meaning of the words but the second level of meaning, which varies according to the genre being used. This extension of the symbolic character of language may be regarded as a second level of symbolism.

Deeper levels of meaning in language have been acknowledged for a long time in Christian scholarship. They are found as early as St. Paul himself, when he interpreted the story of Hagar and Sarah as an allegory of the Old and New Covenants. By the Middle Ages Christian scholars were regularly reading the Bible in four different modes: the literal, the allegorical, the moral and the spiritual. The legitimacy of the last three are now questioned and were mostly abandoned by Protestant scholars from the Reformation onwards. What has not been sufficiently recognised, however, is that religious language generally depends on a second level of symbolism.

The symbolic character of religious language was not easy to detect because it was so often found side by side with language used quite literally or at the first level. Let us take the Apostles' Creed, for example. 'Born of Mary, suffered under Pontius Pilate, crucified, dead and buried' are words used at face value, making claims which are open to historical investigation. But the rest of the second article, 'conceived by the Holy Ghost ... descended into hell, rose again from the dead, ascended into heaven, sits at the right hand of God', makes claims which are not open to historical investigation. By using verbs of the same order (conceive, descend, ascend, sit) the impression is given of first level, historical meaning; in fact, these verbs are all used in a second level, or symbolic, mode. 'Heaven', 'hell', 'Holy Ghost' are not names of publicly identifiable places or people; they are symbols. They are words of faith, expressing values and experiences, and do not have external referents other than images in the human mind.

During the long pre-modern period, when the human origin of language was not recognised, language was language was language. There was no call to distinguish between first level statements which described the external world and statements of faith which expressed one's inner world of meaning. Only the former statements, however, used language literally and so were open to public investigation and verification. The latter borrowed the language created to describe the external, public world but used it symbolically to express internal faith, aspirations, subjective interpretation and values.

So until modern times little clear distinction was made in religious language between simple, descriptive (first level) language and metaphorical, symbolic (second level) language. All kinds of descriptions drawn from human activity were applied to God as if they meant exactly the same as in their original setting. Now that it is obvious the biblical language about God resorts again and again to anthropomorphisms, this is commonly explained by saying that we have no other language but human language to talk about what is beyond human conception. One can understand such a view but this explanation is itself an acknowledgement that religious faith uses ordinary language both metaphorically and symbolically. Previously, however, there was all too little awareness of this: words were taken at face value. The 'wrath of God' was of the same order as human anger but just more to be feared. God was even said to have regretted that he had created humankind.

The symbolic character of religious language is not confined to anthropomorphisms. Don Cupitt distinguishes between what he calls descriptive language and expressive language. In the former, language is used at face value to describe external events and scenes as objectively as possible. In the latter, one is speaking subjectively, giving expression to one's own attitudes, values and aspirations. Whereas science, historiography and so on strive to use descriptive language, religious language is predominantly expressive, for it is concerned with inner spirituality.

The pursuit of spirituality and the quest for meaning even led to the creation of symbols which had no counterpart in the everyday human scene – words such as angel, devil, heaven, hell. We can trace some of them back to a this-worldly origin. Heaven originated as the sky, the natural dwelling-place of the sky-god, but it gradually evolved into a symbol for the place or condition of eternal bliss. The Gehenna (or hell of the New Testament) was originally the Hebrew name for the Valley of Hinnom, which is sometimes thought to have been the communal rubbish dump and incinerator for the city of Jerusalem, but had already begun to play a role in Jewish mythology as the entrance to the underworld of the dead.

Medieval theologians, including Aquinas, spent a great deal of time discussing angels, even to the point, it is said, of trying to calculate how many could dance on the point of a pin. Even John Macquarrie devotes several pages to them in his *Principles of Christian Theology* (1966). This supposed order of supernatural creatures has continued to play a part in Jewish, Christian and Islamic thought right down to the present, chiefly because they are referred to in the holy scriptures of these traditions. Yet few words betray their symbolic origin more clearly. In both Hebrew and Greek the word used for 'angel' simply means 'messenger' and eventually came to be used as an abbreviation for the longer and more appropriate phrase 'messenger of God', which is still often found. As ancient kings sent communications through personal messengers, so it seemed appropriate that the King of Kings would do the same. These divine messengers were conceived as living permanently in heaven in the presence of God. Creative human imagination quite naturally supplied them with wings so that, like birds, they could travel to and fro between heaven and earth.

In time a whole mythology developed around the angels. Because they were heavenly creatures they were perfect and sinless, unlike humans. They were associated with beauty and music. They were the bearers of divine truth and this normally meant good news. They were associated with joyful service. We still associate these values with 'angel' at a time when, for most moderns, the term is retained solely for its metaphorical or poetic value. Thus the word has returned to the status with which it began – the status of symbol. But, whereas the symbol originated in a dualistic context, it is now being used in a secular context. This may prove to be a clue as to how other symbols can survive in entirely different cultural contexts. For most people today 'angel' is no longer the name of a class of unseen, invisible beings, yet when we applaud someone for acting like an angel, we are still drawing attention to a spiritual value. Moreover, we are in no doubt that we are speaking metaphorically.

Easily the most important symbolic concept of spirituality that has been created, certainly for the Western world, is 'God'. Many who have no trouble in acknowledging the symbolic character of 'angel' would be not at all happy about treating the word 'God' as a symbol. This word is so important that the next chapter is devoted wholly to it.

CHAPTER 9

God as a
Central Symbol of Meaning

O f all the symbols to which the human psyche has given birth in order to create meaning, by far the most important is the concept of God. In the monotheistic traditions it became the supreme symbol of meaning. In his novel *The Brothers Karamazov* Dostoevsky put into the mouth of Ivan Karamazov: 'What is strange, what is marvellous, is not that God really exists, the marvel is that such an idea, the idea of the necessity of God, could have entered the head of such a savage and vicious beast as man; so holy it is, so moving, so wise, and such a great honour it does to man.'

Just how did the idea of God enter the human head? Until relatively recently few people paused even to ponder the question. After all, as the Bible rightly observed, 'No one has ever seen God!' Yet the reality of God long seemed to be so self-evident that 'only the fool would say to himself, "There is no God"'.[1] John Calvin wrote, about 1535: 'That there exists in the human mind, and indeed by natural instinct, some sense of Deity, we hold to be beyond dispute, since God Himself ... has endued all men with some idea of his Godhead ... There is no nation so barbarous, no race so brutish, as not to be imbued with the conviction that there is a God.'[2]

In the cultural context in which Calvin lived, there was every reason to believe that human knowledge of God went back to the time of Adam and Eve, only a few thousand years ago. If language was assumed to have existed before Adam, then so much more was it to be taken for granted that knowledge of God also had been there from the beginning of time. In the greatly extended cosmic and cultural horizon in which we live today, Calvin's claim is seriously defective. 'The conviction that there is a God' has never been universal to humankind and has been largely confined to the monotheistic cultures. If one thinks it to be self-evident, that serves only to show how much one has already been culturally conditioned. In other words, it is a belief relative to time and place.

Moreover this relativity began to be sensed during the Axial Period. The Greek philosopher Xenophanes (sixth century BC) condemned the Olympian gods for their immorality, poked fun at their anthropomorphic character and argued that animals probably made gods in their own image as much as humans had done. At about the same time the Israelite prophets were scornfully dismissing the gods of the nations as having no reality or substance to them.

During the long period in Western culture when it was assumed that the Bible contained the divinely revealed truth about origins of the world and of humankind, there was every reason to be convinced, as Calvin was, that the very concept of God, being the name of the creator, was older than creation itself. Within this intellectual climate it was assumed that the observations of Xenophanes and the Israelite prophets applied only to the gods of other people. It is only in modern times, when we have come to see that the time-scale of human history and culture has to be stretched out far beyond the limits found in the Bible, that we are able to ask afresh how the concept of God arose in the first place. We find that, far from being older than creation, it is in fact much younger than the human species. Most important of all, the concept of God, like all concepts, has been created by the human mind. Behind the concept of God as now found in Western culture, there lies a long and complex history. Let us now outline 'the history of God', to learn what it tells us about the human quest for meaning.[3]

In their book *The Intellectual Adventure of Ancient Man*, archaeologists H. and H.A. Frankfort sketched what they took to be the view of reality shared by the ancient humankind of the Middle East. Borrowing terms made famous by Martin Buber in his classic *I and Thou*, they asserted that, 'The fundamental difference between the attitudes of modern and ancient man as regards the surrounding world is this: for modern, scientific man the phenomenal world is primarily an "It"; for ancient – and also for primitive – man it was a "Thou".[4] Our early human ancestors knew nothing about an inanimate world. They experienced their external environment as a reality wholly permeated with life, life as fully conscious as their own.

In this scientific age, in which impersonal objectivity has become so dominant, we experience our environment at almost the opposite pole to that of ancient humankind. We run the risk of treating even other humans as impersonal objects. Martin Buber wrote his classic work because of his fear that the rapid growth of the 'It-world' (as he called it) in modern times is in danger of strangling the unique character of the world of personal relations. We need to pause, therefore, to recollect that our relations to other people are on a quite different level from our connection with impersonal objects. Objects have a past and a possible future but they have no presence. People, on the other hand, are known by their presence, a phenomenon which can even transcend time. Objects are completely passive in the face of our activity; with people there is reciprocal activity, in the course of which people may change and mature as a result.

It was with that kind of personal reciprocity that the ancients felt themselves to be encountering their environment. Life was an experience they knew inwardly and subjectively. Therefore, of necessity, they treated the living environment to which they responded as being as personal and as humanly subjective as they were themselves. Not only did they draw little clear distinction between humans and animals but the whole of external reality – mountains, rivers, clouds, storms and so on – were the many faces of hidden personal forces. To be a person was to have feelings and to exert a will. So the external world they encountered operated according to the whims and intentions of a personal will similar to their own.

Drawing on our modern understanding of the human psyche, we would say that the ancients projected their subjective experience on to their environment, yet not in such a way as to be aware

that they were doing so. They simply encountered their environment with awe because of its mysterious movement. The world as
they conceived it (that is, the world they were constructing in their
minds as a result of their existential encounter) was shaped by what
they felt inwardly, and they saw the external world as a mirror
reflection of their inner world.

In time the vaguely defined 'Thouness' of their world was
divided into specific areas and given particular names appropriate
to the function each was believed to perform. In this way the
ancients conceived their environment to be inhabited by a class of
invisible beings, sometimes referred to as spirits, sometimes as
gods. They did not ask *what* caused the storm but *who* caused it. To
them it seemed self-evident that all natural events, such as storms,
were caused by personal wills, such as that of the god who resided
in the storm. (Even today people may explain an event not caused
by humans as due to the 'will of God'.)

The ancients understandably found the natural world full of
mystery and wonder. It was out of the way in which they experienced and interpreted it that the gods came to birth. They were
created by the collective human mind, and became part of the
shared world which the ancients constructed. The process of
conceiving and naming the gods, all made possible through
language, was a way of ordering their world and of providing a
rational explanation of everything they observed and encountered
in nature.

There were common elements in the polytheistic cultures
which evolved, because the external world they all shared was
basically the same everywhere. Most early cultures came to speak
of the earth as a mother and to treat it as such; similarly, they
referred to the sky as father (still reflected in the words 'our
heavenly Father'). Thus not only was human personality being
projected on to external reality (as Xenophanes observed) but so
were human sexuality and human family relationships; they were
believed to be part of the basic structure of the cosmos. In the
world being constructed in ancient culture, which formed the
framework of their shared consciousness, inner human experience

was unconsciously being projected on to external reality.

In the mythology of ancient Greece the earth-mother was referred to as Gaia. She emanated from primeval Chaos, gave birth to Uranus (the sky), then mated with Uranus to procreate the race of beings known as the Titans. These, led by Kronos, revolted against Uranus and ruled the universe until they, in turn, were overthrown by Zeus and the other Olympian gods whom they had brought forth. This complex cycle of myths, as portrayed by Homer, finds a parallel in the mythology of ancient Babylonia. There the primeval watery chaos was represented as two oceans, Apsu (sweet water) and Tiamat (salt water). The union of these two beings brought forth the gods. After a series of complicated conflicts in which Apsu was killed and Tiamat prepared to avenge his death, the young god Marduk achieved a great victory, slew his mother Tiamat and cut her in two, using one half to form the earth and the other half to form the sky.

These are but two examples from ancient times of what was probably a very widespread, if not universal, mode of understanding reality – that is, of constructing an ordered world in which to live. In tribal cultures similar worlds continued until quite recently. The Maori, for example, has retained a respect for the land and for all natural forces which the European settlers often do not share. In the cycle of myths which described the Maori world, Papa (the earth-mother) and Rangi (the sky-father) emerged out of the womb of the primeval night in a very close embrace. It was the gods whom they procreated who forced them to separate and thus allow the light to enter the world between the sky and the earth. Leader of the gods was Tane, the deity of the forests and birds. This primeval event is still reflected in the falling rain and the rising morning mists, which represent, respectively, the weeping of Rangi and Papa over their enforced separation from each other.

As we look back to the birth of the gods in ancient times, from a cultural context which has long abandoned primitive polytheism, we too often fail to appreciate that the 'gods', conceived by human imagination to explain natural phenomena, were just as much concepts of primitive 'science' (that is, knowledge of reality) as they were of primitive religion. Where modern physicists create such terms as electrons, quarks and black holes in order to explain natural phenomena, the ancients created spirits, jinn, angels, devils and gods. The gods formed part of the world which the ancients constructed for themselves. A world (as explained in Chapter 4) is a mental construction. It is an inner world through the grid of which external reality is interpreted and understood. We may feel inclined to refer to the ancient gods as imaginary figures, because they are not part of our world. For the ancients, however, they were very real figures indeed.

It was not just because they were *gods* (a word we commonly associate with religion) that these were key figures in the religion of ancient humankind; it was because, in the world constructed by the ancients, the gods were the most significant bearers of meaning. It was through the gods that the ancients understood who they were and what life was all about. This they expressed in their myths, the stories about the gods. In such a context the gods did have religious significance, even though in the ancient world the primitive equivalents of what we call religion and science formed an indivisible whole.

If the time were to come when people began to ignore, despise or make fun of the gods, their religious significance would decline and disappear. Even if the gods remained part of the furniture of the human world, they would be a far less significant part. Such a time did come. It occurred at the Axial Period and the process took different forms.

Gautama did not deny the existence of the gods. He simply displaced them from the centre of attention, regarding them as irrelevant to his religious quest. Buddhism is sometimes said to be atheistic but that is not strictly true. Buddhism never went out of its way to deny the existence of the gods. It simply ignored them and they eventually faded from Buddhist consciousness. By the same token, as Buddhism permeated certain cultures figures very like the ancient gods began to re-appear. But that is another story and simply reflects how the Axial traditions have always shown a tendency to revert to pre-Axial forms. The fact remains that the

Buddhist tradition, older than Christianity by some 500 years, abandoned the concept of the gods and, by its success in offering a pragmatic means of understanding human existence, demonstrated that the gods were not indispensable to religion.

At the eastern end of the Mediterranean, the questioning of the gods took a different form. Initially there were two such forms and these eventually became synthesised into one. We have already noted how Xenophanes ridiculed the ancient Greek gods of Olympus. He went on to argue for a single, motionless, non-anthropomorphic god who controlled everything by the power of thought. Instead of simply denying the reality of the gods, or bypassing them as the Buddha was to do, Xenophanes retained the Greek word *theos* (god) but radically revised its meaning, thus enabling it to continue to perform the religious role of being the centre of a meaningful world.

This was the method followed by the later Greek philosophers. All of them replaced the plurality of the gods as a class of superhuman beings with the use of *theos* in the singular. This meant that the term tended to be treated as a proper noun or personal name, in the way Zeus and Pluto were personal names. Yet this is not what the philosophers intended. Moreover, they differed in what they chiefly affirmed about *theos*. Plato's *theos* was the essence of goodness, the creative source of everything, to whom were to be attributed the intelligent souls found in humans. (This has to be understood against the background of Plato's theory of 'forms' or 'universals', which later contributed to the other-world of Christian dualism. The 'universals' were non-physical and abstract ideas. Thus Plato's *theos* was the universal, impersonal and eternal 'form' behind the humanly conceived *theoi*, gods, of Olympus.)

For Aristotle, *theos* was even less personal than for Plato, being chiefly conceived as the Prime Mover of the cosmic system. The Stoics, in turn, conceived *theos* as the principle of rationality and order which pervaded all things. For them *theos* was the unity of all reality, so that *theos*, ether, *logos* (reason), soul of the world and nature were largely synonymous terms. The Roman Stoic philosopher Marcus Aurelius (121–180) said in his *Meditations*:

> Providence is the source from which all things flow; and allied with
> it is Necessity, and the welfare of the universe. You yourself are part
> of that universe; and for any one of nature's parts, that which is
> assigned to it by the World-Nature or helps to keep it in being is
> good ... Always think of the universe as one living organism, with
> a single substance and a single soul.[5]

The influence of the Greek philosophers was later to penetrate
deeply into the Christian understanding of God, particularly
through the neo-Platonist philosopher and mystic Plotinus (c.
205–270), who so influenced Augustine. Before looking at the
great synthesis of two cultural streams which took place during
the early centuries of the Christian era, however, we must first go
back to the other, and religiously more dominant, tradition which
contributed to it.

Even before the Greek philosophers gave to the word *theos* a
radically new meaning, a parallel transition was taking place in the
tiny nation of Israel at the instigation of their prophets. The 'gods'
as a class of beings were eventually and somewhat scornfully
banished from reality in favour of one supreme being, an invisible
spirit known only through speech. The transition took place in
stages over several centuries. Out of a milieu of cultures practising
polytheistic nature religions the Israelites began to tread a new and
distinctive path. At first they did not deny the reality of the gods
which other nations worshipped but they restricted their own
worship to one god, whom they knew by the proper name of
Yahweh: 'Yahweh our God is one' (Deuteronomy 6:5); 'You shall
have no other gods besides me' (Deuteronomy 5:7). (The situation
in which each nation is reckoned to have its own god is not pure
monotheism and is sometimes referred to as henotheism.)

Through most of the period of classical Israel, 1000–597 BC,
the Israelite prophets were fighting the last remnants of polytheism
among themselves, warning their people not 'to go after other
gods to their own hurt'. Only by the sixth century BC was the
prophetic voice proclaiming that their god Yahweh was the only

god who had any reality. 'Turn to me and be saved, all the ends of the earth! For I am God, and there is no other' (Isaiah 45:22). This Yahweh was conceived originally as the one who had liberated the Israelites from slavery in Egypt and led them into the land of Canaan. Only later did the Israelites extend their conception of Yahweh to be the creative source of all that exists, the maker of heaven and earth, the ultimate explanation of all mysteries and the key to the meaning of human existence.

It is important to observe that the Israelites, in spite of their demolition of 'the gods' as a class of beings, retained the actual Hebrew word for 'the gods', *elohim* (still plural in form), but gave it a new connotation, just as the Greek philosophers had done with *theos*. The word has a double use in the Old Testament. When it refers to the gods of the nations it is intended to be treated as plural, but when it refers to Yahweh it is intended to be treated as singular.

Just as *theos*, being only one and not a class, tended to be treated as a personal name though not intended as one, so the translation of *elohim* as 'God' has given the impression of being a personal name. In the Bible, however, often this did not take place. There we find the word *elohim* frequently attached to people – as in 'the god of Israel', 'the god of Abraham', 'my god', 'your god'.

In this usage 'god' is not a personal name. Though the word originated in ancient polytheism where it referred to a class of beings who had personal names, here it is being used with a subtle but important difference. In the transition taking place in the Axial Period, both in Greece and in Israel, we see the word god being increasingly used in an abstract and hence symbolic way to refer to whatever values a person or a nation treated as supreme. Moreover, it implied that if you were to ask, 'Where shall I find the god of Abraham?', the appropriate answer would be, 'Watch how Abraham lives his life and discern what he appears to regard as of ultimate concern to him; that is all you will ever know of the god of Abraham. His god consists of the values he lives by and the goals he aspires to.' (This point is taken up later.)

It is relatively easy for us in modern times to concede that the 'gods' were the product of the collective human imagination. We tend to lose sight, however, of the fact that the concept of God as found in later monotheism was a refinement of what originated there. This refinement was of a quite radical kind, owing much, as we have seen, to both the prophets of Israel and the philosophers of Greece. So convincing did this revised concept of God become that eventually it spread throughout the Middle East and Europe in one or other of its three major forms: Yahweh the *Elohim* of Judaism (often referred to as 'The Name'); the trinitarian *theos* of Christianity; and Allah of Islam. These three forms of monotheism dispelled the remnants of polytheism wherever they could; that was the one thing they had in common.

It was only to be expected that this divine One would come to be conceived in personal terms, partly because the earlier 'gods' had been conceived as sharing in all the human emotions and motivations, and partly because the values which are of ultimate concern to us humans arise out of our nature as persons and our personal relations one with another. It was unthinkable that these features would not be found in the very nature of God, the chief difference being that God was conceived as one who possessed personal qualities raised to an infinite degree. The correlation between the personal character of God and that of humans was specifically acknowledged in the biblical affirmation, 'God created humankind in his own image or likeness'.

Whereas in Greece *theos* was chiefly related to the whole universe and to nature, in Israel *elohim* was chiefly related to the history and fortunes of people, in particular the people of Israel. As the dominance of the Exodus story in all of Israel's early traditions shows, Yahweh the god of Israel was primarily conceived as the god who brought them out of Egypt, who led them to Canaan and eventually established the kingdom and dynasty of David. Only subsequently was he linked with the creation myths. Thus God, as portrayed in the Bible, was the 'Lord of human history' even more than he was the 'maker of heaven and earth'. Whereas the gods of the pre-Axial cultures were believed to manifest themselves in natural phenomena, the God of Israel was conceived as making his will known through the (partly legendary) patriarchs as spiritual leaders, the prophets as spokesmen for God, and the Davidic kings as those anointed to rule.

It was this understanding of God as being particularly concerned with human beings which the early Christians inherited from Jewish faith, and which they took with them into the non-Jewish world of Graeco-Roman culture, where it became synthesised with Greek philosophical thought during the first 500 years of Christian history. What eventuated as the classical Christian understanding of God owed almost as much to Plato as it did to the Israelite prophets. The transcendental, other-worldly, unchanging God of Plato was united in uneasy tension with the immanent, this-worldly, humanly-feeling God of Israel. The tension was prevented from falling apart by the formulation of the symbolic doctrines of the trinity and the incarnation.

These two doctrines show clearly just how far the Christian understanding of God had diverged from the pure monotheism preserved, and still affirmed, by Jew and Muslim. The Christian concept of God was expanded to contain the whole system of belief, which the creeds set forth within the framework of the holy trinity. To synthesise the changeless, abstract *theos* of Greek theology with the incarnation of the god of Israel in an historical person, God came to be spoken of as 'three *hypostases* in one *ousia*' (the Greek version) or 'three *personae* in one *substantia*' (the Latin version). If that were not complex enough, the Creed of Chalcedon (451), in particular, reads like a verbal conundrum, describing Jesus Christ as 'truly God and truly man ... consubstantial with the Father according to the Godhead, and consubstantial with us according to the Manhood ... to be acknowledged in two natures, inconfusedly, inseparably; the distinction of natures being by no means taken away by the union, but rather the property of each nature being preserved, and concurring in one Person and one Subsistence'.

The Christian holy trinity (itself a complex verbal symbol) was a far cry both from the god of Plato and from the god of the Israelite prophets. It is little wonder that a substantial minority of Christians rejected this verbal formula even in the fifth century and no wonder at all that, since God could be understood only through a maze of abstract philosophical terms, the ordinary medieval Christian turned in devotion to the saints and the Virgin Mary.

In theological circles, as time went on, and perhaps out of a desire for philosophical precision, the 'God of the philosophers' gained ascendancy over the 'God of Abraham, Isaac and Jacob' (as Pascal so neatly put the contrast); this was further emphasised in the thirteenth century when Aquinas embraced a further contribution of Greek thought, this time from Aristotle. During the later medieval period the original purpose of the doctrine of the trinity tended to be lost sight of. The humanity of Jesus was reabsorbed into his divinity. The humanness and immanence of the biblical God was surrendered to the cosmic changelessness of the Greek *theos*.

By the seventeenth century the deists were reducing the god of the philosophers to the far-distant creator who took no interest in human affairs. This was a stepping-stone, first to agnosticism, then to atheism. As the age of modernity began it was becoming increasingly difficult to support the 'god of the ancient philosophers' on purely rational grounds. Yet, as theologians attempted to stem the tide of atheism which began to flow from the late eighteenth century, they so often strangely ignored the doctrine of the trinity. They have been left defending the god of Plato and Aristotle even though, in the disintegration of the classical synthesis, the Greek component has proved more vulnerable than the biblical component. To understand why this is so we now need to go back to what some claim as the first seeds of the age of modernity.

William of Occam (c. 1300-1349), a Franciscan scholar at Oxford, was the most brilliant exponent of the philosophy called nominalism. This denied that Plato's 'universals' had any reality at all except in human thought. Universals such as 'goodness' were simply names created by the human mind – hence the term nominalism. The implication was that, if Plato's god (being 'goodness') was a 'universal', it too was a name created by human thought. Occam never put it as bluntly as that, of course, and would not have lasted long had he done so; yet that is what his position was destined to lead to. The philosophy of nominalism eventually aided the rise of empirical science and did much to usher in the modern world. We shall look at two significant steps on the way.

Luther was a nominalist. We find this reflected in his Large Catechism:

> A god is that to which we look for all good and where we resort in every time of need; to have a god is simply to trust and believe in one with our whole heart ... the confidence and faith of the heart alone make both god and an idol. If your faith and confidence are right, then likewise your god is the true god. On the other hand, if your confidence is false, then you have not the true god ... whatever your heart clings to and confides in, that is really your god. [6]

Already we find in the phrases 'a god is that to which we look for the good' and 'whatever your heart clings to and confides in, that is really your god' an acknowledgement of how subjectively the term 'god' was being used. Luther still wanted to distinguish between a presumed 'true god' and the false gods which one's heart might cling to; he probably assumed that the testimony of the holy scriptures provided the necessary criterion for making that distinction. But this eventually broke down at the point where the human origin and character of holy scripture became clear in the nineteenth century.

Not surprisingly, therefore, it was the nineteenth-century theologian and philosopher Ludwig Feuerbach (1804–72) who most fully drew out the implications of Occam's nominalism to conclude that 'God' is a humanly created concept. [7] The argument runs like this: the concept of god originated as a class of mythical beings in ancient polytheism; it was subsequently radically reinterpreted by Plato to be a universal; universals can now be seen to be humanly created names which possess no ontological existence; the Christian 'God' is consequently a name or concept created by human thought. 'To ask whether there is a God', said Feuerbach, 'is to ask whether the universal has an existence of its own.'[8] To the nominalist who acknowledges the human origin of universals, and of all the abstract terms of human language, the answer has to be in the negative. Feuerbach concluded that 'God' was an unconscious objectification of all that the human mind felt to be of worth. 'God' had been created by human imagination to contain, symbolically, the highest human aspirations and values. 'By his God thou knowest the man, and by the man his God; the two are identical.'[9]

In the previous century Voltaire, a deist, had made the famous observation, 'If God did not exist it would be necessary to invent him.' What Voltaire did not realise was that God *had* been invented, out of the necessity to find meaning. 'God' was a humanly created symbol. All talk and discussion about God (theo-logy means god-talk) is really an exercise in human self-understanding. By referring to the God-symbol we are discussing the meaning of human existence. 'God' is the symbol most central or basic to meaning. In the long history of the word 'God', Feuerbach may be taken as marking a turning-point as radically significant as those marked by the Israelite prophets and the Greek philosophers.

In sketching the history of God we have come on a very long journey. It started with the gods of ancient polytheism. It passed through a refining process in which the many gods were replaced by the One God, and the One God was so far beyond human conception that strict monotheists, such as Jews and Muslims, often preferred to speak of God simply as 'The Name', 'The One' or the bearer of 'The Ninety-nine Beautiful Names'. Christians spoke much more of the *attributes* of God than of the *being* of God. The most authoritative theologians adopted the *via negativa*, which acknowledges that it is impossible to say what God *is*, only what God *is not*.

At last we have reached the point where we can acknowledge that 'God' is a word, a very important word, a symbolic word. It has no external referent which is open to public confirmation. The word 'God' has become a functional term whose content depends on what we (subjectively) put into it, and this process, as we have seen, had its beginnings in the Bible. The word 'God' has a function, but no content or meaning except that which we supply. When we use this word we are affirming something about ourselves. It is a religious symbol which has the meaning we choose to give it. The content with which we invest it is the set of values and aspirations which we (subjectively) find laying a claim upon us. What those are depends on the world we have constructed, both individually and collectively.

This may be clearly illustrated by the fact that, at the collective level, Jews, Christians and Muslims, while all claiming to be monotheists, have never agreed on the question of who the true God is. They cannot be said to worship the same God for the only criterion we have for determining identity is the 'attributes' of God. The attributes constitute the content of the word 'God' and we humans are the ones who determine those attributes – that is, we are the ones who attribute the qualities in question. For the Jews, God is the One who delivered their forebears from slavery, gave them the land of Israel, and providentially continues to preserve their identity. For the Christians, God is the One who became incarnate in Jesus Christ. For the Muslims, God is the One who appointed Muhammad as the last of his prophets and through whom he delivered the Qur'an. In each case the attribute is a *sine qua non* of the tradition in question, yet in no way can it be reconciled with the others. Without these attributes the word 'God' is bereft of meaning. We have a hint of this in a dictum of an early Pope, Sixtus I (c. 117–127), 'God is not the name of God, but an opinion about Him.'

We are able to see that 'God' is a word, or concept, which has had a long history in the course of which it has undergone some radical changes and has been understood in widely variant ways. But this quite basic symbolic word appears now to have lost its validity. As John Macquarrie has well said:

> There was a time in Western society when 'God' was an essential part of the everyday vocabulary ... But in the West and among

educated people throughout the world, this kind of God-talk has virtually ceased ... People once knew, or thought they knew, what they meant when they spoke of God, and they spoke of him often. Now in the course of the day's business we may not mention him at all. The name of God seems to have been retired from everyday discourse. [10]

We shall now examine why this is so.

CHAPTER 10

When Symbols
Cease to Bear Meaning

Religious symbols are born out of the human quest for meaning. It is not easy to explain how and why symbols come to birth. One cannot even readily prophesy whether or not something is likely to assume the role of a symbol. Symbols simply rise out of the cultural environment and by the time a symbol is recognisable as such it has, of course, already come to birth. Perhaps the best we can do to understand the conception and gestation of symbols is point to the creative power of the collective unconscious. As a person constructs a world, and a society constructs a shared world, the collective unconscious appears to respond to the deep human need to find unity and purpose in human experience, and does so by leading the conscious to focus attention on objects and words which have some potential to mediate or reveal the meaning which satisfies that need.

Whatever has a beginning, however, is likely also to have an end. Whatever comes to birth eventually faces the crisis of death. Though we may not be able to explain very adequately how symbols are born, we can observe, as we look back, how they eventually die, sometimes reaching great power before showing signs of decay. All through human history there has been a coming and going of symbols. That is the way human culture has evolved.

Sometimes symbols are suddenly and deliberately destroyed. Sometimes they simply fade away as we grow beyond them. Today we are witnessing a gradual decline in the great symbols of the post-Axial traditions. Symbols of very long standing appear to be in their death-pangs. Indeed, whole symbol systems are under threat and showing signs of dissolution. We must examine how this has come about and then explore the possible responses to the death of the major symbols which have provided meaning for our forebears. The undermining of the traditional symbol systems is a global phenomenon but we shall draw examples chiefly from the Christian tradition.

Religious symbols, whether objects, rituals or words, have always faced two dangers. The first occurs when the symbol becomes mistaken for that intangible something, such as ultimate meaning, that it has had the power to transmit. The other danger occurs when the symbol loses the power to transmit anything but itself. In both cases the religious symbol ceases to function as a symbol should. In the former, we have crass idolatry, defining idolatry (using the words of Paul Tillich) as 'calling something ultimate which is less than ultimate'. In the latter, we suffer a sense of the loss of ultimacy and our existence feels threatened by meaninglessness. A religious symbol is performing its role successfully when it is instrumental in assuring us of ultimate meaning. It does this by holding the seen and the unseen in perfect, if uneasy, balance.

Let us look at the danger of idolatry first. The triple-stranded Middle Eastern religious tradition, which is composed of Judaism, Christianity and Islam, saw idolatry as its most serious threat. This is often forgotten today when atheism and so-called unbelief are widely regarded as the most serious threat. Common to Jew, Christian and Muslim in the pre-modern world was chiefly their militant rejection of the 'gods'. It was not the belief in no god at all but the belief in too many gods which they jointly regarded as their main religious rival. It is too often overlooked, therefore, that the monotheism common to these three really began with the denial of the gods, which is a kind of relative atheism. That is why the First Commandment of the Decalogue reads, '*You shall have no other gods but me*', and why the simple Islamic creed, the Shahada, asserts '*There is no God* but the true God'.

Since these ancient gods had been given visibility in images and other art forms, the emergence of monotheism led necessarily to iconoclasm, the wilful destruction of all such images. The natural corollary of the First Commandment was the Second Commandment: 'You shall not make for yourself a graven image, or any likeness of anything that is in the heaven above, or that is in the earth beneath, or that is in the water under the earth'. This strong prohibition of images meant that the most sacred symbols of the pre-Axial cultures were dealt a death-blow by the rise of monotheism.

As a result of this prohibition Christians and Muslims have destroyed and defaced images and other sacred objects wherever they have spread their influence. As noted earlier, there is considerable doubt today as to whether the people of pre-Axial cultures were quite as guilty of crass idolatry as their accusers maintained. With the gift of hindsight, we may now concede that neither tribespeople nor the ancients rarely ever *wholly* identified their stone and wooden images with the spiritual beings they worshipped; they could well have regarded them as genuine religious symbols, though it is anachronistic to project such a distinction back to their time. Nevertheless, it was this monotheistic rejection of other gods which led to the widespread destruction of that ancient mode of religious symbols.

Judaism and Islam have been stricter with sacred images than Christianity. That is why Islamic art came to depend almost exclusively on design rather than on the representation of living creatures. Any visual representation of God is unthinkable in Islam, and even the human form has traditionally been excluded. Christianity, on the other hand, has tended to stray rather more from the strictly iconoclastic path on which it originally set out. It held out against the use of icons and images until about the eighth century. It was John of Damascus (c. 675–749) who was chiefly instrumental in turning the tide in their favour. He argued that icons and religious pictures are necessary for illiterate people as aids to devotion, and they simply tell, in picture form, the sacred story which the literate can read in the Bible. The matter was settled at the Seventh Ecumenical Council in 787. From that time onwards the medieval church consistently tried to draw a clear distinction between idolatry, defined as the *worship* of images, and the legitimate *veneration* of icons or images of Christ, the Virgin

Mary and the saints. In view of their warning that no divinity or power resided in the images, we could say that they were defining them as genuine religious symbols.

In practice, however, the fine distinction between worship and veneration, between idol and symbol, is hard to preserve. Holy objects easily come to be treated as charms and fetishes. The common expression 'Touch wood!' is a survival from the practice of touching the sacred cross to preserve oneself from calamity. The bread of the eucharist came to be identified so completely with the body of Christ that not only did it come virtually to be worshipped as God in visible form, as exemplified in the rituals of the reserved sacrament and the monstrance, but the doctrine of transubstantiation was developed to provide a philosophical way of explaining how, by a miracle, the bread and wine became quite literally the body and blood of Jesus Christ. In many and various ways medieval Christianity strayed from the path of genuine religious symbolism into the very idolatry which, by its own central prohibition, it so strongly condemned. For wherever religious symbols become identified with what they symbolise the subtle shift from symbolism to idolatry has taken place.

At the Protestant Reformation the rejection of idolatry was reasserted; yet it was not without great resistance, even within Protestantism. So strong was the religious devotion associated with the holy communion that not even Luther or Calvin was willing to go as far as the Swiss reformer Zwingli and actually speak of the bread and wine of the eucharist as symbols. While rejecting the Roman Catholic doctrine of transubstantiation and all veneration of the sacramental bread and wine, they nevertheless wished to associate these elements with what they called 'the real presence' of Christ. The full ferocity of Protestant iconoclasm was directed against the elaborate imagery retained by Roman Catholicism from medieval times and it reached extraordinary lengths among the English Puritans, who even destroyed the stained glass windows of churches. Even as late as the early twentieth century some Protestants would not allow a cross within their churches, regarding it as superstitious popery.

In religious circles today, however, there is a much more positive appreciation of the legitimate role of visual symbols and there
is greater readiness to refer to them as symbolic. The bread and
wine of the eucharist, for example, are consciously treated by the
majority of Protestants, and perhaps most Catholics, as symbols
rather than as supernatural objects. We could speak of this process
of continuing to use symbols, even while acknowledging them to
be symbols, as the *re-cognition* of symbols. The objects in question
are being *cognised* as symbols (and not treated as idols or fetishes)
and being *restored* to the legitimate status of symbol, possessing the
power to embody and transmit some ultimate meaning.

The symbolic character of religious language has been proving
more difficult to acknowledge. Conservative Christians, for
example, who would not dream of venerating an icon or sacred
image, nevertheless have shown themselves strongly attached to
particular words, concepts and dogmatic beliefs, refusing to accept
them as symbolic. Let us take two examples which have been the
source of much debate, and which are often resorted to as touch-
stones to determine whether a person or a set of convictions can be
termed genuinely Christian.

The first is the phrase 'the Son of God', as traditionally applied
to Jesus Christ. To say 'Jesus was a Jew who was reared at Nazareth' is an historical statement open to public investigation and
confirmation or denial. To say Jesus is 'the only Son of God' is not
an historical statement but a confession of faith. It is an expression
of the value and significance which Jesus holds for the person
making the statement. It is a personal, subjective statement not an
objective fact open to public investigation. It uses a term which, in
its literal meaning, refers to relationships of human kinship; when
applied to God it is necessarily metaphorical or symbolic, having
been removed from the context which gave it its primary meaning.
In any case this symbolic term was already in general use before it
came to be applied to Jesus in a special way. It was a symbolic way
of evaluating saintly people. We find it in the New Testament:
'Blessed are the peacemakers, for they shall be called sons of God'
(Matthew 5:9), where 'son of god' is a metaphorical synonym for

'godly person'. Like all symbolic terms, it can be interpreted in a variety of ways. When it came to be applied to Jesus, first as a way of honouring him and later as a way of affirming his supposed uniqueness, it was changing in usage but it still remains symbolic.

The second example has to do with the resurrection of Christ. It is surprising how much it is still assumed, even by theologically literate people, that the term 'resurrection from the dead' has a very clear and definable meaning. Once again, the term originated quite some time before the Christian era, as a consequence of the eschatological myth of the last judgement. It was of necessity, therefore, a mythical or symbolic term from the beginning and open to a wide variety of interpretations. This diversity is amply demonstrated within the pre-Christian Jewish writings. That is why the New Testament itself is also far from uniform in the way the term is understood. The Gospel of Mark even reports how the disciples questioned 'what the rising from the dead meant'. Paul, Mark, Luke and John all seem to have understood the resurrection of Jesus in different ways. [1]

Because of the symbolic character of the term 'resurrection', and the variety of ways of interpreting it, the early Christian community developed a number of legendary stories in order to provide it with more explicit meaning. These had mythical components; for example, the discovery of the empty tomb becomes the context within which an angel delivers the news of the resurrection. Some of these stories speak of the risen Christ as if he were a spiritual figure who could appear and disappear at will; others speak of the risen Christ as if he were a resuscitated physical body who could eat food. Each of these stories can speak quite powerfully if read as a complete unit and understood symbolically. If read literally, as though they took place in the same kind of world we find ourselves living in, they soon begin to raise problems. This is not only because angels are sometimes found playing the key role, as in Mark's story; it is because these stories are told to fit the mental world constructed and shared by people in the first century. It was a world in which the dead were conceived as dwelling under the earth and in which it was possible to reach the throne of God by ascending high enough into the sky. The mental picture of the resurrection reflected in these stories is a journey of ascension from the underworld up into the heavens.

In modern times the resurrection stories have often been read as if they were historical, rather than symbolic, and have been appealed to as a means of proving the resurrection of Christ on the basis of historical testimony. That is, confessions of faith expressed in symbolic terms have been unwittingly transferred to another literary genre, that of first-level historical testimony. This puts the cart before the horse. Stories which arose to express faith are being turned around to explain why the faith arose in the first place.

The modern attempts to prove the resurrection of Christ on rational grounds not only set out from a grave misunderstanding of the symbolic nature of the term 'resurrection', but fail to see how essential to faith are both visual symbols and symbolic language. Paul Tillich observed that the first step towards the non-religion of the Western world was made by religion itself, when it tried to defend its great symbols by treating them as literal stories instead of accepting them as symbolic. It is vain to defend the great verbal symbols of religion by simply denying their symbolic status. That way leads to idolatry.

Nevertheless, it is true that the great symbol systems of the religious traditions are disintegrating and the great symbols are losing their power. The current crisis faced by traditional Christianity is due to the decline of the dualistic view of reality. The other-world of the dualistic picture which has been slowly dissolving from Western consciousness was in fact an elaborate system of symbols. Heaven and hell symbolised the issues of ultimate personal destiny. God on his heavenly throne symbolised the unity, purpose and worth of the universe we live in. The Last Judgement symbolised the issues at stake in every decision we make, great or small. The Christ figure symbolised our need to be saved from the worst we can do to ourselves.

These great symbols are no longer pregnant with meaning as they once were. This brings us to the second great danger faced by symbols, the opposite of idolatry. Symbols may die. If symbols lose their power to transmit meaning and die, they cease to be symbols; they revert to their mundane existence in much the same way as, at the end of his dream, Scrooge's ghostly visitor turned into the bedpost.

What, if anything, is to be done about the death of symbols? Nothing needs to be done wherever symbols have died (or been killed) simply because they have proved false and harmful (as with the Nazi swastika) or where they have outlived their usefulness owing to changing cultural conditions. It is a different matter, however, with those symbols so basic that they provided people with their sense of identity or their purpose in life. The loss of such symbols results in the threat of meaninglessness, as when Nietzsche explained nihilism as resulting from the 'death of God'.

Few have understood and explained the symbolic nature of religious language and religious figures more clearly than Paul Tillich.[2] He was scornful of people who referred to symbols pejoratively with such comments as 'It's only a symbol!', insisting that it is only through symbolic language that we are able to give verbal expression to ultimate meaning in human existence. But even Tillich had to concede that when we become aware of the phenomenon of symbolism in religion we can no longer relate to symbols with quite the same innocent simplicity as the pre-moderns. It is as though, relative to our pre-modern forebears, we have had the scales removed from our eyes and we become convinced we are in closer touch with the real world than they were. We have moved from the state of childlike innocence to face the hard, and somewhat chaotic, facts of reality. We are like children who have realised that the story of Father Christmas is not literally true. Yet if they look back, at first with nostalgia for the magic that has vanished, and later with the depth of mature wisdom, they will realise that the story symbolises in dramatic fashion the joy and excitement of giving and receiving.

We have already touched on this problem when discussing myths in Chapter 2. Myths are a special kind of symbolic story. It is the same with symbols generally. Since the advent of modernity, we have become aware of our symbols in a way that our predecessors were not. In speaking of myths as the symbolic stories of faith, Tillich suggests that, 'A myth which is understood as a myth . . . can be called a "broken myth".'[3] Instead of referring to symbols, acknowledged to be symbols, as 'broken symbols', it may be preferable to use a more positive term such as 're-cognised symbols'.

Can the re-cognising of symbols help us to steer a path between the idol and the dead symbol in such a way that symbols may still be a means of guiding us to a meaningful existence? This possibility will be explored in Chapter 15 in relation to the very important verbal symbol of God. But here let us first see what it is about the traditional use of the God-symbol which has to die before it can rise to new life as a symbol.

The first requirement is simply to acknowledge the symbolic character of the word 'God' and to dispense with the notion that it names an objective reality, however unseen and transcendent. Certainly, rejecting the external objectivity of God is a form of atheism in that it denies the legitimacy of a particular way of understanding 'God'. In this sense, monotheists were atheists from the beginning; the first Christians were even accused of atheism by those who remained faithful to the ancestral Roman gods. The monotheists, in turn, regarded their accusers as superstitious idolaters. Similarly, in the transition to global culture, those who conclude that 'God' is a symbolic term tend to regard the objective theism of tradition as idolatry and superstition. (Superstition may be defined as the survival of an earlier religious belief after the dissolution of the 'thought-world' to which it belonged.)

Paul Tillich, for example, maintained that, 'It is as atheistic to affirm the existence of God as it is to deny it.'[4] The reason is that 'existence' applies only to objects, which might or might not exist; even to ask the question 'Does God exist?' implies an objectivity which is inappropriate to God. God is not such an object. Tillich insisted that 'God' is not the name of an objective supernatural being but a symbolic word which refers to whatever concerns us humans in an ultimate way. We cannot express or talk about whatever concerns us ultimately except by means of symbols. 'Faith is the state of being grasped by an ultimate concern', Tillich said, and 'the fundamental symbol of our ultimate concern is God'.[5]

Similarly, Gordon Kaufman maintains that theology has always been a human activity which draws on the power of the human mind to imagine, idealise and conceptualise. But, whereas previously this activity occurred unconsciously, we are now able to see that this is what we humans have been doing all along. Henceforth, he believes, we must quite consciously construct or refashion our religious symbols. This activity he calls third-order theology in contrast to first-order theology (where the gods were taken to be real and active spiritual beings) and second-order theology (which acknowledged the symbolic character of religious language but simply accepted this in the form in which it had been handed down). 'The symbol of God claims to represent to us a focus for orientation which will bring true fulfilment and meaning to human life. It sums up, unifies, and represents in a personification what are taken to be the highest and most indispensable human ideals and values', writes Kaufman.[6]

In similar fashion Don Cupitt draws a distinction between what he calls a realist and a non-realist view of 'God'. The realist view interprets the word 'God' as a first-order descriptive term which means there must be an actual or an imagined objective referent, such as a supernatural spiritual being. The non-realist view interprets the word 'God' as a symbolic term belonging to the expressive second-order mode of language appropriate to religion. So, for Cupitt, 'God is the mythical embodiment of all that one is concerned with in the spiritual life.'[7] He insists that we still need myths and religious symbols with which to express our quest for meaning and spiritual fulfilment but in modern times we are being forced to acknowledge the mythical and symbolic character of our religious language.

As the prophets warned of the dangers of idolatry, so the interpretation of 'God' as the symbolic embodiment of the cluster of values we have come to regard as supreme is a warning of the danger of idolising any one of our values. That such a danger exists can unfortunately be exemplified only too frequently from both the Christian and Islamic traditions. People who sincerely believed they were faithfully obeying the will of God have performed the most horrific atrocities, such as the burning of witches, the torturing of heretics, the execution of apostates, the ostracising of homosexuals. Thus, the reason the fundamentalists are so convinced even today that they know exactly what is in the mind of God on any particular subject is that this is really what is in their own minds but they have unconsciously projected their thoughts on to God. The unconscious projection of one's thoughts on to a supposed divine being quickly leads to fanaticism, and the history of religion is littered with examples.

In his widely read *Honest to God* John Robinson perceptively pointed out that in modern times the ancient practice of idolising *metal* images of the gods has been transformed into the idolising of *mental* images of God.[8] By realising that the images and values embodied in the term 'God' are *ours* (and we acknowledge our own fallibility), we are less likely to attribute to them an absoluteness they do not deserve. The importance, therefore, of having a basic symbol as our ultimate point of reference in our quest for meaning is that it effectively relativises every *thing* and prevents us idolising, or treating as absolute, any object, idea, doctrine or ideology.

Tillich, Cupitt and Kaufman have argued in their respective ways that 'God', understood as a symbol, is religiously and ethically more important to us than the objectivised, realist 'God'. As the original monotheism emancipated humankind from subjection to the ancestral deities, so the re-cognising of 'God' as a symbol emancipates us from subjection to any object less than ultimate. They contend that we need a symbol, such as God, as a point from which we may continue to subject everything else to critical examination. Without such a symbol we easily become subject to things (such as wealth) or systems of ideas (such as religious doctrines or political ideologies) which become our gods or taskmasters. In order to make sure 'God' remains a symbol and does not itself become a kind of fixed idea we may, with Tillich, have to speak of the 'God beyond God'.

The second requirement for the resurrection of the God-symbol is to reject the rigid structure of polarities which have become part and parcel of the dualistic view of reality associated with an objective deity:

Earth	Heaven
Creature	Creator
Humanity	Deity
Subject	Ruler
Submission	Authority
Powerlessness	Power
Ignorance	Knowledge
Imperfection	Perfection
Sinfulness	Sinlessness
Under Judgement	Seat of Judgement
Profane (secular)	Holy (sacred)

In the dualistic Christian world, all of the right-hand qualities came to be associated with God and, where appropriate, were affirmed as divine attributes; hence the emphasis on God's omnipotence, omnipresence and omniscience. All the left-hand qualities were associated with humanity. As Feuerbach so pertinently remarked, the holier and more powerful God was conceived to be, the more powerless and sinful humanity found itself to be.

That in itself was bad enough, but it was not all. As feminists have more recently pointed out, God was conceived as male – the heavenly father. Since the heavenly father was male, men and not women shared one important characteristic with God. So men began to bask in the glory of at least some of the values on the right-hand side, the praiseworthy values, leaving the left-hand qualities to be associated with females, and thereby downgraded as negative and harmful. It was men rather than women who were taken to have been made in the image of God. Paul could not have put it more plainly when he said, 'As God is the head of Christ and Christ is the head of man, so man is the head of woman' (1 Corinthians 11:3), the reason being that it 'was not the man who was deceived but the woman' (1 Timothy 2:14).

So it is not surprising that the most serious condemnation of traditional monotheism has come from feminist thought. The transfer of the seat of sacred power from the earth to the heavens, and the demise of the earth-mother occasioned by the victory of the heavenly father, upset the balance of values in the gender relationship. In the pre-Axial cultures male and female values were conceived to be in a state of complementary harmony. In the myths which formed the ancient mode of understanding reality the gods were at least equally balanced by the goddesses. In some of the myths of origin the goddess even preceded the gods, since it was from her cosmic womb that the universe was assumed to have come to birth.

The Israelite prophets, in banishing ancient polytheism, effectively desacralised the natural earthly forces. By doing so they made the role of the earth-mother redundant; all power subsequently rested with the father in heaven. At this point monotheism, almost of necessity, became male-oriented or, as we now say, patriarchal. It led to a gross imbalance in Judaeo-Christian culture by which the male was glorified and the female downgraded, an imbalance of which we are only in the latter part of the twentieth century becoming aware.

The maleness of God the father and also of his only son Jesus Christ has been appealed to within the Christian tradition, both in the past and continuing into the present, as the reason why all who serve God at the altar must also be male. The maleness of God has led to the oppression of women by male domination. Patriarchy permeates the biblical heritage, so that for as long as the Bible continues to be taken as establishing the norms for Christian faith and practice it cannot help but foster and preserve male rule.

Similarly, the almightiness of God has prompted humans, and particularly males, unconsciously if not consciously, to affirm power and strength as supreme values. The macho image, so admired by many, has its counterpart in the all-powerful God, who can devastate the earth with thunderbolts, send plagues to punish the wicked and cause all the earth to tremble. We have seen it vividly expressed from ancient psalms to modern hymns.

Likewise, the omniscience of God has motivated humans to believe they were following a divine path in seeking ever to increase their knowledge of the world and so gain greater mastery over the earth and all physical forces. It certainly motivated the pioneers of modern science. They were often devoutly Christian and tended to conceive God as the great mathematician, the designer of the cosmic machine and the fount of all knowledge.

The needs of the coming global culture are bringing to an end the era of undisputed male dominance, of the uncritical admiration of physical power and of the unfettered pursuit of knowledge without thought for its moral consequences (the development of nuclear weapons being a case in point). The time for glorifying the Almighty (male) God who supposedly rules from on high is now over, as is the non-symbolic use of the term 'God' to name a supposed objective beneficent being of creativity, knowledge and power.

Popper's three world model helps us to do justice to the nature and role of religious symbols, including the God-symbol. They find their place in World 3, the world created by the collective human psyche. They do possess a reality but it is a World 3 reality and not a World 1 reality. They are symbols, just as words are symbols, and their function is to provide order and meaning for human existence. As Cupitt said, 'What is new in modern times is that the advance of consciousness has compelled us to admit the mythological character of much of our own religious thinking.' [9]

Symbols, and systems of symbols, cannot be over-valued. The creation of World 3 has enabled our species to evolve to the state we experience today. The symbol systems of World 3 enabled our forebears to order their day-to-day experience in a meaningful way and to construct worlds which enabled them to experience a sense of personal fulfilment in human existence. It is the collective unconscious which holds the key to the birth and the death of symbols.

But the advent of modernity is causing the erosion of the traditional symbol systems, and the slow collapse of the very worlds for which they provided meaning. Many of the traditional symbols were created to suit a cosmology which has become outdated. We have been moving to a very different cosmology, one which calls for either new symbols or a radical reformulation of the old ones. We have entered a period of radical cultural transition. To this we turn in Part III.

The Creation
of the Global World

CHAPTER 11

The Demise
of the Christian World

Each of us lives in a world we have personally constructed, though usually we are not aware that we have done so. Further, we have been able to construct our own personal world because we, in turn, have already been shaped by the culture into which we were born; our personal world is largely drawn from the shared world which has given our culture its identity and coherence. This shared world is the result of a long and complex cultural evolution and has been collectively constructed by all of our ancestors. There have been as many shared worlds as there have been human cultures.

Just as the shared worlds of pre-Axial cultures were threatened, relativised and then either absorbed or displaced by the shared worlds which evolved in post-Axial civilisations, so the latter are now in turn being stripped of their claims to absoluteness and becoming relativised by the birth-pangs of still another kind of shared world; for convenience it can be called the global world (see Introduction). This will be more fully discussed in the following chapters but first we must observe how the traditional shared worlds, particularly the Christian world, are showing signs of dissolution as a result of the emerging global world.

All of the shared worlds which evolved after the Axial Period are being similarly undermined, but at different rates. We shall look specifically at the Christian world, chiefly because it is the one from which the new global world has, like a chrysalis, begun to emerge. It is consequently the one with which the global world has most in common. The Islamic and the other non-Christian cultures are equally threatened by the emergence of the global world but because it has penetrated them from the outside, they are inclined to regard it as a foreign enemy. That is why Islam, for example, is currently trying to resist the inroads of the global world by treating it as the destructive influence of the decadent West, which must be resisted and eliminated to allow the restoration of a healthy Islamic civilisation.

It is, by contrast, the culture of the Christian West which has been, unintentionally, giving birth to the global world. There is thus an inherent relation between the Christian world and the global world. That the Christian world is now facing its own demise is evident from the way in which our age is already being spoken of as the post-Christian era.

Chapter 3 outlined how the Christian world came to be constructed on the basis of the Christian story. Let us now look briefly at the Christian story. Of course it can be told in many ways; and through the centuries it was continually being added to and changed. This is only the simplest of outlines, and it follows the chronology supplied by the Bible.

> In the beginning, a few thousand years ago, God made the earth and everything in it, giving priority and dominion to the human race. There was trouble from the time of our first parents onwards, resulting in selfishness, hatred, cruelty and murder. God determined to rescue the human race from its own self-destroying practices and chose a people, the descendants of Abraham, Isaac and Jacob, to be a beacon of light in a dark and fallen world. Even his chosen people failed to walk in the path he had provided. So God sent his servants, the prophets, to recall his people to their responsibility; still his chosen people failed and had to be punished by being exiled for a time from the Holy Land he had provided for them.
>
> At last God sent his own son to be born in human flesh. So by divine design Jesus was born of a virgin at Bethlehem and reared at Nazareth. Some time after reaching maturity he became an itinerant teacher and healer, who impressed the crowds by his homely wisdom and his deeds of love. He called twelve men to be his disciples. They listened eagerly to his teaching of the imminent coming of a new era, the kingdom of God; they acclaimed him to be the Messiah long awaited by the Jews. After only a short ministry, during which time he aroused the antagonism of the priests and scribes,

Jesus was put to death by crucifixion by the Romans. At first, shattered by this calamity, the disciples returned to Galilee in despair. But Jesus rose from the dead, appeared to his disciples, and ascended into heaven. The Apostles had their faith restored and received new power by the gift of the holy spirit at the feast of Pentecost. They were commissioned to go out and preach the gospel, awaiting expectantly for Jesus to return from his seat at the right of God, at which time he would judge all people and establish the righteous in the new kingdom.

(There was no standard version of this later part of the story and it was this section which went through the greatest change and adaptation in the first few centuries. It will be further discussed in Chapter 14.)

The Christian world was constructed on the basis of this story. Jesus became the central figure in this world and was acclaimed to be wholly divine and wholly human. His birth in Bethlehem cut time in two. His death on the cross was seen as the key to salvation, being variously construed as a victory over Satan or as a sacrifice to God. Jesus was acclaimed to be wholly unique and the saviour of the world. Confirmation of this was found in his virginal conception, his performance of miracles, and his resurrection from the dead.

The construction of the world shared by Christians took place over a long time, rather like a medieval cathedral, and reached the peak of its development in the High Middle Ages. The process was too complex to describe here but we can sketch what this world was like just before it began to disintegrate.

As already observed in Chapter 4, the Christian world was dualistic, consisting of the tangible, visible, material world here below and an unseen spiritual world associated with the sky above. The tangible world was experienced as a kind of two-dimensional flat earth. It had been created by God specifically to be a dwelling-place for humans and it remained under the providential control of its all-powerful divine creator. But this world was destined eventually to pass away, for it was a fallen world. It was a world under judgement as a result of the wilful disobedience of our first parents. All humans too were under judgement; having been born in a state of sinfulness, they were already due to be condemned to eternal punishment unless saved by divine grace. The divine judgement would be pronounced after death when their souls entered the spiritual world.

The unseen spiritual world was conceived as being divided into three domains: heaven, purgatory and hell. Hell, ruled by Satan, was the sphere of eternal punishment for the damned. Heaven, the dwelling-place of God, was the sphere of eternal bliss for the blessed. Purgatory was an intermediate sphere where one continued to suffer for one's (minor) misdeeds, until one was purged of everything preventing one from entering heaven. In the popular view purgatory was the domain one was most likely to enter on leaving this temporal world at death: only the saints were thought to be already fit to go straight to heaven.

To avoid the everlasting tortures of hell and ensure at least a place in purgatory it was necessary to be in communion with the church. The church had been founded by God through his son Jesus Christ to be the vehicle of divine grace; by it alone could humans be saved from the hell they justly deserved because of their sinfulness. The church dispensed divine grace through the sacraments; these mediated the forgiveness which God freely offered to the faithful and the penitent. Thus excommunication from the church had become a penalty more serious than death itself.

The Christian community consisted of the church triumphant in heaven and the church militant on earth. Within the latter the authority to dispense the sacramental grace was reserved to ordained clergy; this placed great power in their hands. In exercising the right to excommunicate from the church, the Pope, as the supposed successor to St. Peter, had a power greater than that of life and death. Known as the power of the keys, it rested on the appeal to the words spoken by Jesus (according to Matthew 16: 18–19): 'I tell you, you are Peter [*petros*] and on this rock [*petra*] I will build my church, and the powers of death shall not prevail against it. I will give you the keys of the kingdom of heaven, and whatever you bind on earth shall be bound in heaven and whatever you loose on earth shall be loosed in heaven.' Thus in the Christian world the church was easily the most powerful institution.

Human existence on earth was viewed, therefore, as a preparation and testing-place for life in heaven. Every decision taken should be made in the light of how it related to one's final destiny. The church, being the divinely appointed vehicle for divine revelation, was the only reliable teacher and guide. It possessed a monopoly of the knowledge of truth and morals. Fear of excommunication was a very effective means of preserving uniformity, consistency and stability; heresy was treated as a crime more heinous than murder.

Such was the world as conceived and shared by Christians. Built into it were safeguards for its preservation and perpetuation. The Christian world induced great confidence and was, in its time, powerfully convincing. In every village, market town or city there stood the church or cathedral, occupying a central position. It was a monument in stone, visibly manifesting the character, permanence and might of the Christian world.

The typical church building of Eastern Orthodoxy is particularly illuminating in portraying the Christian world in miniature. The walls of its largely square base represent the earthly limits of north, south, east and west. The large domed ceiling (often painted blue) represents the heavenly domain, and the chandelier suspended from it portrays the saints who shine in heaven. The sanctuary, representing the meeting-place between heaven and earth, and entered only by priests, is hidden from the common gaze by the screen or iconostasis, for only the very holy are permitted a glimpse of heaven while they are still on earth. The corner of the sanctuary where the eucharist is prepared is even thought of as the manger of Bethlehem, where the incarnation took place.

In Eastern Orthodoxy heaven and earth were thus thought to be relatively close. In the Western church, by contrast, it was not the immanence but the transcendence of God and his heaven which was paramount. So the church building, rather than representing heaven within it, simply pointed to the heavenly places far above by means of a tall steeple. The church building was a refuge of safety in the wicked and fallen world. (In early times the church had been imagined as a ship on the stormy sea; that is why Western churches remained elongated, their central section being called 'the nave', from the Latin word, *navis*, for ship). One entered this refuge or colony of heaven from the west (representing darkness) and immediately encountered the baptismal font. In baptism one received spiritual renewal and was given a place in the company of people preparing for their eternal destiny. Within the church one looked steadily towards the east (representing light), and the nearer one moved towards the altar and sanctuary the holier was the ground on which one trod. (This was an area reserved for males in general and for priests in particular; the Christian world was predominantly masculine, as in the terminology of God the *father* and Jesus Christ the *son*.)

It was not only in space but also in the dimension of time that the Christian world was viewed and experienced through the grid of symbolism. The Christian story ordered the passing of time, marking it by the many annual festivals and innumerable saints' days. In the seasons of the Christian year, from Advent to Pentecost, one lived through and experienced afresh the initiating events of the story on which the Christian world was founded. The annual Christian festivals served as a continual reminder of the duties and aspirations which were expected of everyone living in the Christian world, and which gave identity to Christian culture.

In the Christian world as experienced in medieval Christendom, therefore, the Christian symbol system permeated every aspect of society, having created a fully integrated and homogeneous culture. It shaped the way people both lived and thought. It determined the patterns of human behaviour, both ritualistic and ethical. It was at the leading edge of human thought and enquiry, and the best minds of the day were fully immersed in it. It had led to the establishment of the Western-style university, which originally grew up around the theological schools of Paris, Oxford and Heidelberg.

The Christian world described above is now at an advanced stage of disintegration. The seeds of this process can be traced back at least to the fourteenth century but not until the Protestant Reformation did it manifest itself publicly. What then sparked off an explosive situation was undoubtedly the challenge by Luther to the authority of the Pope; the latter, as we have noted from the power of the keys, was in many ways the foundation stone on which the whole edifice of the Christian world had come to rest (at least in Western Christendom). But the Christian world did not come tumbling down all at once, partly because the Reformation affected much less than half of Christendom and partly because the Protestant reformers had no intention of destroying anything but idols. Their intention was to *reform* the church or (to continue the metaphor) to *reconstruct* the Christian world in the light of the Bible, which they interpreted as the original plans of the divine architect.

Like the opening of Pandora's box, however, the Reformation led to much more than the reformers ever envisaged. Once they had removed the foundation stone which guaranteed the unity and the truth of the Christian world, it was only a matter of time before the structure would disintegrate, consisting as it did of an unseen spiritual world holding a dominant position in relation to the visible tangible world. It was out of Protestantism that the global world was destined eventually to emerge; even to this day stubborn resistance to the global world is to be found more in Catholicism than in Protestantism.

The reformers themselves unwittingly took the first bold step in dismantling the Christian world by their abolition of purgatory. Since purgatory was the domain of the higher world which most people expected to enter when they died, its sudden disappearance from the Christian world was more significant than it might appear from this distance in time. The reformers abolished purgatory because it had no warrant in holy scripture and because the medieval church had found it to be a very effective mechanism for raising funds. It had to be condemned, therefore, as a vain human invention and no part of what God had revealed.

What was not fully realised at the time was that the abolition of purgatory was a step towards secularisation. Perhaps unintentionally, it turned human attention back to this-world. It had the effect of upgrading the importance of everything one does during this earthly life, for it implied that, since there is no intermediate state between death and the final judgement, one's death closes off all further options concerning one's final destiny. There is no second chance: on death one is consigned immediately either to heaven or to hell. Thus attention became more focused on life in the here-and-now and the importance attached to everything one does. That is the basis of this-worldliness or secularisation.

Heaven and hell and all the other aspects of the Christian world remained intact for both Protestant and Catholic for quite some time. They were chiefly concerned with debating just how the grace of God operated through the institution of the church to ensure personal salvation in the other world. The next steps in the dissolution of the Christian world came somewhat more gradually and as a result of the four Copernican revolutions in thought (as outlined in the Introduction). These led to the radical shift in consciousness, which has been accelerating since the mid-nineteenth century.

During the last decades of the nineteenth century doubt began to surface quite openly among Christian thinkers regarding the objective reality of hell and of the person of Satan. Considerable theological debate took place over these questions, with the more liberally minded people finding they could no longer reconcile the notion of condemnation to eternal punishment with the affirmation of an almighty and all-loving God. Sermons threatening fire and brimstone for the unrighteous began to be heard less frequently. For increasing numbers of Christians, hell began to disappear from the Christian world as they now envisaged it.

Friedrich Schleiermacher (1768–1834), sometimes judged the first modern theologian, warned that 'the ecclesiastical doctrines of the Last Things [return of Christ, resurrection, last judgement, eternal blessedness] could not have ascribed to them the same value as the other Christian doctrines'.[1] Since his time, Protestant theologians became increasingly cautious in what they were prepared to say, not only about hell, but also about heaven, or even about any form of post-mortem existence (or what is popularly referred to as life after death). By the middle of the twentieth century heaven, like hell before it, was losing its former objective reality in Western consciousness. It was becoming the butt of jokes rather than of serious discussion. The term retained some metaphorical or poetic value in times of bereavement, but little more.

When the highly acclaimed theologian John Baillie wrote about personal human destiny in his book, *And the Life Everlasting* (1934), he found himself forced to acknowledge that 'the only knowledge we can have of eternal life is that which comes to us through our present foretasting of its joys. All that we know of the other life *there* is what we know of it *here*. For even here there is *another* life that may be lived [and] ... this other life is the life everlasting'.[2] This is but one step away from saying that there is no other life but the one we live here and that the term 'eternal life' more properly refers to the highest quality of life which it is possible to experience here.

Thus step by step the supernatural domains of the medieval Christian world have been dismantled, leaving the Christian tradition with some very great problems. The Christian gospel of salvation had long been preached on the assumption that people either already shared the Christian world-view or else could be readily convinced by it. How the institutional church mediated the divine grace for the benefit of one's eternal destiny assumed prior conviction in an unseen, supernatural world. With the coming of the global world these assumptions can no longer be made. Thus a good deal of traditional Christian teaching has become increasingly out of touch with, and irrelevant to, the global world. As Don Cupitt has aptly said, 'When we go to church we re-enter a medieval universe which, so far as the outside world is concerned, finally passed away over three centuries ago.'[3]

Signs of the dissolution of the Christian world are evident in the ebbing of Christian allegiance. Regular attendance at church began to decline in the nineteenth century. Most people in the

Western world continued to think of themselves as Christians and even to hold many of the Christian beliefs but they were becoming less committed to them. Even without realising what was happening they were beginning to undergo a shift in the way they experienced reality; the shared global world was displacing the Christian world. This explains why nearly half of the population were still to be found attending church on any particular Sunday in 1850, but more than a century later the proportion has decreased to ten per cent or less (though it varies from country to country).

The symbols giving visibility to the Christian world no longer enjoy the high public profile they once possessed. Of the annual Christian festivals, Advent, Ash Wednesday, Lent and Whitsunday were the first to disappear from public celebration. Then Easter tended to become a purely secular holiday. Only Christmas has remained as a community celebration, yet with minimal reference to any Christian content – so much so that occasionally there is a movement to try to put Christ back into X-mas. There still remains, but only just, the division of time into a seven-day week, which Christians and Muslims inherited from ancient Israel. There, every seventh day was celebrated as a commemoration of creation, God having rested on that day after the creation of heaven and earth in six days. During this century the weekly sabbath day of rest has been invaded, first by sport, and more recently by commercial trading.

The great medieval cathedrals, which once gave such awe-inspiring visibility to the Christian world, now strikingly symbolise, in a negative way, the extent to which the once-glorious Christian world is fading from view, leaving only the shell of its former self. The cathedrals attract a steady stream of tourists who come to admire the marvels of medieval architecture and perhaps look back with nostalgia to the so-called 'ages of faith', but not the large congregations of regular worshippers for which they were originally built. The cost of keeping the fabric of the buildings in repair has become an impossible burden for the tiny congregations who now use them and who have, unintentionally, become a 'society for the preservation of historic monuments'.

Not only is active participation in Christian ceremonies now declining quite fast, but organised Christian communities or churches now cover a very wide spectrum in both belief and practice. The One, Holy, Catholic and Apostolic Church, which once constituted the community of Christians, was for centuries both unified and also co-terminous with society. Today this is no longer so: the many Christian denominations into which the church has become fragmented find themselves to be private religious communities living within the larger society, which is increasingly secular in its public life. These fragments of the once-great church have lost much of the former capacity to be catholic or universal and have developed sectarian characteristics; this applies even to the so-called mainline churches.

During this century new Christian divisions have emerged, which cut right across the denominational divisions from former times. These new divisions stretch from the radicals at the left to the extreme conservatives at the right. They were observed in 1923 by Kirsopp Lake, a biblical scholar of international repute, who wrote a book entitled *The Religion of Yesterday and Tomorrow*.[4] In it he made a prophecy which has turned out to have shown remarkable foresight. Writing shortly after the rise of the fundamentalist movement in the USA, he noted that in the mainline Protestant churches there were to be discerned three main groups, whom he called the fundamentalists, the traditionalists and the experimentalists (among whom he numbered himself). He prophesied that the traditionalists would force out the experimentalists (today we would call them the radicals) and then they themselves would gradually be re-absorbed by the fundamentalists. Thus, he said, the mainline churches would shrink from left to right. This phenomenon is particularly noticeable today in the English-speaking world. In relation to the intellectual climate of society at large, the churches have become increasingly conservative and defensive of their identity. As the churches grow smaller and more conservative, we find in them the last remnants of the Christian world. These remnants exist like islands of the past in the fast-flowing tide of secularisation which is giving rise to the new global world.

For a while it seemed as if the crisis which had struck the Christian world could be met by simply eliminating from the body of Christian doctrine a few selected beliefs and concepts. These were the overt relics of the former Christian world which were most blatantly out of kilter with the emerging global world. Leading spokespeople for liberal Protestantism adopted this procedure, chiefly between 1850 and 1930. It led, of course, to an increasingly truncated set of doctrines, which deservedly attracted the criticism of reductionism. It reached its extreme in some winter lectures of Adolf von Harnack, widely distributed in 1900 under the title *What Is Christianity?*. The purpose of Christianity, as Harnack saw it, was to call all humankind into a universal community of brotherhood, where all were united by their common love of God and of their neighbour.

Further into the twentieth century it became clear that the solution offered by Protestant liberalism was too superficial to be satisfactory. The offending supernaturalistic elements were not just a few cosmetic additions which could be easily dispensed with. It was coming to be recognised that the whole of the Christian message was set in the framework of a world which had largely passed away. A much more radical solution was called for.

During World War II a leading New Testament scholar, Rudolf Bultmann (1884–1976), published an epoch-making essay, 'New Testament and Mythology',[5] in which he asserted that the Christian message had become incredible to modern humankind because it presupposed a mythical world which now belongs to past history. He asked what possible meaning could be given to such phrases of the creed as 'descended into hell' and 'ascended into heaven', when 'there is no longer any heaven or hell in the traditional sense of those words'.[6] He argued that it was a matter not of eliminating these terms and concepts but of interpreting them. Bultmann proposed a programme of 'demythologising', a word he coined to refer to the task of re-interpreting the essential message of Christianity into thought forms appropriate to the world in which we live – that is the global world. The more liberal and radical people within the churches have for some time, often

without knowing the word, been doing their own demythologising of the sermons they hear, the hymns they sing and the
ceremonies they share in.

But the crisis faced by the Christian world refuses to go away,
and it is not just a crisis for the Christian world. A Dutch Roman
Catholic, W.H. van de Pol, wrote in his book *The End of Conventional Christianity*:

> The crisis which mankind all over the world finds itself in today is
> a crisis of hitherto unknown proportions, depth, and significance. It
> is radical. It reaches everyone and everything. The new mankind
> which will be born of this crisis will be a different and new
> mankind in thought and action. The way of thinking, the way of
> experiencing existence and all reality, and therefore the religious
> aspect of being-human, are in our time subject to a radical
> revolution. [7]

It is this which is here called the global world and which we
shall explore further in the coming chapters.

Before we do so, however, there is one further question to be
discussed. How is it possible that the Christian world, which was
experienced by so many people and for so long as real, convincing
and absolutely true, can now be undergoing an almost complete
dissolution? The answer to this question takes us back to all that
was said in Part I about the way worlds are constructed.

There we discussed the primacy of language. With language we
tell stories. With stories we construct worlds. In the Christian
world now, we are observing those steps in reverse. The Christian
world is disintegrating because the Christian story on which it is
based is losing its power. All stories have their day, though some
last much longer than others. Just as the stories which excite our
imaginations and grip us wholly as children often cease to do so as
we grow beyond them, so, on a much larger scale, stories which
underpin the destiny of a family, a tribe, a race, a civilisation,
eventually lose their power to convince.

Over the last two centuries the Christian story, on which the
Christian world was built, has been falling apart, and for several

reasons. The new cosmology and the evolutionary view of origins undermined the first part. The Bible fell from its pedestal as it came to be studied as a set of documents of human origin. As biblical scholarship began to distinguish between history on the one hand and legend and myth on the other, it undermined confidence in the second part of the story. Encounter with other cultures increased the awareness of cultural relativity and undermined the exclusive and absolute claims made for Jesus Christ. Jesus came to be seen as an attractive Jewish teacher who showed some originality, rather than as a divine figure. He too was a man of his own time and not the centre of history; he could no longer be acclaimed as the one and only saviour of all humankind.

As worlds are constructed out of stories, so stories are built out of words. The key terms in the Christian world – purgatory, hell, heaven, fall, last judgement, angels, resurrection, ascension into heaven, holy trinity, and even God – remain words. They have been very important words, words which helped to create a meaningful world for those living within it. Some of these words will remain because of their capacity to mediate meaning. But in the meantime new ideas and new words have come into being, arising out of a new form of consciousness. Out of these new words a new story is beginning to be told and on the basis of this story a new world is emerging.

CHAPTER 12

The New Story of the Earth

Every world we humans construct is based on a story. The demise of the Christian world has come about, as we have just seen, as the Christian story on which it was based first came to be questioned and then to be replaced by a new story. It is the latter which forms the basis of the emerging global world. It is no accident that the first serious signs of the crisis now faced by the Christian world appeared in the nineteenth century, for it was then that biblical criticism began to cause the erosion of the biblical story, and the Darwinian theory of biological evolution opened the way for the new story of the earth and human origins. Let us look at this new story.

Stories are made with words. New words make possible new stories. The new story, which has become basic to the global world, began with a new word or idea: the notion of evolution in its broadest sense of change and development from within. This, more than anything else, has been responsible for the demise of the Christian world and the birth of the global world. It is the key to the new story and hence to the new world. For this reason the total rejection of biological evolution by fundamentalists is understandable even if it is wrong.

Yet the pioneer thinkers who contributed so much to the telling of the new story were themselves the products of the Christian world. They were influenced, unconsciously if not consciously, by the Christian story, if only because it had for so long permeated Western culture. It is altogether appropriate, therefore, that one of the first to attempt to tell the new story (or myth) of our time in the most comprehensive way was a man equally committed to both the Christian heritage and the modern scientific enterprise.

He was the Jesuit palaeontologist Pierre Teilhard de Chardin, and he told the story in *The Phenomenon of Man*. This is not a scientific work (though he thought it was) but it does contain a lot of scientific material, some of it now dated. What makes this book so epoch-making is the grandeur of its story-like epic vision. This, along with other current material, will be drawn on as we now sketch the earth's own story.

In the beginning, more than fifteen billion years ago, time, space and all matter (or energy) burst into existence in a cosmic event of unique character, popularly known as the 'Big Bang'. Since nothing (not even time) preceded it, it has become meaningless to ask what led up to it or why it occurred. The universe, in all its complexity and mystery, just is; and it is as old as time itself. Moreover, it is a universe, or unitary whole, whose various components exist, and can be adequately understood, only in relation to the whole. Time, space and basic matter form a cohesive whole; they cannot exist in absolute isolation from one another.

The universe is not static and changeless. Because time is one of its essential components, the universe is continually undergoing change. It is evolving from within itself. The universe cannot be explained from sources outside itself for the universe has no outside. The universe, if we wish to explain it, can be explained only from within; it must be allowed to be self-explanatory. The universe explains itself by its own story, and it is on the basis of what we humans have found about that story that we are now constructing the global world.

In manifesting continual movement and change the universe shows a great capacity to be self-creative. It displays a strong tendency to form itself into all sorts of new and complex designs, by what Teilhard chose to call the process of 'complexification'. (Scientists now find it useful to speak of four different categories of force operating within the universe: gravitational, electromagnetic, weak nuclear and strong nuclear. They search for a unified 'theory of everything' which would explain all four as different aspects of a single force or form of energy.)

By the process of complexification, not only do the unstable forms of sub-atomic matter stabilise into the forms we call atoms, but the atoms in turn, under the right conditions, join themselves into molecules made up of different kinds of atoms, which constitute entirely new substances. Molecules can become so complex that when they contain millions of molecules we need to refer to them as megamolecules.

The very complexity of the megamolecule is the key to the next evolutionary stage, the advent of life. For our understanding of the story of the universe from this point onwards, however, we are largely confined to the earth for our knowledge. Whether there is life elsewhere in the universe must be left an open question, for to date we have no evidence of it. The sheer immensity of the universe strongly points to the probability that there is, yet life as we know it depends on so many particularities that we must still seriously contemplate the possibility that earthly life is unique.

The universe was more than ten billion years old before the planet earth was formed, possibly when a fragment became detached from the nuclear furnace we call the sun, and quickly crystallised into stable matter. Or its formation may have been due to the assembling of stellar dust, resulting from the earlier explosion of giant stars. In any event, an imaginary galactic observer of four billion years ago would have thought the earth to be as lifeless as all the other planets of our solar system appear still to be. Yet from this earth over aeons of time have evolved all the innumerable genera and species that we now know to have existed at some time or other.

The process by which a previously lifeless planet became a living planet is so extraordinary that we find it almost impossible to accept. Yet the theory of biological evolution, taken to its logical conclusion, leads us to the view not that the countless forms of planetary life were suddenly created out of nothing by divine command, nor that they arrived from outer space, but that they evolved from the earth itself. In other words the almost infinite variety of living organisms now *on* the planet are in fact an integral part *of* the planet.

Admittedly, the evolution of planetary life took place by a process we do not yet adequately understand. It is not surprising, therefore, that many people still refuse to accept it, though this is partly due to the inability of our tiny minds to appreciate the enormous length of time during which evolution has taken place. One of life's ironies is that the very people who claim to believe in divine miracles are most resistant to the notion of evolution; they insist that this is a miracle too outrageous for them to accept. They prefer to retain the Christian story which states that God created all living forms by divine *fiat*.

A particular difficulty we humans have in accepting the awe-inspiring miracle of evolution is that we have for so long drawn a clear division in our minds between all living creatures (including ourselves) and the lifeless planetary mass beneath our feet. This absolute distinction is reflected in the line drawn between organic chemistry and inorganic chemistry, and has led contemporary scientists to theorise that the first living forms, simple though they were, must have come to this planet from outer space. Such theories cannot be ruled out.

Difficult though it may be for us to grasp, however, the simplest and most adequate explanation of the origin of planetary life is that the earth, like the universe, contained the potential for life within itself at the time of its formation. When the conditions were right, the apparently lifeless earth gave birth to life. So it is quite appropriate for us to think of the earth as alive, as a living planet, as a kind of living organism albeit a very complex one. Moreover we humans, like all other creatures, are a part of this living planet in much the same way as the cells of our bodies and the corpuscles of our blood are living entities within each complete human organism.

The transition of the earth from being an apparently lifeless planet to a living planet occurred so long ago, of course, that it remains shrouded in mystery. In view of the aeons of time over which biological evolution has been operating, the initial transition from non-life to life is unlikely to have been a sudden event. The scientists who opt for an extra-terrestrial origin of life suggest that the earth, while still young, was seeded by organic molecules, rather like amino acids, which had resulted from chemical processes in space during the billions of years before the earth existed. John Gribben asserts that 'only the most blinkered Earth-chauvinist would try to argue that life got started from scratch on our own planet'.[1] But however and wherever it took place, the importance of the transition from non-life to life can hardly be overemphasised.

Teilhard de Chardin sketched in his all-encompassing narrative of evolution what we could legitimately call the biography of the living earth. To this end he divided the story into four sections called Pre-Life, Life, Thought, Survival (the future). He set out to show how each successive stage derived wholly from what had preceded it. Thus everything which has evolved was possible because of what was already there. Life itself, including even human consciousness, was potentially present from the beginning within the basic material of the earth (and hence of the universe).

What makes something alive? An entity may be said to be living if it is capable of reproducing itself. The cell may be regarded as the smallest granule of life, just as the atom is the smallest granule of stable matter. Yet even the virus satisfies this definition of a living entity. So the line between non-life and life may turn out to be an almost arbitrary one which we humans draw where we think fit, and the virus may be as close to that line as we can get. Teilhard drew attention to the complexity of such tiny living entities as the virus and the cell, for they contain millions of atoms.

It was in the capacity of earthly matter to unite into ever more complex patterns that Teilhard believed he had found the key to the advent of life, and later to the dawn of consciousness. From atom to molecule, to megamolecule, to cell, to multi-cell, to micro-organism, to macro-organism, to animal, to vertebrate, to primate, to anthropoid and finally to human, he contended, the level of consciousness has been steadily rising with every increase in the degree of complexity.

The degree of complexity which makes the primates so

important is to be found in their advancing cerebralisation. Whereas the other animals have tended to lose versatility as their limbs and teeth came to be used for, and permanently locked into, highly specialised activities, it was not so with the primates, in whom the evolutionary process of complexification concentrated on the brain. It is in the brain that the nervous system has become unbelievably complex, thus providing humans with the greatest degree of versatility to be found among all earthly organisms and giving rise (as we saw in Chapter 5) to the creative human psyche.

This has meant that the next stage of the evolving earth advanced through one particular species, *Homo sapiens*. For only in the human species did abstract thought or mental reflection come to birth. We have already discussed in Chapter 5 how Teilhard referred to this radical transition as noogenesis and how he judged it to be as significant as the transition from non-life to life. Yet, in spite of these two successive stages of transition, evolution forms a single, continuous process always in the same general direction, and with increasing complexification.

The arrival of human self-reflection has meant that the earth is enveloped by a new kind of sphere. For a long time in the early stages of the evolving earth there was simply the barysphere (the heavy core), the lithosphere (the earth's solidifying skin), the hydrosphere (the oceans) and the atmosphere (the air). Then came the first significant transition, the emergence of the biosphere; this is a thin film of life, a planetary envelope, which has formed where the atmosphere meets the hydrosphere and lithosphere. The second significant transition brought into being the noosphere, the envelope of thought in which we humans live and move and have our being, and without which we would not be human. What Teilhard called the noosphere is very similar to what Popper has referred to as Worlds 2 and 3, World 2 being the actual sphere of human consciousness and World 3 the sum of all of its products.

Humankind came so silently into the world, and so long ago, that they were already sprawling all over the world from Africa to Beijing before they left traces (still extant today) of where they had been. The emergence of human culture, while lengthy when compared with the life-span of an individual, is actually very recent in the life-span of the planet. The basis of human culture (World 3) is language. That is why, in this book, we started with language. It was language which led to the level of human self-consciousness that we now all share. It also led to the creation of our human worlds.

Although human culture has emerged so very recently in geological time, it is changing at a much faster rate than the previous stages of evolution and still accelerating. 'The human being is now discovering', wrote Teilhard, 'that he is nothing else than evolution become conscious of itself . . . The consciousness of each of us is evolution looking at itself and reflecting upon itself.'[2] (This idea, incidentally, first came from Julian Huxley and was eagerly adopted by Teilhard.)

But 'evolution' simply refers to the way the living planet has continually changed from within. So, in view of the fact that all life, including humankind, has evolved out of the planet, it would be truer to say that it is the earth itself which is now becoming conscious of itself, and it is doing so chiefly through the medium of human consciousness. The more we humans recover the sense of our own earthiness and of our complete oneness with the planet, the more we are able to say that the earth is a thinking organism and we humans constitute the chief organ through which it thinks.

The extraordinary capacity for complexification and creativity which has been potentially present in the earth from its beginning has had maximum opportunity to flourish through the human species. The very long age in which the great reptiles roamed the earth was a striking demonstration of the maximum size to which earthly creatures could profitably grow. But were the dinosaurs aware of who they were and what they had achieved? Almost certainly not. The earth's capacity to produce diverse living forms was simply blundering along blindly, as if trying out everything; in that case, sheer size and brute strength were being pushed to the limit.

With the advent of the human species and the birth of the

noosphere the earth's creativity moved in a different direction, in which the very idea of purpose and/or meaning was at last able to surface. This section of the earth's own story we have already covered in Part I. Starting with language, and going on to stories and worlds, the human species evolved the highest form of consciousness we know, and it created the culturally based worlds in which to live. These worlds of thought together constitute the noosphere of the earth.

These many human worlds, collectively, constitute the earth's awareness of itself – that is, the earth's self-consciousness. Metaphorically they may be loosely regarded as the current state of consciousness of the earth itself. Because this totality of human consciousness currently exists in more than five billion individual centres, which are not only different from one another but often in conflict, we are able to contemplate this totality only from our own exceedingly restricted and individualistic standpoint. Yet, by virtue of our growing acquaintance with the content of the noosphere on the global scale, we are able to grasp some outline of it in our imaginations.

That is the new epic story of the earth on which the global world is based. It is not entirely new for there are important links with the traditional story, and it has been emerging out of the Christian world based on the traditional story. For example, even the biblical tradition has long said that we humans 'came out of the ground; we are dust of the earth and to dust we return'. That has now become transformed into something like this: 'By a very long and complex process we individual members of the human species have evolved out of the material substance of the earth. Each of us is a tiny segment of the earth's "dust", which has become self-conscious. Our self-consciousness has been made possible by our geological history, our genetic history and our cultural history. From this history we came, and back into this history we go.'

The new story also reflects the old story in that it assumes a linear view of time, in the course of which evolutionary change takes place in stages or eras. The biblical story of creation apportioned the created objects to six successive days on a kind of rising scale. (That is why biblical literalists keep trying to re-interpret the biblical material to make it fit the time-scale of the new story.) The books of Moses divided human history into successive stages, marked by an increasing decline in the average length of human life. Under the influence of Zoroastrianism, these stages were later translated into millennia, each with its own characteristics. (That is why biblical literalists also make so much of the coming new millennium.) Of course the new story has been extraordinarily magnified in its dimensions of time and space; whereas the old story thought in terms of millennia, the new story unfolds over billions of years.

Also of great interest, and perhaps of some surprise, is the link the new story has with the pre-Axial section of the old story. Even the Bible reflects the pre-Israelite nature religions in which the ancients thought of themselves as the children of the earth-mother. They were able to think of the earth as a divine mother because they lived very close to the earth, and were continually aware of how much they depended on her for life and sustenance. So, in their myths, the earth became personified and treated as a great mother, from whose womb all forms of life had come. The burial of the dead in the earth was seen as the return to the womb.

It appears, therefore, that the new story of the earth, in reminding us of the earthly matrix from which we have evolved, is reviving in us some aspects of very primitive human thought. How, then, did we come to imagine ourselves to be spiritual beings rather than earthly creatures?

It was in the Axial Period that the strong link with the earth came to be broken. Robert Bellah has called this break 'the phenomenon of religious rejection of the world characterised by ... the exaltation of another realm of reality as alone true and infinitely valuable'.[3] As language had enabled our ancient forebears to develop their ethnic cultures, so it enabled them at the Axial Period to question what they had achieved and partially to reject it. It further enabled them unconsciously to project their inner world of meaning on to external reality as another world, unseen but preferable to the one they inhabited. They came to see themselves as more properly belonging to that external spiritual world, thus divorcing themselves more and more from the earth. It was as if emerging self-consciousness was leading humans to believe they deserved something better than what this earth could provide. (Today, however, that may be judged by some as a state of mind bordering on hubris.)

Zoroaster taught that this world is the scene of a cosmic battle between good and evil and, though we humans are free to choose and are responsible for our ultimate destinies, it is to the other-worldly life of bliss beyond the great judgement that we must set out sights, and not on the pleasures of this world. The Buddha diagnosed human existence in this world as eternally subject to suffering; the only relief from it was to be found through the way of enlightenment which led to nirvana (the blowing out of the candle of life and the entry into an other-worldly state of bliss). Plato taught in the *Phaedo*[4] that we humans are in essence immortal souls who are temporarily imprisoned in our bodies, as in a tomb, so that only by eventual disentanglement from this physical existence can they return to the eternal world of spirit elsewhere. Thus pure knowledge is to be attained only after death, when the soul has become separate from and independent of the body.

The earliest biblical myth of origins, in Genesis 2–3, reflects an intermediate position. There it is God and not the earth which creates human life, even though it is out of the dust of the earth that he did so. Moreover, God is quaintly portrayed as living on the earth himself, even to the point of regularly taking a post-siesta constitutional in the garden after the heat of the day was past.

It was the Israelite prophets who, in pioneering the post-Axial Judaeo-Christian tradition, urged people to abandon the former gods of nature in favour of a transcendent heavenly deity. The more God came to be conceived as ruling from a heavenly throne, the more humans saw themselves distanced from the earth. Unlike the animals, humans imagined themselves to be made in the image of God, enjoying a status in relation to the earth which was not unlike that of the heavenly king.

This transferral of the seat of power from the earth beneath to the heavens above encouraged the Israelites to believe that henceforth humans had been given 'dominion over the fish of the sea and over the birds of the air and over every living thing that moves upon the earth'. Because God in his heaven came to be differentiated absolutely from the earth he was believed to have created, it followed that nothing on earth was to be given any kind of worship. 'You shall not acknowledge any other gods but me. You shall not make any graven image, any visible likeness of any thing that is in the heaven above, or that is in the earth beneath or that is in the water under the earth', ran the commandment, which was originally directed against the images of the gods of nature. The worship or veneration of anything at all in the natural world was thus strictly forbidden.

The ancient bond with nature which humans had experienced from the beginning of human culture was thus effectively broken by the rise of Judaeo-Christian monotheism. The gods of nature were deposed as objects of worship and replaced by YHWH, the Maker of Heaven and Earth and the 'Lord of human history'. Thus, the sacred power which, in the ancient cultures, had been conceived as permeating the natural world was in Israelite tradition being withdrawn from nature and seated in a supernatural world above. The natural world was becoming wholly desacralised; the natural forces were denuded of sacred power and humans had no need to fear them any more.

When this biblical heritage from ancient Israel became synthesised, first with Zoroaster's myth of the last judgement and later with Plato's analysis of the human condition, it led to the fully fledged dualism which has marked both Christianity and Islam. The transfer of the seat of sacred power from the earth to the heavens has had significant and long-term consequences. It sealed the demise of the earthly mother and completed the cosmic triumph of the heavenly father. In the three religious worlds of Judaism, Christianity and Islam, and particularly in the latter two, the heavenly world took precedence over the earthly world and the heavenly father has reigned supreme for up to 2500 years.

Thus our Christian forebears came to think of the earth as a lifeless thing beneath their feet and to see themselves as creatures whose true destiny was in a heavenly realm above. The lowly view they had of the earth is reflected in some of the uses we give to the word 'earthy' to this day. From Plato to Descartes, the earth and all physical reality was judged to be inferior to the human soul or mind, in which rationality and/or the essential self was thought to reside.

The conviction that humans were made in the image of God and had been given dominion over the earth underlies the scientific and technological enterprise to this day. The Christian tradition at last freed humans to explore this physical earth, uninhibited by any emotional or religious attachment to it. The scientist has tended to study everything but himself. To preserve scientific objectivity the scientist has tried to keep his or her own presence out of the field of study; in other words, the scientist has tried to study the world from the vantage point of the supposed divine creator, imagined as being external to, and superior to, the earth.

Yet we must acknowledge that the evolution of the dualistic world has not been without its benefits. As just noted, there is a direct correlation between the desacralisation of the natural world and the rise of the modern scientific enterprise. Modern science evolved in the Western world instead of elsewhere as an indirect consequence of Christian culture. Jacques Monod, for example, suggested that the reason why science occurred in the Christian West rather than in any other civilisation was the fundamental distinction it made between the domains of the sacred and the profane.[5]

One can hardly dispute the tremendous value to all humankind of the immense and still rapidly escalating body of reliable knowledge which the scientific enterprise has in total made available to us. From Roger Bacon, through Francis Bacon, Galileo, Newton and Darwin to Einstein, the scientific study of the universe we live in has been an enterprise we cannot possibly reject. For better or for worse, it has given us the materials with which we have been composing the story of the earth.

The feminist theologian Rosemary Radford Ruether suggests that we need scientist-poets who can retell this 'story of the cosmos and the earth's history, in such a way that can call us to wonder, to reverence for life, and to the vision of humanity living in community with all its sister and brother beings'.[6] It is on the basis of this new story that, for better or for worse, the global world is already coming to birth in the collective consciousness of humankind.

CHAPTER 13

The New Global World

'Man is entering a new phase in his and her self-consciousness, planetary, pluralist and historical; and human society a new phase of global conflict or community. The ideas for our new life together must themselves be new', wrote W. Cantwell Smith.[1] This new phase in human self-consciousness is as yet far from universal, but it is spreading around the globe. In spite of some efforts at resistance, it is taking shape in more and more people, even if only subliminally as yet. This new phase is related to what was referred to earlier as the Global Phase in human culture. As a result, a new kind of shared world – the global world referred to earlier – is being constructed in more and more human minds.

The new shared world has become predominant in Western culture, manifesting itself particularly in the scientific community (for reasons that will be discussed presently) but reflected also in literature, the arts, politics, economics, the mass media and all the activities in which we engage on an international or global scale. It is only because this shared global world is already spreading widely that intercultural and international activities have been able to take place as much as they have. In many Westerners the global world has already largely displaced the Christian world which preceded it. In others it is threatening and undermining the last remnants of the Christian world and causing the latter to be relativised and/or privatised. Because the global world first emerged in the West it is still somewhat less pervasive in non-Christian cultures such as the Islamic, Hindu and tribal, but there are signs nevertheless that it is infiltrating quite rapidly, chiefly through general education and the mass media.

The global world shares a common body of scientifically

based knowledge. Because of that it has four chief characteristics: it has become global in horizon, secular in character, humanly based and subject to rapid change. What is here meant by each of those terms may become clearer as we examine them in turn.

It is the significant increase in the body of objective knowledge which has made possible the human construction of the global world. World 3 of Popper's model has been rapidly expanded by this type of knowledge. Being open to public scrutiny, it is universal to the human species and is not the special preserve of any one ethnic group or any one religious tradition or ideology. (There is no such thing as Christian chemistry, Maori physics, communist biology or feminist mathematics.) It is commonly referred to as scientific knowledge, but the word science, which etymologically means simply 'knowledge', is a shorthand way of referring to all knowledge which has been attained by the scientific method. This means, among other things, that it has stood up to various tests which have attempted to show it to be false. Popular thought often has it that scientists prove something to be true, when it is nearer the mark to say that scientists are always trying to falsify what they or others believe to be true. When they cannot falsify it (always assuming that what they are testing would have been possible to falsify), they then have some confidence in believing that it *is* true.

The true scientist is essentially a doubter, not a dogmatist. Yet it requires considerable courage to doubt what is assumed to be true and absolute by the culture in which one has been nurtured. Such courage is itself an expression of faith. Faith and doubt are not the polar opposites they are often taken to be. So, in a sense, the people who pioneered the global world were treading a path of faith, and that has been an essential link with the Christian path of faith out of which they came. A second link is found in what chiefly motivated the pioneering scientists: their search for knowledge. This too was already embedded in the meaning system of the Christian world and is exemplified in John 8:28, 'You will know the truth and the truth will make you free'.

It was the exercise of both doubt and faith on the part of a few unusually free and creative individuals which led to new paths of faith at the Axial Period, even though, as time went on, those new traditions themselves tended to crystallise into dogmatic ideologies. It was a fresh wave of doubt and creative imagination which enabled some pioneer thinkers to cross the threshold which led into the modern phase of global culture. The global world may be said to have evolved out of the faith to doubt. [2]

Doubt and creative imagination still remain the foundation of the scientific enterprise. This was too easily forgotten in the first flush of success which attended the development of empirical science in the eighteenth and nineteenth centuries. There was a noticeable tendency to treat science as a new god which spoke with absolute and final authority. Extremely valuable though science is, it cannot reveal the final and infallible truth in the way divine revelation was thought to have done in the Christian world. Science depends on the inductive method of reasoning. It does not prove something to be true but is continually testing theories, both new and old, to see whether they are false. Positive results lead not to certainty but to varying degrees of probability. Consequently the rapidly increasing body of objective knowledge which is being amassed by science never reaches finality but is always open to change.

Because there is no finality even in the scientific enterprise, the scientist goes forward in faith. But as the body of objective knowledge grows larger, and coheres into a consistent whole, confidence in its reliability grows stronger. Even so, from time to time, there is a significant new discovery, causing what is called a paradigm shift in the way scientists interpret their data. The accumulating and universal body of objective knowledge is drawing people of all races and cultural beliefs together into common ways of thinking and it is these which constitute the raw material of the global world we share.

The new shared world is therefore *global* in its horizons, in that it extends to all humans right round the globe. People are less and less able to ignore what goes on outside their own narrow parochial interests and are being drawn into an increasing awareness of global events. Wherever there is radio, television, printed news and cinema, people are being forced to think of themselves as living in an international global community. The welfare and destiny of the people of all nations are becoming increasingly interconnected. Increased international trade makes us increasingly interdependent. National economies are becoming dependent on the global economy.

Although the previous ethnic and ideological boundaries still exist, they no longer set the limits to how people live and think in the way they used to. The global world relativises all earlier boundaries and increasingly passes them by. Consequently, the shared worlds which were previously dominant within those boundaries, and which were often regarded as absolute and primary, are being rendered relative and secondary to the global world.

Unlike the dualistic character of the Christian world, the new global world is monistic. That means that the universe is conceived as essentially one, even though its dimensions of time and space are so enormous as to be, for all practical purposes, infinite. It means further that the former rigid dividing line between matter and spirit has been eliminated; in the global world reality is experienced as psycho-physical in that the more obviously physical earth has the capacity to bring forth first life and then thought. This monistic or one-worldly character of the global world is the reason for calling it *secular* (or this-worldly). And the body of objective knowledge which forms the raw material for our common construction of the global world is secular knowledge.

The third characteristic of the global world is that it is *humanly based*. In this new shared world, the culture, values and beliefs by which people live are openly and consciously acknowledged to be of human origin. As all forms of life, including humans, have slowly evolved out of the earth, so language, culture, religion and objective knowledge have been created by the activity of the collective human mind, drawing on both imagination and rationality. As the scientific enterprise started with the faith and courage to doubt inherited traditions, so all kinds of traditions, being human in origin, are now being examined more critically than ever before. Wherever they have the intrinsic power to commend their worth they are retained, but where they do not they are either quickly discarded or allowed gradually to wither away. This means in turn that the global world is one of accelerating cultural change. There has been more change in the last 400 years than in the previous 1500 years. There has been more change this century than in the previous 400 years.

The global world not only brings change; it is itself continually *changing*. We must keep remembering that worlds are what we humans construct, and consequently they have always been subject to change. Because our forebears were unaware that they were constructing their world, and they identified their world with the presumed objective reality, it was possible for them to assume that their world was fixed, unchanging and absolute. That is exactly how the Christian world was experienced for so many centuries. But the more we become aware of the way we construct our world, the more we come to acknowledge that the global world can never be static, final and impervious to change.

The body of objective knowledge out of which we construct it is itself never complete. It always remains partial and is continuously being added to and revised. There is no permanent fixed point from which we can view reality. That was one of the consequences of the Copernican revolution. The global world remains relative to the human standpoint. It can never be more than a human construction of the presumed objective universe, based on our ever-developing body of objective knowledge. It remains a world centred on the human species, just as our own personal appropriation of the shared global world remains centred on ourselves. So the new global world which we humans of all races and cultures have been constructing, and which sets the outer limits of our shared consciousness, is global, secular, humanly based and changing.

The birth of the new global world, with its open acknowledgment of the human role in the construction of human cultures and shared worlds, has meant that everything previously regarded as fixed and absolute is now seen to be relative. There may be 'truths', 'facts', moral values and objective knowledge which we believe we can affirm with confidence, but they all lack absoluteness. There can be no known absolutes because of the methods by which we come to know anything. The area of philosophy which deals with this is called epistemology. The philosopher D.W. Hamlyn concludes his essay on the history of epistemology by asserting that it is an illusion to suppose that we can ever arrive at knowledge which is absolutely indubitable and that 'much of the history of epistemology has depended on this illusion'.[3]

While the absence of absolutes may at first sight be thought a great loss, it has nevertheless proved to be an unexpected boon. It has led to a great burst of freedom for human thought and social change, such as has never been experienced before on such a scale. This freedom may be, and certainly has been in some quarters, assessed as a mixed blessing. It has given rise to a large crop of new social problems, but it has also led to a series of emancipations. Social strata, stretching from royalty to slavery, were once thought to have been ordered by divine decree. The recognition that these social distinctions are of human origin has spelt the end of absolute monarchy, slavery, white supremacy and male domination. All social, racial and individual distinctions have become relativised to the more important goal of ensuring equality of rights and opportunity to all human beings.

The advent of the global world is causing 'closed societies' to give way to the 'open society'. In pre-modern times all humans lived in what may be called a *closed society*, of which there were many: tribal cultures, early kingdoms, Christendom and Islam are all examples. In a closed society there is social pressure to conform, though its strength varies from one to another. In a closed society the shared world is experienced throughout the society in a remarkably homogeneous way. The world each individual lives in is largely identical with that of his or her neighbours. The Maori lived in the Maori world, the Christian lived in the Christian world, the Muslim in the Islamic world and so on. The shared world gives identity and a strong sense of cohesion to the culture of that society, and the individual depends for his or her personal identity on the identity of the culture. So people describe themselves by saying, 'I'm British!', 'I'm a Maori', 'I'm a Christian', 'I'm a Muslim' and so on. Members of a closed society who transgress its traditional beliefs or practices endanger the identity of that society and are ostracised, exiled, excommunicated or even executed.

In the global world this is not so. The closed society is being replaced by the *open society*, in which we have become more emancipated from external authority, such as the authority of the church, the authority of the ruling classes, and of course the authority of past tradition. We are much freer to think for ourselves, to make our own decisions, without having our beliefs and behaviour patterns imposed on us by an external authority. The beliefs, lifestyles, patterns of behaviour and social institutions in Western society have never been so fluid as they are today, nor have they existed in such diversity. Not only are they changing quite fast in comparison with the pre-modern world, but they have become so much more personalised, varying from person to person. There is much more room for individual development and creativity in today's open society than there was in the previous closed societies.

By the same token, the open society manifests much more diversity than do closed societies. Tolerance (within limits) becomes an acclaimed virtue in the open society, which not only tolerates diversity but at times even rejoices in it. Religious faiths show tolerance and understanding of one another which would have been impossible before the coming of the new global world. Diverse religious groups live side by side in what is now called religious pluralism. When the Protestant Reformation fragmented the Western church, it led to bitter religious wars. On this side of the Enlightenment, most Christian groups have come to have mutual respect for one another and are finding ways of fuller co-operation, though only rarely re-uniting. Even 'world faiths' (to use a relatively new term) are recognising they have a common field of interest.

What makes it possible for diverse religious convictions to be held by people living in the same society is that, often without realising it, they have already accepted the broad outlines of the global world. This is reflected in the name chosen to describe the movement by which religious groups have been drawn into closer association with one another: 'ecumenical', which is derived from the Greek term for 'the whole of the inhabited world'. The global world takes ecumenism to its limits, and includes all faiths just as it includes all races. Christians and Muslims can justifiably claim that their intention was to become global and include all races in their respective worlds, be they Christian or Islamic. The difference is that they now find themselves in a global world which has emerged in spite of them rather than because of them.

The advent of the global world is the great new event of human history. We have long been accustomed to fastening on significant events as a way of ordering time. The ancient Romans dated their calendar from the supposed foundation of Rome. The Islamic world based its calendar on the date of Muhammad's Hijrah from Mecca and the establishment of the first Islamic society at Medina. Christians, of course, fastened on the birth of Jesus Christ, and came to regard it as such a decisive event for the destiny of humankind that they made it the centre of history, measuring everything from before or after that date. In the Western world we carry on the practice of naming our years by this method (though, ironically, we name the days of the week after the names of the pre-Christian gods).

As the Christian world fades away, however, we are being forced to acknowledge that, not only does history not really have a centre, but there may be historical and cultural events which are even more significant for the destiny of the human species than the birth of Jesus of Nazareth. In 1946, for example, after the world had been stunned by the first use of a nuclear weapon of war, a Christian theologian, Henry Wieman, referred to the bomb that fell on Hiroshima as an event which cut history in two in a way that was more abrupt, decisive and revolutionary than the birth of Jesus. [4]

Nuclear weapons, however, are simply alarmingly dramatic examples of the transition to modernity, which with the Axial Period may be regarded as the two most significant points in the evolution of human culture (these have already been discussed in the Introduction and in Chapter 7). As the Axial Period gave rise to the cultural traditions which have provided the meaning systems for humankind for more than 2000 years, the advent of the global world, which is currently threatening those traditions, is the great new event of human history.

Not only is this event giving us greater freedom and diversity than ever before, but it is now forcing us to see how far we are responsible for constructing the world we live in. The toleration of diversity being promoted by the global world does not immediately result in peace and harmony. First there is the survival, and even resurgence, of the prejudices and animosities which arise from ethnic, national and religious allegiances. Second, the dissolution of the post-Axial worlds, such as the Christian world, results in a noticeable decline in the traditional patterns of moral behaviour, which have given each society its identity, cohesion and stability. As individuals have been freed from the social restraints of the past, their newly found personal freedom has tended to develop into licence. Concerned people all round the earth are deploring what seems to them to be the moral decay of the social behaviour required within the former (closed) societies.

This brings us to the consideration of a vital difference between the global world and all previous worlds. The raw material from which the latter were constructed consisted of the common knowledge contained within the local cultural tradition, coupled with individual personal experience; both of these had a fairly large subjective component which reflected the value system of those concerned. Each of the traditional worlds evolved a meaning system which provided restraints on human behaviour and a common motivation. The global world, by contrast, is based largely on the growing body of scientific knowledge, which by its very nature is value-free. (It is now acknowledged that the scientific enterprise is rarely, if ever, completely free of human subjectivity, but at least objectivity is always the ideal being sought.) Just as it is value-free, however, scientific knowledge cannot of itself provide answers to the human quest for meaning. It can supply only the framework within which those answers are to be sought. The global world, insofar as it is based on scientific knowledge, is devoid of meaning.

As Western minds during the nineteenth century came to recognise that meaning and purpose appear to be absent in the emerging view of reality which we have called the global world, an intellectual void began to open up. This was called nihilism, a word coined in Russia but which soon spread through the Western world. It was expressed in Dostoevsky's character Ivan Karamazov, who said, 'If God does not exist, everything is permitted'. Nietzsche used the term extensively to describe the situation which resulted from the dissolution of the Christian world, saying, 'One interpretation of existence has been overthrown, but since it was held to be *the* interpretation, it seems as though there were no meaning in existence at all, as though everything were in vain.' Nihilism began to move through Europe like a spectre, engendering fear and disillusionment.

The very great difference, therefore, between the emerging global world and the many traditional worlds it is undermining and threatening to supersede is that they were meaningful worlds and the global world is not, or at least not yet. Each of the traditional worlds had evolved as an amalgam of the common knowledge of the day and of the symbols which had been humanly created out of the quest for meaning. In these traditional worlds knowledge and meaning were fully integrated into a purposeful, cohesive unity. That is why, in each of them, the meaning system could always draw supportive confirmation by appeal to common knowledge; the two had been woven into a common story. The medieval Christian world, for instance, as outlined in Chapter 11, was a consistent and homogeneous whole.

All the worlds which humans had constructed prior to modernity had been shaped and directed by the quest for meaning. Each had been successfully established because, in their ideal form, current knowledge and the quest for ultimate meaning were in a harmonious relationship. Paul Tillich spoke of such a culture as theonomous, by which he meant that the ultimate meaning of everything (symbolised in the word *theos*, or God) permeated the world one lived in and was transparently clear.

It was in the High Middle Ages that the Christian world came closest to being theonomous. We have already noted that in that dualistic world people experienced the unseen spiritual domain as being as just as real as the tangible earth on which they walked. 'The other world' (also known as 'the eternal world', 'the spiritual world', 'heaven and hell' and so on) was a system of symbols providing meaning to human existence. It was a world which consisted solely of words or mental images and existed only in the collective mind of Christendom. It had evolved over the first thousand years or so of Christian history, and was an essential component of the total Christian world. Although it lacked the empirical or ontological reality of the physical earth, it was far from being merely an illusion as a Freudian psychologist might conclude. It was a world which supplied meaning to earthly human existence.

The reason that the demise of the Christian world has left such diversity, even confusion, in Christian circles today, and that so many of those in the Western world who have abandoned traditional Christianity still suffer from a spiritual void they are unable to explain, is this: the global world, in undermining and displacing the Christian world, has not yet evolved an equivalent meaning system. Thus, even in this post-Christian era, the basic need to find meaning in life leads many to cling to one or other of the remnants of the 'other-world', even though it has to be acknowledged that this 'other-world' no longer possesses the reality formerly attributed to it.

In Part II we explored how the human quest for meaning gave rise to all human cultures and religions. In the past, however, the innate drive for meaning was unconscious. Our ancient forebears experienced the human condition in ways we do not. Until the Axial Period there was very little self-critical examination of the human condition, and even in the Axial Period critical self-reflection was confined to the few. In ancient times the drive for meaning was still largely unconscious and was hidden behind the drive for survival. What ancient cultures achieved unconsciously in the basic drive for meaning we in modern times are now required to do quite consciously. Moreover, the quest for meaning has to be undertaken by everybody and not simply by the few.

With the advent of the global world the quest for meaning has become more of a personal responsibility than ever before in human history. If we are to find meaning in human existence we have to create it for ourselves. Life has become a venture in which each of us is now responsible for creating our own personal meaning system. This fact is not yet widely appreciated or understood, however.

What has been happening so far is that the human species as a whole is still living off the accumulated spiritual capital of the past. The majority of people still draw spiritual support from the traditional meaning system of their past culture, even if it operates only vaguely or is restricted to times of crisis. Indeed, the prospect of facing the meaningless void now opening up in the global world is sending some people back to their spiritual past. That accounts for the resurgence of traditional religion, as evidenced in Christian fundamentalism, Islamic fundamentalism and the rise of old religions under new names. The advent of the global world, which is still religiously neutral, allows us to be pluralistic and competitive in religion. The religious answers of the past continue to provide for us a kind of spiritual smorgasbord from which, as individuals, we are free to choose or ignore, as it suits us.

Those who have rejected all forms of traditional religion may well settle for something less than the quest for ultimate meaning. They give their chief attention to practical activities such as sport, crafts, amassing wealth, social work, politics, raising a family, or even just eating and drinking. Many people, finding themselves in a global world which apparently has no intrinsic meaning, appear to be opting for a more pragmatic response to life. They are not inclined to think much further than the practical activities which demand their immediate attention. Each of these brings some temporary satisfaction and is not to be wholly despised. The 'Eat, drink and be merry' slogan, attributed to Epicurus (341–270 BC), even got a mention in the Bible in Ecclesiastes (8:5), where the Preacher commends these earthly pleasures, saying 'there is nothing better for mankind to do under the sun than to eat, drink and be happy'.

The current transition from the Christian world to the global world has been marked by a renewed and positive interest in the earthy life we live in the here-and-now. We are abandoning the other-worldly hopes and goals that humans developed in the post-Axial traditions. It ill behoves the more heavenly minded to be judgemental of purely secular existence, for we all spend most of our time attending to the immediate concerns of mundane matters. Most people in the past were also content to be carried along by the crowd without concerning themselves too much with the long-term direction being taken. Such direction as was consciously chosen has been due to the seers, prophets, philosophers and artists who have taken the trouble to ask the basic questions about meaning.

The global world now coming to birth has evolved of its own accord, for better or for worse. No one designed it: it lacks any intrinsic design, meaning or purpose. To date it has given us the freedom to make our own personal choice about what makes our life worthwhile, and it has allowed us collectively to blunder along blindly without any clear sense of direction. But this may not last; we need to remember that the global world is still only coming to birth and is in a very vulnerable state.

The traditional worlds of the past evolved to maturity as the collective human unconscious provided for each an appropriate system of meaning. That system often originated with a founding prophet but it was later collectively developed by others, all motivated by the quest for meaning. That meaning was understood chiefly in terms of a spiritual destiny.

Already voices are being raised by people who may some day come to be acknowledged as the seers, prophets and philosophers of the global world. The reason these voices are being raised is that human technology has been developing so rapidly during this century that it is now beginning to produce negative and destructive results. What we took to be the freedom to explore is now being judged as greedy exploitation. What we took to be the welcome expansion of human power and inventiveness is now seen to contain the seeds of our own destruction.

Such voices have begun to warn us of a nemesis looming on the human horizon, brought about by over-population, rapid destruction of animal and plant species, rapid consumption of non-renewable resources, shortage of food supply, pollution of such basic commodities as clean air and water, and general interference with the ecology of the planet.

It is one of the tragic ironies of our time that, at the very moment when conservative Christians are blaming our increasingly anti-social behaviour on the decline of the Christian world, there are others who are subjecting the Christian tradition to harsh judgement; they say it is to be held ultimately responsible for the coming nemesis. If we credit the Christian tradition with having made possible the rise of modern science, we must also debit it with the negative and destructive activities resulting from modern human technology.

In a now-famous article in *Science*, March 1967, Lynn White, professor of history at the University of California, wrote:

> Christianity in absolute contrast to ancient paganism, and Asia's religions, has not only established a dualism of man and nature, but also insisted that it is God's will that man exploit nature for his proper ends. ... Christianity bears a huge burden of guilt for the human attitude that we are superior to nature, contemptuous of it, willing to use it for our slightest whim ... We shall continue to have a worsening ecological crisis until we reject the Christian axiom that nature has no reason for existence save to serve man. [5]

In similar vein, Arnold Toynbee asserted in 1973 that some of the major maladies of the modern world, such as the recklessly extravagant consumption of nature's irreplaceable treasures, could be traced back to a religious cause: the rise of monotheism. This removed the age-old restraint on human greed to exploit nature, which used to be held in check by the pious worship of nature.

Many will think these attacks on traditional Christianity unfair, and already Christian voices are being raised, urging responsible stewardship of the earth's resources. Yet even Tim Cooper, an evangelical Christian now crusading on environmental issues, has conceded that:

> Most Christians envisage leaving the earth when they die and going 'up' to heaven. This 'otherworldly' strand in Christian teach-ing leads many to understand salvation in terms of deliverance from the physical, material, bodily world. The Earth is like a huge airport terminal where we spend what seems to be an unduly lengthy period, overcrowded and a little bored, waiting for the plane to heaven to take us away.[6]

Thus the 'other-worldly' hopes so treasured in the traditional Christian world may now be turning out to be a threat to our planetary future in that they can deflect us from our earthly responsibilities. Earlier Christians could afford to be uninterested in the future of the earth for they saw their own destiny elsewhere. Failure to care for this earth now appears to be endangering the future of those who will succeed us.

Only in the last 150 years has the new story of the earth begun to be told and, as a result, to become the foundation of a new global world being formed in our minds. We now find, perhaps to our alarm, that while we humans had little to do with the story through most of its four billion years, we have now become responsible for how the story is to unfold from here onwards. Since the earth, in a sense, has become self-conscious in us humans, it now has the opportunity to plan its own future. Instead of blundering along by blind chance, as it apparently did in the past, it now has the possibility of moving forward purposively to an even more fruitful future. But will it do so? Or will it, through us, blunder on to disaster? The end of the story of the earth has yet to be unfolded and it increasingly depends on humankind.

CHAPTER 14

The End of the Earth's Story

The story of the earth, as briefly narrated in Chapter 12, was chiefly a story of origins. It still lacks an ending, which means that the story is left unfinished. The end of a story is particularly important, not only because the story is incomplete without it but, even more, because it holds the key to the meaning of the whole. The word 'end' has a double meaning in that it can refer to either 'finish' or 'purpose'. It is the end (or finish) of the story which makes finally clear to us what is the end (or purpose) of the story and whether there is any point in telling it.

Many stories, of course, are told simply for entertainment or to satisfy curiosity. But the kinds of stories on which we construct worlds are much more important. We may call them existential stories on the ground that they are believed to hold the key to the nature of human existence. Existential stories are what were referred to in Chapter 2 as the myths most basic to a culture. The complete existential story of a culture often consists of a collection of stories; these fall into two different categories of myth. Myths of origin tell how things began and why things are as they are. Myths which tell how things will end may be called eschatological, from the Greek word *eschata*, meaning 'the last times', which is found frequently in the New Testament. Eschatological myths symbolically point to the ultimate meaning or significance of what has been created. In asking about the end of the story of the earth we are looking for the eschatological myth to match the myth of biological evolution; such a myth would express the meaning given to human existence within the global world.

The story on which the Christian world was built possessed an eschatological myth which gave meaning to life lived within the

Christian world. The Bible not only starts with myths of origin but ends with an eschatological myth. The fact that the Book of Revelation is so much like a quick succession of weird dream images serves to illustrate that eschatological myths usually have to draw on creative imagination even more than do myths of origin.

Because the basic story on which the Christian world was built evolved over a long time, the end of the story was continually being filled out and readjusted to meet changing circumstances. Even the earliest form of the story has an eschatological component; for the story itself took the form of a journey towards an end. It was a very simple story, telling how Abraham, the symbolic father of the Jewish people, set out to go to a new land of which he knew nothing. Thus the Judaeo-Christian story originated as one oriented towards a future goal. The horizon within which the story unfolded was no more extensive than the area over which nomadic tribes migrated, for it was being told at a time when there was no awareness of planetary or cosmic horizons such as we have today.

The primary version of the Judaeo-Christian story, even though it is placed chronologically after the Abraham story, is also in the form of a journey. It took shape around the historical events by which Moses led the Hebrew slaves from Egypt through the wilderness to the Promised Land. In that form the story has remained the solid foundation of the Jewish world right down to this day. As we have already seen in Chapter 3, continuing Jewish existence is based on that story which is relived each year. The story forms the framework of the Pentateuch, Five Books of Moses, which became the foundation of holy scripture. It is particularly important to observe that the story ends at Mount Nebo: at that point Moses viewed from far off the land of promise which he himself was destined not to enter. Thus for Jew and Christian the story of that journey became symbolic of the meaning of life, the crossing of the Jordan became a symbol of death, and Canaan the symbol of the ultimate spiritual goal, which was always to lie ahead.

It was only after the Judaeo-Christian story had become

enlarged to include cosmic origins, as now found in the opening chapters of Genesis, that we find the prophet Jeremiah sowing the seeds of a new and more extensive eschatological myth. In the following striking words he envisioned a different and much graver end to the story of the earth as a whole:

> I have seen what the earth is coming to,
> and lo, it is as formless and empty as when it began.
> And I have seen the heavens;
> their light has gone, only darkness is left.
> I have seen the mountains and they are quaking,
> and the hills are shaking to and fro.
> I looked and there is not a human to be found,
> and all the birds of the sky have fled.
> I looked and the garden-land has become a desert
> and all its cities are in ruins. [1]

In this vision of the end of the world, Jeremiah used the same words – 'formless and empty' – which are found at the beginning of the Bible to describe the formless void before creation began. They are the only two places in the Hebrew Bible where these actual words are used together.

This myth of an imminent cosmic end persisted in Jewish thought, especially in times of national crisis, and it took new forms, eventually providing the background for the rise of Christianity. The Jewish people had suffered oppression for so many centuries under the foreign rule in turn of the Babylonians, the Persians, the Greeks and the Romans that by the time of Jesus there was a widespread Jewish hope that God would finally deliver them by a cataclysmic upheaval of cosmic dimensions. It was in this context that Jesus began to proclaim the coming of the kingdom of God. It is most explicit in such Gospel chapters as Mark 13, Matthew 24 and Luke 21, where we read, for example:

> And when you hear of wars and rumours of wars, do not be alarmed; this must take place, but the end is not yet. For nation will rise against nation, and kingdom against kingdom; there will be earthquakes in various places, there will be famines; this is but the beginning of sufferings ... But in those days, after that tribulation,

the sun will be darkened and the moon will not give its light, and the stars will be falling from heaven, and the powers in the heavens will be shaken. And then they will see the Son of man coming in clouds with great power and glory. And then he will send out the angels, and gather his elect from the four winds, from the ends of the earth and to the ends of Heaven.[2]

One of the great achievements of modern New Testament scholars is to realise that the whole of the New Testament is permeated by the conviction, held by the first Christians, that they were living at the 'end of the age' (the *eschata*). Christianity came to birth amid the expectation of the imminent end of the heavens and the earth. It was explicitly referred to in Revelation 21: 'Then I saw a new heaven and a new earth; for the first heaven and the first earth had passed away'.

This primitive Christian eschatology left a permanent deposit in Christian doctrine in the expectation of the imminent Second Coming of Jesus Christ, as expressed in the credal phrase 'He shall come again with glory to judge both the living and the dead', and this has been revived by Christian preachers in times of crisis. (It seems ironic that the sandwich-board fundamentalist who displays his sign in Hyde Park declaring 'The End is Nigh' is closer to the original emphasis of New Testament eschatology than that which came to dominate classical Christianity.) The reason why this eschatological dimension of the New Testament virtually became lost, and had to be rediscovered by modern scholarship, is that from the second century onwards the Christian story began to develop a rather different version of the end. The imminent end-of-the-world eschatology tended to become hidden from Christian consciousness in favour of a more personalised eschatology dependent on the evolving dualistic world-view; by this view 'the next world' no longer needs to be cataclysmically introduced for it already exists and, at death, one is personally translated into it.

However, in both the primitive and the medieval forms of the end of the story, what was really vital was the concept of final judgement. It was this which was declaring that human existence had moral significance and is ultimately meaningful. By the same token it was the eventual decay of the traditional eschatology in recent centuries which has been leading, step by step, to the demise of the Christian world, as we have seen in Chapter 11. For the birth of the global world has been accompanied by a growing threat of meaninglessness, sometimes extending to nihilism and existential despair.

In the spiritual vacuum opening up because the Christian story was slowly losing its end, and in the absence of any satisfactory end (or purpose) to the earth's story, it was entirely appropriate that the person who had most vividly unfolded the new myth of origins for the global world should also attempt a new eschatological myth. Teilhard de Chardin extrapolated from his story of the earth's past what he took to be the basic and enduring trends which would continue into the future. On this basis he envisioned a mind-boggling evolving future.

There is a significant difference, however, between Teilhard's eschatological myth and those of Jeremiah and the primitive Christians. The latter attributed the coming cosmic upheaval to the will of the divine creator who existed outside of all he had created. The cataclysm they expected was interpreted as an act of divine judgement on the wilful wickedness of humankind, consistent with that reflected in the myth of Noah and the great flood. Such an act of divine judgement would demonstrate that this is a morally controlled universe in which good finally does prosper, with the consequence that the righteous have nothing to fear from the upheaval.

But Teilhard had dispensed with the myth of a creator God existing outside of the universe. For him the universe was itself an evolving, self-creative and self-spiritualising whole. Consequently the end of the story of the earth was already present in seminal form within the evolving process; one simply had to understand what the basic trends were and project them into the future. The end of the great story of the earth (which Teilhard called Omega) was already present in the beginning of the story (which he called Alpha). Teilhard was impressed by what he saw as the inner consistency of the evolving universe and by these terms he linked his vision with the New Testament eschatological myth. He loved to quote Revelation 22:13: 'I am the Alpha and the Omega, the first and the last, the beginning and the end.'

Most people regard Teilhard's futuristic sketch as fanciful science fiction mingled with pious Catholic devotion. The Jewish anthropologist Raphael Patai understandably says in his book *Myth and Modern Man*, 'Teilhard embarks on a mythical-eschatological fantasy voyage that easily dwarfs every previous vision of the ultimate end of humanity.'[3] Yet, provided we acknowledge that every eschatological myth must draw on creative imagination, Teilhard's vision is not without its merits. He believed the human habitation of the earth is now reaching a decisive point where convergence (or coming together) must replace divergence (continual division) and willing co-operation must replace competitive rivalry. In the long era of divergence on the planet the number of species multiplied and it was the fittest which survived. In the coming era of convergence, made necessary by the finiteness of the earth, humans must now learn how to live in harmony with themselves and with the earth or they will perish.

Teilhard felt confident of the coming advent of global harmony because of the continuing operation of the same cosmic forces which, in the past, had led to complexification and heightened consciousness. The same trends which led from the megamolecule to the organism would now lead human individuals to cohere and form an even more complex living organism. It would be a social organism in which individuals, while continuing to enjoy personal identity and freedom, would willingly respond to a common goal for the good of the whole. He looked hopefully to the time when the billions of centres of human consciousness would, by the process of complexification, become 'a harmonised collectivity of consciousnesses equivalent to a sort of super-consciousness'.[4]

Should some such phenomenon ever evolve, it would indeed constitute a centred self-conscious earth, operating through the vast number of individual human consciousnesses. The noosphere, as Teilhard called the vast collection of human consciousness and its products, would gradually develop its own centre in a way analogous to the unifying role of the self in the human psyche. (As a devout Catholic, Teilhard conceived this centre of human consciousnesses as the cosmic Christ.) Of course we are still very far from such a unification of humanity at present, yet Teilhard's vision may be regarded as the kind of spiritual goal which, for the coming era, could be the equivalent of the kingdom of God for the early Christians or the place of heavenly bliss for the medieval Christian; both of these goals were equally visionary in their time.

Teilhard did not stop with just the planetary future. In an awe-inspiring way he envisioned the vast cosmos evolving towards an ultimate Omega point. It is of course myth, an eschatological myth, and not the scientific projection which Teilhard took it to be. Even as myth his vision is less than fully convincing. Teilhard developed it in the cultural context of immense optimism with which the Western world entered the twentieth century. Science and technology were growing so rapidly that there seemed to be no limit to what humans would eventually achieve. The 'sky was the limit', so far as human technology was concerned, and the sky itself has no limits. As we near the end of the twentieth century the unlimited optimism so dominant at its beginning is being dampened, and sometimes even replaced, by an ominous pessimism about the human future.

There are, of course, good scientific grounds for prophesying that in the far distant future the earth will become uninhabitable as the sun finally exhausts its nuclear fuel and swells out to be a red giant which will swallow up the earth. Estimates place that as far ahead in the future, some four billion years, as the origin of the earth lies back in the past. This kind of end to the earth's story is not likely to keep us awake at night. It may raise theoretical questions as to whether the universe as whole has any ultimate significance but it does not have an existential import for the foreseeable human future.

It is not the far distant end of the planet with which we are to become concerned but an end which may be no further away than the twenty-first century. The scenario of the earth's story which is much more alarming, and which, unfortunately, is all too possible, is that the humanisation of the earth, instead of moving on to a fruitful future, will come to a tragic end long before the earth is swallowed by a dying sun. Not only is there no guarantee of future progress for humankind but there is today far less confidence about the global future than there was at the beginning of this century. We are now receiving some alarming signs from the earth. They are early warning signals of a living earth which is beginning to feel the pressure of the machinations of the human species it has brought forth. They are the equivalent in the global world of the prophetic warnings from an angry God in the kind of world in which both Jeremiah and the early Christians lived in.

First, there is the human population explosion, which is now expanding exponentially. It took one thousand centuries for the human population to reach 1.65 billion. It took only one century for this figure to rise to 5 billion. Demographers estimate that by the year 2025 it will be 8.5 billion. In spite of claims that the earth can theoretically sustain a population of 10 billion, there is already a sizable proportion of humankind which is either starving or undernourished.

Second, massive development of human technology is leading to the rapid exhaustion of the earth's non-renewable resources, such as oil, gas, coal and uranium. The increasing demand for power for both manufacturing and transport is leading in turn to mass pollution of air and water, the two most basic commodities on which human existence depends.

Third, by destroying the rain-forests and (unintentionally) increasing the deserts, we humans are interfering with the delicate balance of interdependent forces on which planetary life has hitherto depended. What has evolved over millions of years we now have the power to destroy in a few decades, either knowingly or unknowingly. We have greatly speeded up the extinction of living species. We appear to be depleting the ozone layer which protects us from the harmful effects of the sun's radiation. We are increasing the amount of carbon dioxide in the air, which has the effect of changing climatic conditions and of producing global warming.[5]

Only in the nick of time, if not already too late, have we stumbled on the mystery of ecology. The word ecology was invented as recently as 1873 to refer to the mutual relations which exist between all living organisms and their environment. The word has come into common use only since the middle of this century and we are still a long way from recognising its implications. There are two things in particular about ecology which we have to take very seriously in considering the future of planetary life.

The first is that the destiny of any living species is completely dependent on the particular environment in which it has evolved. Take away that environment, and the species dies immediately. A species and its environment have to be viewed as a living whole, a symbiotic life-field. If the environment changes too radically the species declines and becomes extinct. It is probable that the dinosaurs came to a relatively sudden end because of a rapid environmental change even though the reptiles had dominated the earth for 200 million years. We humans are rapidly destroying the environment on which many forms of animal and bird life depend, and many species are already extinct.

The same ecological principle applies to the human species itself. We too can live and thrive only in an environment of a particular kind, the kind which has enabled us to evolve both biologically and culturally to be what we are. Even though the human species may possess greater powers of adaptability than many other species, our destiny still depends on a life-supportive environment. If we change our environment too radically, we too go the way of the dinosaurs.

The second important aspect of ecology is an extension of the first. Just as a species and its environment must be treated as a whole, a life-field as it were, so all life-fields are inextricably joined to one another by a complex set of mutual inter-relationships. All forms of life from the virus to the human species, including the fish of the sea, the birds of the air and everything which moves on the earth, form a living whole. The biosphere, or thin layer of life enveloping the globe, is a unity. We are part of it. It is at our peril that we interfere with it in any drastic way.

The attitude of the so-called primitive cultures towards the powers of nature was much healthier than ours, even if it was reached by trial and error rather than by scientific knowledge. They respected the natural forces and, as we have seen, worshipped them as personified gods. They acknowledged that there had to be limits to human interference with nature and they clearly marked these with various taboos and totem rituals. Similarly, the ancient Indian mind was more aware than we Westerners have been of the unity of all life, whether in the smallest insect or in the gods. In Hindu thought, life in all its many forms was to be treated with holy respect. This was reflected in the Hindu eschatological myth, which we refer to as reincarnation or rebirth. For them, it may be said, the end of a person's story and the end of the earth's story were inextricably linked.

An appreciation of global ecology is only beginning to surface in modern human consciousness. Until it takes hold of us and changes our scale of values and our economic planning, we remain morally and spiritually inferior to primitive humankind in spite of our urban sophistication. Already a great conflict is beginning between those who want to exploit the earth for short-term gains and those who want to conserve the natural resources of the earth so that their use will be sustainable. We are becoming increasingly aware that political and economic power at the moment rests largely with those who are too often ready to opt for short-term gains rather than the long-term goals of sustainability.

Some steps towards resacralising the earth have already been made. We have even taken the concept of 'sanctuary' out of the church building and given it back to the earth, as in bird sanctuaries, fish sanctuaries and so on. But there is very much more to be done. The momentum of the past is so powerful that already it is almost beyond halting. It will take all the collective will we humans can amass to halt our exploiting, polluting and destructive way of life and, of our own free choice, turn our collective energy into avenues which respect the earth, preserve life and promote harmony in the ecosphere. The ecosphere has become the God 'in whom we live and move and have our being'. Indeed, the care of mother earth, and all which that involves, is to a large extent replacing the former sense of obedience to the heavenly father (this is further explored in the final chapter).

The nemesis now appearing on the earth's horizon is approaching with alarming speed. Is it possible for some five to eight billion people to change the direction of our global life in the relatively short time left, especially when most of them are as yet hardly aware of the dangers facing our future? It already seems an impossible task. The words of imminent judgement uttered by Jeremiah and the early Christian preachers in their times have become surprisingly relevant in the global world.

Arnold Toynbee, in *Mankind and Mother Earth*, the last book he wrote before his death, said:

> Within the last two centuries, Man has increased his material power to a degree at which he has become a menace to the biosphere's survival; but he has not increased his spiritual potentiality; the gap ... has consequently been widening ... an increase in Man's spiritual potentiality is now the only conceivable change in the constitution of the biosphere that can insure the biosphere and Man himself, against being destroyed.[6]

Toynbee was convinced that the present threat to humankind's survival can be removed only by a revolutionary change of heart in individual human beings, and that only religion can generate the will-power needed for such a task, understanding religion to be the 'human being's necessary response to the challenge of mysteriousness of the phenomena that he encounters in virtue of his uniquely human faculty of consciousness'.[7]

Similarly Lynn White, also critical of traditional Christianity, believes that religion, rather than science and technology, holds the answer to the ecological crisis. The crisis will continue, he says, 'until we find a new religion, or rethink our old one ... Since the roots of our trouble are so largely religious, the remedy must also be essentially religious, whether we call it that or not.'[8]

Whether the imminent challenges the human species now faces will lead to the rise of anything which could be called a religion is partly a semantic question: what do we mean by religion? A distinctive feature of the global world is that we humans have become much more autonomous; we now acknowledge diversity of viewpoint and refuse to be pressured into uniformity by external authority. It is extremely unlikely, therefore, either that any one of the traditional world religions will ever become the universal religion of humankind or that any new religion at all comparable with them will arise to fill the need.

We may gain a clearer idea of what might eventuate in religion by looking back again to the Axial Period. The Axial religions by no means wholly eliminated the ethnic allegiances on which the pre-Axial ethnic religion was built; they did, however, relativise them, and many pre-Axial symbols, rituals and beliefs were transformed to serve the Axial religions. Similarly, in the transition to modern times, the new set of global imperatives stemming from the condition of the earth itself may continue to draw inspiration and encouragement from the pre-modern religious traditions even though they have now been relativised.

For example, eschatology operates at two different levels: the personal and the collective. In the ethnic cultures, the preservation and identity of the ethnic group took precedence over that of the individual. In the post-Axial traditions, however, there was much more emphasis on the personal destiny of the individual; the end of one's own personal story became paramount, particularly in Buddhism and Christianity. In the global age, the destiny of all life on earth must take precedence over one's personal destiny; the challenges now facing the human species as a whole have to be faced and solved collectively, if they are to be solved at all. It appears that only a carefully planned response by the human species as a whole is likely to be effective and such a plan will rest on a widely accepted diagnosis of the global problems coupled with commonly accepted goals. But this need not prevent the individual person turning to those ideas and practices, both ancient and modern, which make most sense to them for their own personal destiny, provided these do not conflict with planetary goals. Such a way allows for some degree of autonomy and diversity at the personal level, while still fostering unity at the collective level.

As the new set of global imperatives becomes more clearly understood and appreciated by humanity as a whole, they will, let us hope, have the power to generate a collective response which manifests the character of religious zeal. It may be so different from religious phenomena of the past that many will not wish to call it religion, at least at first. Yet, if religion is defined in the broad terms discussed in Chapter 7, then it is not inconceivable that the growing sense of urgency engendered by the current planetary trends will motivate us to create a new collective expression of 'a conscientious concern for what really matters', of 'an ultimate concern which contains the answer to the question of the meaning of life'. Such a new expression would constitute a meaning system appropriate to the global world; it would take fully into account both the beginning and the end of the global story.

New values and meaning systems are not created out of nothing. An axiom of the story of the evolving earth is that the seeds of each new developing phase are already present in what has gone before. We have previously discussed the links between the global story and the Judaeo-Christian story and the indubitable fact that the global world was born out of the Christian world. This does not mean, however, that it is only the Christian tradition which can contribute to a meaning system for the global world.

W. Cantwell Smith, in *Towards a World Theology*, explored the ways in which people of all cultures and all paths of faith could work towards a common global objective. He wrote:

> My aspiration is to participate Christianly in the total life of mankind ... And I invite others to do so Jewishly, Islamically, Buddhistically, or whatever – including humanistically. It will not be easy to build on earth a world community. It will not be possible, unless each of us brings to it the resources of his or her own mind, and his or her own faith. [9]

The most which any of us can hope to contribute to the meaning system of the global world will be limited to the particular tradition which has shaped us. This book quite obviously reflects the Christian culture of the West out of which it has come; it is from within those acknowledged limits that, finally, we shall now explore some of the ways in which the Judaeo-Christian tradition may be rethought to contribute to the 'new religion' of the global world, thus motivating people to create the most fruitful and meaningful end to the story of the earth.

CHAPTER 15

A Focus of Meaning
for the Global World

'Now that the Christian world has collapsed, the moment has arrived for faith to open itself to the full meaning and reality of the [global] world', thus (slightly adapted) wrote Thomas Altizer when, along with others in the 1960s, he discussed the death of the God of Christendom and the advent of the post-Christian age.[1] In 1979 he sketched a 'study of the radical reversal of the Christian consciousness', in which he said, 'We are still only at the threshold of understanding a new and revolutionary world of faith. We will fully enter the threshold only when we acknowledge that a revolutionary transformation of faith has already occurred.'[2]

If one were to limit Christian consciousness to that found within the circles of traditional Christianity one would find little evidence to support Altizer's claim that 'a revolutionary transformation of faith has already occurred'. But if one were to include the mass of post-Christians, people who have been shaped by the Christian past and who still live by what they often call 'the Christian values' even though they no longer observe the traditional church practices, then one would have a clearer idea of what Altizer may be referring to. The final chapter of this book is an attempt to understand this 'revolutionary transformation of faith'; it reflects some of what is going on in post-Christendom outside the churches rather than within them.

Just as primitive Christianity took root inside the Jewish world but outside the circle of Jewish officialdom, so the continuation and transformation of the Christian cultural tradition, in a form appropriate to the global world, may already be taking shape outside of Christian officialdom. The official church leaders have in too many cases anchored themselves so firmly to the past that they are no longer free to provide spiritual leadership for the global world. It is tragically ironic that the theme of 'death and resurrection' is at the heart of the Christian tradition and yet, at the very time when traditional Christianity is required to become dead to its former self in order that it might be resurrected in a 'post-Christian' mode, its official leaders are determined not to let the old Christianity die. Jesus, after all, is dead. He did really die and the first Christians dramatically emphasised the fact by referring to his descent into hell (or underworld of the dead). So Altizer discussed the process he believed the still evolving Christian tradition must now go through under the title of *The Descent into Hell*.

But if traditional Christianity *were* now allowed to die, how could it possibly be recognised again in its resurrected form? That, of course, was a problem with the resurrection of Jesus also; even the New Testament Easter stories reflect ambiguity, as when Mary mistook Jesus for the gardener. Re-cognition of Christianity would be provided by the reappearance of certain symbols, motifs, values and so on which have given identity to the classical form of Christianity. They could be verbal symbols such as the God-symbol, motifs such as the incarnation, and the importance of such personal qualities as faith and self-sacrificial love. Whether they do so reappear remains to be seen. We are here simply exploring how the Christian tradition may help to provide a focus of meaning (or new kind of religion) for life in the global world.

In the cultural traditions which developed out of the Middle East it was the word 'God' on which faith focused for the creation of meaning. What this word symbolised became the object of faith; or, alternatively, whatever people trusted themselves to in an ultimate way, and in which they found the meaning of their life, they came to refer to as their God. But can this symbolic word continue to be a focus of meaning for the global world? We have already observed in Chapters 9 and 10 how the traditional way of understanding this symbol has been fading from modern consciousness. Many conclude that the God-symbol is tied to a meaning which has now outlived its usefulness and that it must be relegated to the burial ground for dead symbols.

Yet, if we simply abandon the God-symbol we may have to invent another verbal symbol to take its place as a focus of meaning. As Karen Armstrong well said at the conclusion of her exhaustive study of the history of God: 'Human beings cannot endure emptiness and desolation; they will fill the vacuum by creating a new focus of meaning ... if we are to create a vibrant new faith for the twenty-first century, we should, perhaps, ponder the history of God for some lessons and warnings'.[3]

The God-symbol has already been understood in a wide variety of ways during its long history, as we have seen earlier and as Karen Armstrong makes abundantly clear. For this reason there are others who believe that the God-symbol cannot be abandoned. Martin Buber was certainly aware that we live in a post-theistic age and even wrote a book called *The Eclipse of God*; yet he contended that it was because the word has been so used and misused in the past, and had meant so much to people, that it could not be given up.

This suggests that the God-symbol may perhaps be reconditioned in order to become the 'new focus of meaning', provided that we learn how to use it very carefully and in an entirely new way. Gordon Kaufman has already provocatively said, on behalf of the Christian community, that if we are 'to help provide meaning and orientation for life in today's world', we 'must be prepared to enter into the most radical deconstruction and reconstruction of the traditions we have inherited and this includes the most central and precious symbols of these traditions, *God* and *Jesus Christ*'.[4]

In Chapter 10 we observed some steps already being taken in the re-interpretation of the symbol by Gordon Kaufman and Don Cupitt. They suggested, for example, that, though the word 'God' can no longer be used to name an objective spiritual being, it can usefully continue to function as an ultimate point of reference or a unifying symbol. But we must be quite clear what we are doing. We are no longer assuming that the word 'God' names some metaphysical reality whose nature we are trying to discover or understand; rather, we are using a word for its functional value and are then proceeding quite consciously to determine what values should be associated with it.

The functional use of the word 'God' is already deeply embedded in our language. In continuing to use it in this way we are simply acknowledging openly that, apart from whatever metaphysical associations the word may have had in the past, it has also long functioned as a focus of meaning. 'God' is a verbal symbol, and God-talk (or theology) is a language which has been humanly created to help us create meaning for human existence.

Today we are in a better position to see that meaning is something we humans create, for meaning depends on language and language is a human creation. There is no meaning or purpose intrinsic in the physical earth itself, except what we create for it. As Nietzsche said, '*We* invented the concept "purpose"; in reality purpose is lacking.' The most we can say about the earth is that, through us humans, it has manifested a drift towards meaning.

Let us put this another way. The earth's potential for life was present in the universe from the beginning. Similarly, the earth's potential for purpose has existed within it for more than four billion years. But it seems to have been largely a matter of chance as to when, or even whether, that potential for meaning would ever come to be realised in the earth, as it has done through the evolution of human life and culture. Jacques Monod has spoken for many experts in biology when he forcefully asserted that the evolutionary process has proceeded by pure, blind chance and not by prior design.[5] So it has been only very recently, on the scale of geological time, that this process has, by accident, produced the human species.

But now that the human species is here, even though it may have arrived only by an almost infinite succession of chance events, a new set of conditions exists on the earth. In pre-modern times the earth's potential for meaning was still being pursued only in an unconscious way by our human forebears. Meaning slowly evolved out of the collective human response to the demands of planetary existence and came to be expressed in language, stories and finally the beliefs and practices of the many various religions.

But, whereas our forebears were unaware they were the creators of language and meaning, we have now reached the stage in cultural evolution where we are forced to acknowledge how much unconscious human creativity has occurred in the past, and how dependent we are on it for our current human existence. It means further that, if there is to be a meaningful future for humans and for this planet, we now have the responsibility to create it, quite conscious that we are doing so.

If we are going to use the God-symbol we have inherited from past tradition to talk about the central focus of the meaning we must now create, it is clear that we have to learn how to use this symbol in an entirely different way. First, it will be by deliberate choice on our part that we continue to use the word, whereas originally it came into use as the product of the creative unconscious. Second, we shall be using it as a functional term which enables us to establish a point of reference – that is, a focus of the meaning we seek to create; previously it referred to a supposed objective reality. Third, we shall need to determine the values, aspirations and goals to be associated with the symbol; this is what traditional theologians were always doing unconsciously when they spent their time discussing the attributes of God. (It should be noted that even they were wary of ever broaching the question of the 'being' of God.)

In consciously enunciating the values to be identified with the God-symbol, we are not free to make an arbitrary choice. The way we understand the nature of the global world, along with the conditions it sets if human existence is to continue and prosper, will largely guide us in our choice of values and goals. Thus the complex nature of reality, as we see it through the lens of the global world, is supplying us with the materials with which we must create a meaningful future. For this reason there is a sense in which God, understood as the focus of meaning, still 'speaks' to us out of the earthly environment in which we live. At the same time, the human quest for meaning, and the internal spiritual imperative which encourages us to create meaning, may be construed as the God within us.

With the gift of hindsight we can now appreciate, as the majority of our forebears did not, that the first steps in this re-orientation of the God-symbol began to be taken soon after the Renaissance, which was the first sign of the coming global world. The earliest prophetic voice to herald modernity was that of Giordano Bruno (1548–1600), as he revolted against the medieval notion of a transcendent God, dwelling in a heavenly sphere absolutely separated from nature and the earth. He conceived the universe, not as something created by an external divine force, but as an infinite living organism having the principles of all its activities within itself. As he saw it, the universe constitutes the whole of reality and is that in which all things live. 'The true philosopher', said Bruno, 'differs from the theologian in this, that the former seeks the infinite Being, not outside the world, but within it.'[6] How modern all this sounds today!

It is surprising that Bruno could so extricate himself from the dualistic Christian world by which he had been conditioned from birth. Such an intellectual transition is perhaps more understandable in the case of Spinoza (1632–77), for being Jewish he had retained more of the sense of the absolute unity of ultimate reality. The Jews had never developed a dualistic world to the degree that Christians had done. They had never accepted the Christian doctrine of the Fall, even though it had been based on their scriptures. They remained more ready than Christians to accept human mortality, and their scriptures had even declared God to be 'the creator of evil along with good'.[7]

So, reacting against the dualism of body and mind then being philosophically expounded by Descartes (1596–1650), Spinoza contended that there is only one reality and this may be called either God or nature. He contended that God or nature is the sum total of all that is real. God (or nature) is infinite in extent but contains within itself all finite things and beings. Spinoza said, 'Whatever is, is in God, and without God nothing can be or be conceived'. This means that 'The human mind is part of the infinite intellect of God', and 'the love of God for man and the intellectual love of man to God are one and the same'.[8]

Bruno and Spinoza were both too far ahead of their time to be tolerated by either church or synagogue. Yet they were already pointing to the re-orientation of the notion of God which is now becoming necessary. Not surprisingly, therefore, their ideas resurfaced in the early nineteenth century. Schleiermacher wrote, 'Offer with me reverently a tribute to the *manes* of the holy, rejected Spinoza. The high World-Spirit pervaded him.'[9] He then expounded an understanding of the God-symbol in terms of that domain of human consciousness which he called God-consciousness, 'To feel oneself absolutely dependent and to be conscious of being in relation with God are one and the same thing.'[10]

Schleiermacher in turn influenced Feuerbach, who exclaimed, 'Spinoza hit the nail on the head ... Spinoza is the Moses of modern freethinkers and materialists.'[11] Feuerbach (as we saw in Chapter 9) took the re-orientation of the God-symbol an important stage further: 'God' is an idea; ideas are words; words express meaning. So we use the word 'God' to express meaning. Thus Feuerbach made a sharp distinction between the wrong and the right way to use the word God. It is wrong to use the word God to name a supposed metaphysical being. It is right to use the word God as a symbol. It is a symbol of the very essence of humanity, coupled with what humans deem to be the essence of the physical world. (Feuerbach's first book, *The Essence of Christianity*, emphasised only the first component; he added the second in his later book *Lectures on the Essence of Religion*.) Thus, even for Feuerbach, God symbolised both something external to the human condition as well as something internal to it.

Feuerbach was almost wholly rejected in his own day; he was seen as an atheist and an enemy of Christianity. As the ideas of Bruno and Spinoza were rejected in their own time but revived centuries later, so those of Feuerbach, condemned except by a few in the nineteenth century, have resurfaced and spread in the late twentieth century. They are very close to those currently being expounded by Don Cupitt, Gordon Kaufman and others, which were discussed in Chapter 10.

Thus important steps in the re-orientation of the God symbol had already begun at the leading edge of Western thought even before the notion of biological evolution surfaced in the same culture and re-directed human attention ever more intently to the earth. What Teilhard de Chardin did was synthesise it all into one harmonious story. For this task he had received a great stimulus from his teacher, the Nobel prize-winner Henri Bergson (1859–1941), and his book *Creative Evolution*, in which he said, 'God has nothing of the already made; He is unceasing life, action, freedom'. [12]

It was to the living, evolving earth itself that Teilhard turned to find his new meaning for 'God'. He wrote in a little essay on 'The Spiritual Power of Matter':

> I bless you, matter, and you I acclaim: not as the pontiffs of science or the moralising preachers depict you, debased, disfigured – a mass of brute forces and base appetites – but as you reveal yourself to me today, *in your totality and your true nature* ... I acclaim you as the divine *milieu*, charged with creative power, as the ocean stirred by the Spirit, as the clay moulded and infused with life by the incarnate Word ... Raise me up then, matter, to those heights, through struggle and separation and death; raise me up until, at long last, it become possible for me in perfect chastity to embrace the universe. [13]

Since Teilhard's novel views were so distasteful to Catholic authorities that he was not permitted even to publish them during his lifetime, it is hardly surprising that any revived veneration of the earth has been forced to manifest itself outside the circles of traditional Christianity rather than within them. Yet the participants in and supporters of Greenpeace and all other conservation and environmental movements show to their respective causes a zealous commitment of a distinctly religious character. Even more like a religious doctrine is the contention of the scientist James Lovelock that the earth should be viewed, not as an inanimate sphere of rock and soil on the surface of which living creatures move about, but as a living whole which we must treat with a respect bordering on worship. In his book, *The Ages of Gaia: A Biography of the Living Earth*, he suggested that we think of the earth in terms of the Greek myth of the earth-mother Gaia (see Chapter 9).

Ever since we humans began to realise how all living creatures depend on and interact with the environment, we have been learning how to treat creature and environment as a living whole. The sum total of these life-fields (as discussed in Chapter 14) leads us to view the earth itself as a kind of complex super-organism. One of the ways of defining an organism, as opposed to a machine, is that the organism has self-adjusting and -regulating mechanisms. There are several ways in which the earth manifests such self-adjusting mechanisms. The land masses, the oceans and the atmosphere interact like a gigantic cybernetic system. The climate and surface environment, for example, control the life of the plants, animals and micro-organisms that inhabit it, while these in turn affect the climate. Moreover, on this model, the earth has some vital organs. As we humans have heart, lungs and liver, so in a sense does the earth. They are the regions of more intense biological activity, such as rain-forests, soil and coastal seas. This does not mean, however, that the earth has any special interest in us humans; indeed, if humans become too troublesome, the earth's self-regulating mechanisms may themselves result in our elimination from the planet.

Since Lovelock thought of himself as an agnostic he was at first surprised when people took his model so seriously that they appeared to be making a kind of religion out of it. Yet on reflection he conceded that people do need a religion to live by and the notion of the earth as a living planet could clearly be related to more personally than a machine, a scientific analysis or an idea.

But Teilhard's revolutionary religious views, and Lovelock's revival of the Gaia myth, have been treated with great suspicion, if not outright condemnation, by traditional Christian circles. They have been seen as laying the foundation of a new and dangerous rival religion, to be countered in the same way as the nature religions were condemned in the ancient world. Even the well-known liberal Protestant theologian Emil Brunner wrote, as recently as 1952, 'Man's decisive position above Nature, however, is attained in the fact that he does not worship it as divine . . . So long as man regards Nature as divine (as is the case throughout the pagan world) *he is not really its master*, he has not really risen above it, and he *is also not really capable of being truly human*' (italics added). [14] Thus the traditional Christian view – that humans should master the earth – dies hard!

Yet, if it is true (as Toynbee and White contended) that Christian monotheism, in encouraging human domination of the earth, was indirectly responsible for the planetary predicament we now face, and that only a new kind of religion can provide us with the motivation we need to respond adequately to it, then perhaps the general emergence of such things as 'green consciousness' and the Gaia model are the first signs of such a religion.

Further, in Teilhard's vision of the evolving earth we find the continuation of the re-orientation of the God-symbol begun by Bruno, Spinoza and Feuerbach. As Gordon Kaufman wrote:

> We must now conceive God in terms appropriate to our modern understanding of ourselves and our world . . . [that is] in terms of the complex of physical, biological and historico-cultural conditions, which have made existence possible, which continue to sustain it and which may draw it out to a fuller humanity. [15]

If there is to be any satisfactory reconstruction of the God-symbol to mediate to us the bewildering complex of forces on which our existence depends, it is clear that we must shift our attention away from the heavens above to the earth beneath. A growing sense of our utter dependence on the earth, accompanied by a sense of reverence for the earth, does look like the revival of the long-lost worship of the earth-mother (as implied by the Gaia hypothesis). Since the worship of the heavenly father finally vanquished the worship of the earthly mother during the Axial Period, it appears that the transition to modernity is to some extent reversing that cultural shift.

This reversal was strikingly expressed in a remarkable confession made by Teilhard de Chardin, devout Catholic though he was, at the time the story of the evolving earth was taking shape in his creative imagination and before he actually wrote his *magnum opus*:

> If, as the result of some interior revolution, I were to lose in succession my faith in Christ, my faith in a personal God, and my faith in spirit, I feel that I should continue *to believe* invincibly *in the world* [by which he meant the earth]. The world (its value, its infallibility and its goodness) – that, when all is said and done, is the first, the last and the only thing in which I believe. It is by this faith that I live. And it is to this faith, I feel, that at the moment of death, rising above all doubts, I shall surrender myself.[16]

So in the global world our attention is being forced away from the heavens to the very earth on which we live. Nietzsche sensed this when he put into the mouth of his prophet Zarathustra, 'I entreat you, my brothers, *remain true to the earth*, and do not believe those who speak to you of superterrestrial hopes.'[17]

The meaning system (or religion) which is appropriate for the global world must therefore clearly focus on the earth. We have evolved out of the earth and we remain dependent on it for our well-being and our future. It is not from outer space that we humans have come but from the earth on which we walk. We are earthlings. We are not only dust of the earth, but it is the earth itself which, in ways which can only reduce us to awe, has been the matrix of all living forms. We humans have come forth from the earth as from a cosmic womb. We are utterly dependent on the earth for our continued existence. It is the earth's atmosphere (or breath) which we breathe to live. It is the earth's oceans on which we depend for the water we drink. It is the earth's fruits which continually provide the food which nourishes and sustains us. We cannot even venture out into space the tiniest distance without taking with us a little bit of the very earth itself.

But this does not mean that we should simply venerate the earth in the way the ancients venerated the earth-mother Gaia. We are to value the earth, but not to worship it as an object from which we stand apart. And it is certainly not what Teilhard had in mind. That is why the thrust of his work was directed to what he called 'the phenomenon of man'. While remaining part of the earth, we humans are also the thinking envelope of the earth. So the rest of the earth, including all other living creatures, have now become dependent to some degree on what we choose to do and how we choose to live. To value the earth is also to value ourselves and our human future. Conversely, we cannot adequately value ourselves without equally valuing the earth.

This paradoxical relationship we have with the rest of the earth constitutes a new kind of mystical union. Mysticism is the name of a particular strand of religious thought and experience, which has made itself present in most religious traditions. It has regarded union with ultimate reality (in whatever form that was conceived) as the highest spiritual goal for humans to reach. The ultimate reality itself, whether referred to as God or not, has usually been conceived as wholly spiritual and non-material in form. The medieval mystic Meister Eckhart (c. 1260-c. 1328) expressed his mystical understanding of God in the form of this paradox: 'The eye with which God sees me is the eye with which I see him: my eye and his eye are one.'

However, the form of mysticism towards which we may be moving is somewhat different. Since the dichotomy between matter and spirit has been transcended in the global world, the ultimate reality is now to be conceived as being neither wholly spiritual nor wholly physical; it is psycho-physical. Similarly, each of us, though traditionally referred to as body and soul, is a psycho-somatic unity, which in turn is an integral part of the vaster and more complex whole. In human self-consciousness we attempt to visualise the whole of which we are a part, even though, as we have seen, our mental picture of the whole is a world we have ourselves constructed.

As Kaufman has aptly pointed out, any attempt to rehabilitate the God-symbol in today's cultural context must allow for the fact that 'human existence has, in part, created itself in the course of creating an unfolding history' and 'the divine activity which has given us our human being must apparently be conceived now as inseparable from, and as working in and through, the activity of the human spirit itself'.[18] The creativity within the collective human psyche is all of a piece with the creativity within the self-evolving universe. If we use the God–symbol to refer to this creativity, then, in a manner not unlike that of the mystics, we may say that the God within us and the God outside of us are one and the same God.

It is quite anachronistic, however, to project back into the beginning of the universe, or even of the earth, the kind of purposive, designing activity which has now manifested itself in human consciousness. All we can say is that from the beginning the universe and the earth had the potential for purposive action, even though the activity shown by the universe through aeons of time has been blind and unplanned. Only by an almost infinite number of chance events, coupled with the outworking of its own internal structures, has the universe stumbled on a way of incarnating itself on this particular planet in a particular mode of being, within which self-consciousness, free choice and purposive-ness have become a reality. That constitutes the extraordinariness of the phenomenon of man! Something like this may have occurred in countless other places in the universe, of course, but to date we humans are the only creatures we know of who are aware of themselves as being the living incarnations of that distinctive mode of being.[19]

We are at last able to appreciate the main thrust of Feuerbach's *The Essence of Christianity*, largely ignored by his detractors when they so quickly dismissed him as an atheist. Feuerbach saw himself as the new interpreter of Christianity, bringing to light its true essence for the new age coming to birth. For this purpose he fastened on the incarnation, the central doctrine of Christianity, and turned it upside down; or rather (as he would have said) he turned it the right way up. For Feuerbach the incarnation was a mythical event of inestimable symbolic significance. It could quite properly be called the gospel, or good news, because it was the event which enables us to understand the true significance of the human condition by causing the dissolution of the dualistic way of understanding reality. Feuerbach argued that the reason why 'God' could become incarnate in human flesh (a paradox which traditional Christianity had never adequately explained) was that 'God', before being unconsciously projected out into heavenly space, had originated as the highest values and aspirations conceived by humans. Similarly 'heaven' was the unconscious projection of the kind of earth humans would like to be living on. Because these were projected into the dualistic 'other-world', however, they had had the devastating effect of throwing the human condition into disunion with itself, and of destroying forever the possibility of improving human existence on earth. Humans became alienated from their higher selves and the 'world to come' was placed out of reach of earthly existence. Thus there did exist a gulf which needed to be bridged, but it was traditional Christian doctrine which, in part, had created this gulf, interpreting it as humankind's sinful rebellion against God's authority.

The mythical event of the incarnation bridged that gulf, enabling the human condition to be restored to its intended wholeness. The gulf between humans and their 'God' has been obliterated. The holy city has descended to earth, 'God' now dwells among humankind where he belongs (as indicated in Revelation 21:3), and the mythical throne in heaven has been vacated. Traditional Christianity, as Feuerbach saw it, had unfortunately denied the truth of the incarnation instead of affirming it, by the way it had made the man Jesus divine and returned him to heaven to sit at the right hand of God. True Christianity, on the other hand, affirms that there is only one life for us humans; it is here on earth, where we ourselves, by means of the incarnation, have had restored to us the capability and responsibility to manifest divinity by the way we love and respond to one another.

Thus the central Christian doctrine of the incarnation may now be seen as having vaster consequences than traditionally thought. It is not just in one human person, Jesus of Nazareth, that 'God' is to be found incarnate, but in the human species as a whole. This is the significance of Jesus' parable of the judgement in which the judge declared, 'Whatever you did to the least of my brothers you did to me.' In similar fashion the Johannine Christ may be interpreted as speaking not of himself as a unique individual, but of himself as embodying humanity, when he said, 'I and the divine Father are one.'

The doctrine of the incarnation, as expounded by Feuerbach, does not mean that each human individual is an incarnation of God but that the human species *as a whole* is in the process of becoming the fleshly manifestation of God – that is, the creativity and potential for goodness and purposive action to which the God-symbol refers. As Feuerbach understood humanity, it could not be embodied exclusively in one individual. He insisted that we can be humans only in community, drawn together by strong bonds of love. He expressed it thus: 'The essence of being human is contained only in the community and unity of man with man; it is a unity, however, which rests only on the reality of the distinction between I and thou. Man for himself is man (in the ordinary sense): man with man – the unity of I and thou – is God.'[20]

It was this, incidentally, which inspired Martin Buber to write his famous spiritual classic *I and Thou*. There he fastened on personal encounter, one with the other, as the experience in which one can again speak meaningfully of God. He insisted that God is not an objective being and it is idolatrous to speak about God in that way. All that we owe to the human creativity of the past, including all that was discussed in Part I about language and story, has to be appreciated before we can even begin to understand the new meaning of God. As Buber said, 'God embraces but is not the universe; God embraces but is not the Self. On account of this which is unspeakable I can say Thou. On account of this there is I and Thou, there is dialogue, there is language, there is spirit and there is, in eternity, the word.'[21]

This brings us back to where we began – language. The global world now coming to birth in human consciousness began with language. Language and humanity, as we have seen, evolved together in a symbiotic relationship. Language makes possible relationship and community; community makes being human possible, as both Feuerbach and Buber acknowledged. Through language, story and the creation of a world, human consciousness has come to pursue its own quest for unified, meaningful and purposive existence. Complexity is the key to this emergence of meaning and purpose. It is because we humans are much more complex entities than a star or even a galaxy (in spite of their enormous difference in size from us) that we are capable of acting purposively and creating meaning for ourselves.

Even all this, however, we see and understand only from within the mental boundaries of the worlds which we humans have created and are still constructing. In the quality of human consciousness we are beginning to share in the global world, we see ourselves as possessing the potential for rationality and purposive action. Yet the evolution of life on this planet appears itself to be directionless, blind and amoral; it was only because it manifested a cosmic drift towards complexity and meaning that we have reached our present state. Much of that blind and purposeless activity unfortunately still remains in the human condition. This is why we humans, when we act, have the capacity to be both evil and good, irrational and rational, destructive and constructive. In Christian teaching it was traditionally called sin; we may prefer to call it self-centredness and perverse stupidity.

For this reason, however, it is misleading to assume that, because the future of the earth is now largely in our hands, the way ahead is assured. Far from it! There is no guarantee that we humans shall ever manage to produce a united effort to cope with the global nemesis now appearing on the horizon. There is no guarantee that our vision for a more peaceful and harmonious global future will come to fruition. There is no guarantee that love will ultimately win the day. In the global world we find no guarantees, no certainties and no absolutes. In the global world we humans shall have to live more than ever before by the spiritual values of faith and hope.

Christians used to take comfort from the proclamation that the heavenly father 'so loved the world that he gave his only son, that whoever believes in him should not perish but have eternal life'. In the global world it is to the earth itself that we look for comfort and inspiration. The earth has not only been the womb from which all life and culture have emerged but it has continued to sustain all life with its fruits. Further, the earth has shown a great capacity for self-renewal, for the regeneration of new life out of death. Indeed it was from this phenomenon that the Christian tradition originally inherited its central motif of death and resurrection.

The meaning of human existence will increasingly become one of caring for the earth. Care for the earth entails caring for all life on earth and caring for one another. All the hopes, values, goals and devoted service traditionally associated with heavenly places must be transferred to the earth. The whole earth must become re-sanctified in our eyes; the holy colour must change from heavenly purple to earthly green. This imperative to care must take precedence over lesser loyalties and over all differences of race, nationality, gender and personal beliefs. It is the kind of love which is ready to sacrifice individual self-interest for the greater good of the whole. We shall be required to limit our own earthly pleasures and expectations in the interests of the generations yet to be born. Like Moses of old on Mount Nebo looking to the Promised Land, we need to show our concern for a future world that we ourselves shall never enter. This calls for the kind of self-sacrificing love which has long been affirmed in the Christian tradition and symbolised as the way of the cross.

This is no more than a glimpse of the way the Christian path of faith may reappear to serve human needs within the global world. Whether we choose to use the word God, or not, in order to speak about this faith, is a matter of personal choice. The particular words we use, being arbitrary, are relatively unimportant; what is important are the supreme values we come to associate with such time-honoured words as God, and the responsibilities to which those values call us.

If we choose to speak of God, we shall be using this term to focus on all that we supremely value and on the goals which make human existence meaningful and worthwhile; and there is no thing and no place in which we do not encounter this God. All reality is nothing less than 'the body of god' (to use the title of Sallie

McFague's recent book). This God is in the physical earth of which we are a tiny part. Even more, this God is to be found in all living creatures. Most of all, however, this God is rising to self-awareness in the (as yet) confused collective consciousness of the global human community. This is tomorrow's God, calling us from a world yet to be created. But, to create this world, this God has no hands but our hands, no voice but our voice, no mind but our mind, and no plan for the future except what we plan.

Notes and References

INTRODUCTION

1. This model of three phases of cultural and religious development is more fully described in the author's *Faith's New Age* (see Select Bibliography).

CHAPTER 1: IN THE BEGINNING WE CREATED LANGUAGE

1. Benjamin Lee Whorf, *Language, Thought, and Reality*, p. 252.
2. John McCrone, *The Ape that Spoke*, p. 33.
3. Whorf, p. 251.
4. Genesis 11:1.
5. The Prologue is further discussed in Chapter 6.
6. Graham Clarke, *World Prehistory*, p. 28.
7. Richard Leakey, *Origins*, p. 180.
8. ibid., p. 204.
9. Erich Harth, *Dawn of a Millennium*, p. 123.
10. See Jacques Monod, *Chance and Necessity*, p. 123.
11. McCrone, p. 85.
12. ibid., p. 121.
13. ibid., p. 66.
14. ibid., p. 93.
15. ibid., p. 82.
16. ibid., p. 93.
17. Whorf, p. 249.
18. Richard E. Leakey, *The Making of Mankind*, p. 241.
19. Don Cupitt, *Creation out of Nothing*, p. 5.
20. Keith Ward, *Holding Fast to God* (SPCK, 1982), p. 5.

CHAPTER 2: WITH LANGUAGE WE CREATE STORIES

1. Jared Diamond, *The Rise and Fall of the Third Chimpanzee*, p. 137.
2. Mircea Eliade, *Myths, Dreams & Mysteries* (Collins, 1968), pp. 31, 38.
3. Mark Schorer in *Myth and Mythmaking*, ed. Henry A. Murray (George Braziller, 1960), p. 355.
4. Barbara Sproull, *Primal Myths*, pp. 2–3.
5. Mircea Eliade, *Myth and Reality*, pp. 5–6.
6. See the author's *God in the New World*, Chapter 16.
7. Don Cupitt, *What Is a Story?*, p. 77.

CHAPTER 3: WITH STORIES WE CREATE WORLDS

1. Paul Tillich, *Systematic Theology*, Vol. III, p. 61.
2. Don Cupitt, *What Is a Story?*, p. 99.
3. Paul Tillich, *Systematic Theology*, Vol. I, p. 189.
4. Richard Leakey, *Origins*, pp. 185–8.
5. Whorf, *Language, Thought, and Reality*, pp. vi, vii.
6. ibid., p. vii.
7. See David Rosenberg and Harold Bloom, *The Book of J* (Vintage Books, 1991).
8. To avoid the Christian bias these terms imply, it is now preferable to use the religiously neutral terms BCE (Before the Common Era) and CE (Common Era) for BC and AD respectively.
9. Hebrews 11:2 (author's translation and italics).
10. Quoted by Karl Popper and John Eccles in *The Self and Its Brain*, p. 3.
11. Ecclesiastes 3:11.

CHAPTER 4: THE COMPOSITION OF OUR WORLDS

1. Bruce Gregory, *Inventing Reality*, p. 183.
2. ibid., p. 198.
3. See Thomas Kuhn, *The Structure of Scientific Revolutions*, 2nd ed. (University of Chicago Press, 1970).
4. Karl Popper and John Eccles, *The Self and Its Brain*, p. 11.
5. ibid., p. 15.
6. ibid., p. 450.
7. ibid., p. 11.
8. ibid., p. 458.

CHAPTER 5: THE CREATIVE SOURCE OF OUR WORLDS

1. Georg Wilhelm Hegel, *Lectures on the Philosophy of Religion* (Kegan Paul, Trench, Trubner, 1895), vol. II, p. 302.
2. Darryl Reanney, *The Death of Forever*, p. 73.
3. McCrone, p. 184.
4. Popper, p. 442.
5. See Chapters 12 and 14 for a fuller discussion of Teilhard de Chardin's views.
6. Teilhard de Chardin, *The Phenomenon of Man*, p. 183.
7. Carl Jung, 'The Structure of the Psyche', in *The Collected Works of C.G. Jung*, Vol. VIII, p. 158.
8. Tillich, *Systematic Theology*, Vol. I, p. 189.

CHAPTER 6: THE HUMAN QUEST FOR MEANING

1. Since even Teilhard de Chardin, although believing in orthogenesis, had to concede that evolution often appears to be directionless, his invention of

the term 'cosmic drift' has suggested the use here of 'drift towards meaning'.

2. John Macquarrie, *Thinking About God*, p. 77.

CHAPTER 7: RELIGION AS THE CREATION OF MEANING

1. Ludwig Feuerbach, *The Essence of Christianity*, p. 64.
2. Henry Fielding, *The History of Tom Jones* (Penguin Books, 1966), p. 129.
3. Paul Tillich, *Christianity and the Encounter of the World Religions* (Columbia University Press, 1964), p. 3.
4. Carlo Della Casa, 'Jainism', *Historia Religionum*, ed. C. Jouko Bleeker and Geo Widengren, Vol. II, 1971, p. 355.
5. Paul Tillich, *Systematic Theology*, Vol. III, p. 101.
6. Quoted by Karl Jaspers, *The Origin and Goal of History* (Routledge & Kegan Paul, 1953), p. 8.
7. Robert Ellwood, *The History and Future of Faith*, chapter 4.
8. Owen Barfield, *The Rediscovery of Meaning*, p. 11.
9. Deuteronomy 8:3.

CHAPTER 8: SYMBOLS AS THE BEARERS OF MEANING

1. Robert Bellah, *Beyond Belief*, p. 21.
2. Thomas Carlyle, 'Symbols', *Sartor Resartus* (London, 1836).

CHAPTER 9: GOD AS A CENTRAL SYMBOL OF MEANING

1. Psalm 53:1.
2. John Calvin, *The Institutes of Christian Religion*, Book I, Chapter III, paragraph 1.
3. This chapter was already written when I received the excellent book by Karen Armstrong, *A History of God*, in which she relates in great detail how God has been understood by Jew, Christian and Muslim over a period of 4000 years.
4. H. and H.A. Frankfort, *The Intellectual Adventure of Ancient Man*, p. 4.
5. Marcus Aurelius, *Meditations*, translated by Maxwell Staniforth (Penguin Books, 1964), pp. 46, 73.
6. *A Compend of Luther's Theology*, edited by H.T. Kerr (Westminster Press, 1943), p. 23.
7. See Chapter 7 of *Faith's New Age* for a fuller description of Feuerbach's work.
8. Ludwig Feuerbach, *Lectures on the Essence of Religion*, p. 121.
9. Ludwig Feuerbach, *The Essence of Christianity*, p. 12.
10. John Macquarrie, *In Search of Deity*, p. 17.

CHAPTER 10: WHEN SYMBOLS CEASE TO BEAR MEANING

1. For a fuller discussion, see the author's *Resurrection: A Symbol of Hope*.

2. Tillich discussed the importance of symbols in most of his writings, but of special interest is his *Dynamics of Faith* (see Select Bibliography).
3. Tillich, *Dynamics of Faith*, p. 50.
4. Tillich, *Systematic Theology*, Vol. I, p. 263.
5. Tillich, *Dynamics of Faith*, pp. 1, 45.
6. Gordon Kaufman, *The Theological Imagination*, p. 32.
7. Don Cupitt, *Taking Leave of God*, p. 166.
8. John Robinson, *Honest to God* (SCM Press, 1963), pp. 125–6.
9. Don Cupitt, *Taking Leave of God*, p. 166.

CHAPTER 11: THE DEMISE OF THE CHRISTIAN WORLD

1. Friedrich Schleiermacher, *The Christian Faith* (T. & T. Clark, 1928), p. 703.
2. John Baillie, *And the Life Everlasting* (Oxford University Press, 1934), pp. 251–2.
3. Don Cupitt, *Radicals and the Future of the Church*, p. 124.
4. Kirsopp Lake, *The Religion of Yesterday and Tomorrow* (Christophers, 1925).
5. See *Kerygma and Myth*, edited by Hans Werner Bartsch, translated by Reginald H. Fuller (SPCK, 1953).
6. ibid., p. 4.
7. W.H. van de Pol, *The End of Conventional Christianity*, p. 127.

CHAPTER 12: THE NEW STORY OF THE EARTH

1. John Gribben, *In the Beginning*, p. 79.
2. Teilhard de Chardin, *The Phenomenon of Man*, pp. 21, 243–4.
3. Robert Bellah, *Beyond Belief*, p. 22.
4. See Plato, *The Last Days of Socrates*, translated by Hugh Tredennick (Penguin Books, 1954), pp. 108–13.
5. See Jacques Monod, *Chance and Necessity*, p. 162.
6. Rosemary Radford Ruether, *Gaia and God*, p. 58.

CHAPTER 13: THE NEW GLOBAL WORLD

1. W. Cantwell Smith, *Faith and Belief*, p. ix.
2. See the fascinating little book by a philosopher, M. Holmes Hartshorne, *The Faith to Doubt* (Prentice-Hall, 1963).
3. D.W. Hamlyn in *The Encyclopedia of Philosophy* (Macmillan, 1967), Vol. 3, p. 38.
4. Quoted by Gordon Kaufman in *Theology for a Nuclear Age*, p. 15.
5. Lynn White, 'The Historical Roots of Our Ecologic(al) Crisis'. *Science*, Vol. 155, No. 3767 (10 March 1967), pp. 1203–7.
6. Tim Cooper, *Green Christianity*, p. 61.

CHAPTER 14: THE END OF EARTH'S STORY

1. Jeremiah 4: 23–26 (author's translation).

2. Mark 13: 7–8, 24–27.

3. Raphael Patai, *Myth and Modern Man* (Prentice-Hall, 1972), p. 309.

4. Teilhard de Chardin, *The Phenomenon of Man*, p. 276.

5. For much fuller discussion of these issues, see such books as Rachel Carson, *Silent Spring* (Houghton Mifflin, 1962); Richard A. Falk, *The Endangered Planet* (Vintage Books, 1971); E.F. Schumacher, *Small Is Beautiful* (Harper & Row, 1973); Fritjof Capra, *The Turning Point*; Jonathan Schell, *The Fate of the Earth*; Al Gore, *Earth in the Balance* (contains an extensive bibliography).

6. Arnold Toynbee, *Mankind and Mother Earth*, p. 574.

7. ibid., p. 3.

8. Lynn White, 'The Historical Roots of Our Ecologic(al) Crisis'. *Science*, Vol. 155, No. 3767 (10 March 1967), pp. 1203–7.

9. W. Cantwell Smith, *Towards a World Theology*, p. 129.

CHAPTER 15: A FOCUS OF MEANING FOR THE GLOBAL WORLD

1. Thomas Altizer, *Radical Theology and the Death of God*, p. 35.

2. Thomas Altizer, *The Descent into Hell*, pp. 7–8.

3. Karen Armstrong, *A History of God*, p. 457.

4. Gordon Kaufman, *Theology for a Nuclear Age*, p. 13.

5. See Jacques Monod, *Chance and Necessity*, p. 110.

6. Quoted by John Caird in *Spinoza* (William Blackwood and Sons, 1907), p. 78.

7. Isaiah 45:7.

8. John Caird, *Spinoza*, pp. 158, 160, 315.

9. Friedrich Schleiermacher, *On Religion* (Harper & Row, 1958), p. 40.

10. Friedrich Schleiermacher, *The Christian Faith* (T. & T. Clark, 1928), p. 17.

11. Ludwig Feuerbach, *Principles of the Philosophy of the Future*, pp. 23–4.

12. Henri Bergson, *Creative Evolution*, translated by Arthur Mitchell (Macmillan and Co, 1912), p. 262.

13. Teilhard de Chardin, *Hymn of the Universe* (Collins, 1961), pp. 64–5.

14. Emil Brunner, *The Christian Doctrine of Creation and Redemption* (Lutterworth Press, 1952), p. 67.

15. Kaufman, *Theology for a Nuclear Age*, p. 42.

16. Teilhard de Chardin, 'How I Believe', in *Christianity and Evolution* (Collins, 1971), p. 99.

17. Nietzsche, *Thus Spake Zarathustra*, p. 43.

18. Kaufman, *Theology for a Nuclear Age*, p. 40.

19. I am indebted to Kaufman for what he wrote in *Theology for a Nuclear Age* (p. 44), but I have taken his seminal thought a little further.

20. Feuerbach, *Principles of the Philosophy of the Future*, p. 71.

21. See the author's *The World of Relation*, p. 53.

Select Bibliography

Altizer, Thomas J.J. *The Descent into Hell*, Seabury Press, 1979

Altizer, Thomas J.J., and William Hamilton. *Radical Theology and the Death of God*, Penguin, 1968

Anderson, Walter Truett. *Reality Isn't What It Used To Be*, HarperSanFrancisco, 1990

Armstrong, Karen. *A History of God*, Heinemann, 1993

Ball, Ian, Margaret Goodall, Clare Palmer and John Reader (eds). *The Earth Beneath*, SPCK, 1992

Barbour, Ian G. *Myths, Models and Paradigms*, SCM Press, 1974

Barfield, Owen. *The Rediscovery of Meaning and Other Essays*, Wesleyan University Press, 1977

Barrow, John D. *Theories of Everything*, Vintage, 1991

Barrow, John D., and F.J. Tipler. *The Anthropic Cosmological Principle*, Oxford University Press, 1986

Bellah, Robert N. *Beyond Belief*, Harper & Row, 1970

Brandon, S.G.F. *Religion in Ancient History*, George Allen & Unwin, 1973

Buber, Martin. *The Eclipse of God*, Harper & Row, 1952

Buber, Martin. *I and Thou*, translated by Walter Kaufmann, T. & T. Clark, 1970

Capra, Fritjof. *The Tao of Physics*, Fontana, 1976

Capra, Fritjof. *The Turning Point*, Fontana, 1983

Cassirer, Ernst. *Language and Myth*, Harper and Brothers, 1946

Clarke, Graham. *World Prehistory*, Cambridge University Press, 1961

Cooper, Tim. *Green Christianity*, Hodder & Stoughton, 1990

Cupitt, Don. *Taking Leave of God*, SCM Press, 1980

Cupitt, Don. *The Long Legged Fly*, SCM Press, 1987

Cupitt, Don. *Radicals and the Future of the Church*, SCM Press, 1989

Cupitt, Don. *Creation out of Nothing*, SCM Press, 1990

Cupitt, Don. *What Is a Story?*, SCM Press, 1991

Davies, Paul. *God and the New Physics*, Penguin, 1984

Davies, Paul. *The Mind of God*, Penguin, 1992

Davies, Paul, and John Gribben. *The Matter Myth*, Penguin, 1992

Diamond, Jared. *The Rise and Fall of the Third Chimpanzee*, Vintage, 1991

Dobzhansky, Theodosius. *The Biology of Ultimate Concern*, Collins, 1971

Eliade, Mircea. *Myth and Reality*, Harper & Row, 1963

Ellwood, Robert. *The History & Future of Faith*, Crossroad, 1988

Fawcett, Thomas. *The Symbolic Language of Religion*, SCM Press, 1970

Feuerbach, Ludwig. *The Essence of Christianity* [1841], translated by George Eliot, Harper & Row, 1957

Feuerbach, Ludwig. *Principles of the Philosophy of the Future*, Bobbs-Merrill, 1966

Feuerbach, Ludwig. *Lectures on the Essence of Religion*, translated by Ralph Manheim, Harper & Row, 1967

Frankfort, H. and H.A. *The Intellectual Adventure of Ancient Man*, University of Chicago Press, 1946

Frankl, Viktor E. *Man's Search for Meaning*, Simon & Schuster, 1970

Frankl, Viktor E. *The Unconscious God*, Hodder & Stoughton, 1975

Freeman, Anthony. *God in Us, a Case for Christian Humanism*, SCM Press, 1993

Geering, Lloyd. *God in the New World*, Hodder & Stoughton, 1968

Geering, Lloyd. *Resurrection: A Symbol of Hope*, Hodder & Stoughton, 1971

Geering, Lloyd. *Faith's New Age*, Collins, 1980

Geering, Lloyd. *The World of Relation*, Victoria University Press, 1983

Geering, Lloyd. *In the World Today*, Allen & Unwin/Port Nicholson Press, 1988

Gore, Al. *Earth in the Balance*, Plume, 1993

Gregory, Bruce. *Inventing Reality: Physics as Language*, John Wiley & Sons, 1988

Gribben, John. *In Search of the Double Helix*, Corgi Books, 1985

Gribben, John. *In Search of Schroedinger's Cat*, Corgi Books, 1985

Gribben, John. *In Search of the Big Bang*, Corgi Books, 1986

Gribben, John. *In the Beginning*, Viking, 1993

Gribben, John, and Martin Rees. *Cosmic Coincidences*, Bantam Books, 1989

Hart, David A. *Faith in Doubt*, Mowbray, 1993

Harth, Erich. *Dawn of a Millennium*, Penguin, 1990

Hawking, Stephen W. *A Brief History of Time*, Bantam Press, 1988

Joseph, Lawrence E. *Gaia: The Growth of an Idea*, Arkana, 1990

Jung, Carl. *The Collected Works of C.G. Jung*, Routledge & Kegan Paul, 1960

Kaufman, Gordon D. *God the Problem*, Harvard University Press, 1972

Kaufman, Gordon D. *An Essay on Theological Method*, Scholars Press, 1975

Kaufman, Gordon D. *The Theological Imagination*, Westminster Press, 1981

Kaufman, Gordon D. *Theology for a Nuclear Age*, Westminster Press, 1985

Kelsey, Morton T. *Myth, History and Faith*, Paulist Press, 1974

Küng, Hans. *Does God Exist?*, Collins, 1980

Küng, Hans. *Christianity and the World Religions*, Collins, 1987

Küng, Hans. *Global Responsibility*, SCM Press, 1991

Leakey, Richard E. *The Making of Mankind*, Michael Joseph, 1981

Leakey, Richard E., and Roger Lewin, *Origins*, Macdonald and Jane's, 1977

Lovelock, James. *The Ages of Gaia: A Biography of Our Living Earth*, W.W. Norton & Co., 1988

McCrone, John. *The Ape that Spoke*, Picador, 1990

McDonagh, Sean. *The Greening of the Church*, Orbis Books, 1990

McFague, Sallie. *Models of God*, SCM Press, 1987

McFague, Sallie. *The Body of God*, SCM Press, 1993

Mackay, Donald. *Brains, Machines and Persons*, Collins. 1980

Macquarrie, John. *Thinking About God*, SCM Press, 1975

Macquarrie, John. *In Search of Deity*, SCM Press, 1984

Merleau-Ponty, Maurice. *Consciousness and the Acquisition of Language*, Northwestern University Press, 1973

Monod, Jacques. *Chance and Necessity*, Collins, 1972

Nietzsche, Friedrich. *Thus Spake Zarathustra*, translated by R.J. Hollingdale, Penguin, 1961

Peat, David F. *Synchronicity: The Bridge Between Matter and Mind*, Bantam Books, 1987

Peat, David F. *The Philosopher's Stone*, Bantam Books, 1991

Penrose, Roger. *The Emperor's New Mind*, Vintage, 1990

Popper, Karl R., and John C. Eccles. *The Self and Its Brain*, Springer International, 1977

Prozesky, Martin. *Religion and Ultimate Well-Being*, Macmillan, 1984

Reanney, Darryl. *The Death of Forever*, Longman Cheshire, 1991

Roy, Rustum. *Experimenting with Truth*, Pergamon Press, 1981

Ruether, Rosemary Radford. *Gaia & God,* SCM Press, 1993

Schell, Jonathan. *The Fate of the Earth*, Avon, 1982

Sheldrake, Rupert. *A New Science of Life*, Paladin, 1983

Sheldrake, Rupert. *The Rebirth of Nature*, Rider, 1990

Smith, W. Cantwell. *The Meaning and End of Religion*, Mentor, 1964
Smith, W. Cantwell. *Faith and Belief*, Princeton University Press, 1979
Smith, W. Cantwell. *Towards a World Theology*, Macmillan Press, 1981
Sölle, Dorothee. *Thinking About God*, SCM Press, 1990
Sproull, Barbara. *Primal Myths*, Harper & Row, 1979
Teilhard de Chardin, Pierre. *The Phenomenon of Man*, Collins, 1965
Tillich, Paul. *Systematic Theology*, Nisbet & Co., 1953–64
Tillich, Paul. *Dynamics of Faith*, George Allen & Unwin, 1957
Tillich, Paul. *The Courage to Be*, Collins, 1962
Toynbee, Arnold. *Mankind and Mother Earth*, Oxford University Press, 1976
van der Pol, W.H. *The End of Conventional Christianity*, Newman Press, 1968
Whorf, Benjamin Lee. *Language, Thought, and Reality*, Massachusetts Institute of Technology, 1956
Zohar, Danah. *The Quantum Self*, Flamingo, 1991

Index